ASPECTS OF MODERN ART

ASPECTS OF MODERN ART

Aspects of Modern Art

L'ŒIL

THE SELECTIVE EYE III

AN ANTHOLOGY OF WRITINGS ON MODERN ART FROM L'ŒIL

THE EUROPEAN ART MAGAZINE

EDITED BY GEORGES AND ROSAMOND BERNIER

WITH 40 PAGES IN COLOR

G. & R. BERNIER PARIS LAUSANNE

REYNAL & COMPANY NEW YORK

All the material appearing in this book was selected from L'ŒIL.
The texts were originally printed in French and are given in English for the first time.

Published in New York by Reynal & Company Inc. and in Toronto by Macmillan Company of Canada, Ltd

Printed in Switzerland

CONTENTS

I knew Lautrec, Cézanne, Monet...

AN INTERVIEW WITH FRANCIS JOURDAIN BY HENRI PERRUCHOT

Francis Jourdain was born in Paris on November 2nd, 1876. He is now eighty-one, therefore, but he is one of those older men whom it is always a pleasure to meet : the brisk and sturdy figure which greets you with an affable smile has remained magnificently young.

His long life has been an admirably full one. Initially a painter, he soon devoted himself to the decorative arts and displayed in them the audacity and fine taste of a pioneer. For more than a quarter of a century his work in this field was of outstanding importance.

Francis Jourdain's life-story is one of constant renewal. Since 1945, for instance, he has turned to writing and published memoirs, studies, and monographs. Through his close and lifelong acquaintance with the art-world of Paris he has come to know innumerable painters, sculptors and writers. The period of the Salon battles and the Caillebotte bequest, the years when Père Tanguy's shop was filled with unsaleable Cézannes and despised Van Goghs and Toulouse-Lautrec was haunting the Moulin Rouge, the epoch of Degas and Monet and Mirbeau and Zola—all seem to him to have been 'only yesterday'.

One afternoon I went to see him in the apartment in the rue Vavin which he has had for more than forty years, and I listened with intense interest and emotion to his stories of the great masters. The past suddenly moved into the present, and as I sat in his big study I had the feeling that it was only a few minutes since Francis Jourdain had left the people of whom he was talking,—so vivid were the gestures and the tone of voice with which he evoked Lautrec's curiously emphatic utterance and the marked southern accent of Cézanne. I felt that I too might meet then at any moment, and I really believe that if Francis Jourdain had said to me "Let's step along to Le Barc de Boutteville's in the rue Le Peletier", I should have gone and got my hat...

Henri Perruchot: When do you first remember coming into contact with artists ?

Francis Jourdain: *I can't remember a time when I wouldn't have been looking at pictures.*

H. P.: And, of course, your father Frantz Jourdain was president of the Salon d'Automne and had a profound interest in modern art.

F. J.: *Yes. Painters and writers were always in the house. My family were close friends of Daudet, Zola and Goncourt. My father took me with him to exhibitions. I can clearly remember the Palais de l'Industrie, where the Salon was held. That was the great artistic event of the year. Painters spent months getting their things ready for it. Bad art was enthroned there and Puvis de Chavannes' "Le Pauvre Pêcheur" was considered unbelievably daring. My mother often told me that people used to arrange to meet in front of it and "have a good laugh".*

H. P.: When did you first discover the artists whom we admire to-day ?

F. J.: *In 1891. I was fifteen. Two posters made me aware of a whole new world. One was by Bonnard—for 'France-Champagne'. In its form and its use of arabesque it was absolutely new— extraordinary, in the true sense of that word. It was either a masterpiece or complete drivel : there could be nothing in between. At about the same time I saw on the Avenue de l'Opéra another poster. It was being pulled along on a little cart, advertised the 'bal du Moulin Rouge', and represented la Goulue and Valentin-le-Désossé. It was signed 'Hautrec'—or so I thought. It was Toulouse-Lautrec, of course; and I said to myself "I wonder what that's all about ?" I really had the feeling that an unknown world was somewhere round the corner. Soon after that I went with my father to the gallery that Le Barc de Boutteville had opened at 47, rue Le Peletier. I found there more Bonnards and more Lautrecs and also pictures by a score or so of their friends*

and their seniors. My work for the baccalauréat was much the worse for this discovery, for from that day onwards I spent the best part—yes, really the best part— of my time in that gallery !

H. P.: Tanguy and Vollard and Durand-Ruel are famous for the part they played in the art-world of that time, but Le Barc de Boutteville remains comparatively unknown. Could you tell me something about him ?

F. J.: *Le Barc de Boutteville had made a little money by selling old pictures by minor masters. One day Paul Vogler, who was quite a friend of his, got him to go to the Salon des Indépendants. "There's a whole school of very talented young people there", he said. At that time the "Indépendants" were mostly academic painters who weren't even good enough to get into the Salon, but there was one room, just one, in which you could see real painting—and by that I mean the neo-Impressionists, the Nabis, Lautrec, Signac, etc. Le Barc de Boutteville realised that a new and very promising generation was on its way up. He sold his old pictures, repainted the front of his shop and put up a sign : "Impressionists and Symbolists". On the left side of the show-window there was a big notice with the names of all the painters he was interested in. I remember that Manet was at the top of the list. They weren't in alphabetical order, and from time to time he'd add the name of some young chap who was beginning to show what he could do. Monet, Pissarro and Sisley were on the list, of course. I remember that it ended with Willette and Zuloaga, which shows that Le Barc de Boutteville was eclectic in his interests. The painters who made up the interest of the gallery were above all the Nabis and the neo-Impressionists. Bonnard, Vuillard, Lautrec, Maurice Denis, Ranson and Roussel showed their earliest pictures there. Signac and his friends, the neo-Impressionists, liked to keep themselves to themselves and they soon left the gallery.*

An unpublished photograph of Toulouse-Lautrec. It was taken by Guibert, the brother of a friend of Lautrec who for years was close to both Lautrec and his cousin Gabriel Tapié de Celeyran. Lautrec jokingly pretends that his walking-stick is a fishing-rod.

H. P.: Did Le Barc sell many pictures?

F. J: *No. You must remember that at that time the 'connoisseurs' and the enlightened critics were still calling Monet a practical joker, Renoir an ignoramus, Degas a painter of hideosities. Some of them had begun to back-pedal a little, though. As for the wretched Cézanne, everybody thought he'd died years ago and nobody—not even Durand-Ruel, for all his perspicacity—would have dared to show even a sketch from the hand of such a 'pitiable failure'. Le Barc's protégés were almost the only ones to consider Cézanne a great artist. Try as I could, I couldn't get to see one of his "formless beginnings" anywhere.*

H. P.: What were Le Barc's prices like?

F. J.: *They varied from 50 to 500 francs —but only the very largest pictures went up to 500. Two hundred francs was the average price. You could get a water-color for 20 francs: gold francs, of course...*

H. P.: And it was then that you first met the artists who were to become your friends?

F. J.: *Yes, and they were unforgettably kind to me. With a very few exceptions they were simple and natural and as free from pretention as they were from jealousy. I never once heard them talk of the prices they fetched or their standing in the market. Things are very different now: that's why that period of my youth*

Signature of the dealer Le Barc de Boutteville on a letter to Jourdain. Less well known than Vollard or Durand-Ruel, he played a rôle comparable to theirs. He bought mainly Nabis and neo-Impressionists. Bonnard, Vuillard and Lautrec were among his artists.

has such enchantment for me. They lived in their own little circle and thought of nothing but their art. Some, like Monet and Rodin, rarely opened their mouths. When those two came to dine with my parents... I remember that once I saw them bowing and gesturing to one another as to who, as the elder, should go into a room first. There was no way of deciding, for they were born in the same year, 1840, and on the same day, November 14th... Yes, when Monet and Rodin came to dine, they sat in a corner and never said a word. No doubt a certain timidity restrained them from joining in the general conversation, for there were some very brilliant talkers about... Alphonse Daudet, especially: he had a very pretty southern accent and knew how to make the most of it. But even among their own friends Monet and Renoir rarely spoke. In 1889 my father went with Monet and Gustave Geffroy to visit the poet Maurice Rollinat at Fresselines, in the department of Creuse. *Monet loved the Creuse and later went there to work. He never voiced his enthusiasm, but from time to time he would stand still and look hard at the landscape and say to himself "Nom de Dieu de Dieu de Dieu..." During one of these walks Geffroy mislaid his black overcoat, and his friends tried to help him find it. Rollinat suggested that they should climb a hill which gave a clear view over the surrounding country. When they got to the top Monet pointed to a distant speck of black: "There's your coat", he said. "No, no", said the others, "That's a tree-stump". But Monet insisted: "It must be Geffroy's coat", he said, "That particular black does not exist in Nature". And he was quite right—it was Geffroy's coat!*

H. P.: Now, if ever, is the time to quote Cézanne's remark that "Monet is only an eye, but what an eye!"

F. J.: *I also remember the exhibition at which Monet showed his first "Nymphéas" pictures. I was with Signac, and there was one other visitor: Degas. He went from one picture to another with an air of the deepest displeasure, gesturing towards each canvas as if, in his exasperation, he would have liked to tear it apart. Monet appeared, and Signac and I hurried over to say how much we admired the pictures. Degas came up and could hardly contain himself: "I'm going", he said, "I'm beginning to feel dizzy. All these pictures make me dizzy". And he went. And Monet, who was clearly very much hurt—the exhibition represented several years' work—said "Brrr! That old Degas! He's a real terror, isn't he!"*

H. P.: Could we go back to the time when you met Le Barc's painters? You saw a great deal of Lautrec...

This drawing, heightened with water-color, was made by Maurice Delcourt, the wood-engraver, and represents his friend Francis Jourdain. In the background is the poet Henri Levey.

F. J.: *Lautrec was kindness itself. People have often got him entirely wrong. Because he was crippled they made him out to be bitter, sharp-tongued, misanthropic. It wouldn't have been surprising if he'd been malicious, but I don't believe that he*

Puvis de Chavannes: The Poor Fisherman. **1881. Petit Palais, Paris. At the end of the last century this seemed a revolutionary picture. The young Nabis — Sérusier, Maurice Denis, Vuillard — saw it as a model of the 'unassertive color' which was then their aim.**

ever was. He was perfectly simple, loved a joke, and was usually gay and welcoming. I can't think of a better word than 'kindness' or 'niceness' for his chief characteristic. He wasn't in the least vain either of his title, his ancient lineage, his talent, or anything else. He was modest, kind-hearted and a great enthusiast. I can still hear him saying "Well? What d'you think? Pretty good, isn't it? Admirable!" of one or other of the objects which cluttered his studio: the little hamper in which his mother had sent him provisions, or a quarryman's umbrella, of heavy oiled canvas, which Natanson had brought back for him from Poland. Lautrec had a passion for things that had been thought right through: and he liked these objects because they fulfilled their purpose exactly. When he wanted to define his attitude to life he would often use the phase: "Just say what is in your mind". He liked ellipsis in conversation, and never passed judgment. "Know your limits and don't go beyond them: stick to the matter in hand": that was what he was driving at. And he lived up to it. I can see him now: magnificent eyes above a mouth that struck pity and terror.

Doubtless he suffered from some deficiency of the bones. It's been said that he had a man's body on the legs of a child, but I'm not sure that that was quite true. His arms were those of a dwarf. He always wore a hat of some sort, because

he was terrified—so his close friends told me—that someone would give him a pat on the head. This, however well meant, might have been fatal, for—so these same friends said—his fontanel had never quite closed up.

H. P.: What was Lautrec's attitude towards his parents?

F. J: *He had great respect and affection for his mother. She spent several months in Paris every year, and it was on her account that he had taken a little flat in the rue Fontaine; he arranged it himself and decorated it with Japanese prints.*

H. P.: And what about that eccentric gentleman, his father?

F. J.: *I never heard Lautrec make fun of his father. He had, in fact, a certain regard for him and would show, almost with pride, the little bronze animals that his father had sculpted. They were curiously well made, as a matter of fact.*

H. P.: And did you know Gauguin?

F. J.: *Hardly at all, and I never found him very pleasant, as a person. I met him after his accident at Concarneau.*

H. P.: That's to say in 1894-1895, between his first and second journeys to the South Seas.

F. J.: *Gauguin rather liked to play the 'cher Maître'. I remember calling on Durio, the sculptor, who had an unbounded*

9

Van Gogh: « Les Aliscamps. » **One of the pictures which impressed Francis Jourdain on his first visit to 'Papa Tanguy'.**

admiration for Gauguin, and seeing there a canvas which Gauguin had signed "To my disciple Durio..." Just that! That shocked me : it revealed a complete absence of camaraderie. I was not yet sixteen when I wrote for 'La Plume' an article saying that the real inventor of 'Gauguinisme' was not Gauguin but Emile Bernard.

H. P.: That's an interesting point. I'd love to know what you think about this question, which has caused so much controversy among historians.

F. J.: *I haven't changed my opinion. Gauguin went to Brittany because he was tired of impressionist analysis (its objects had never quite satisfied him) and also because he'd had enough of Parisian life. He went, as he said, "in search of a certain sadness", and in order to devise a way of getting clear of realism. Realism had let him down. In 1888, at Pont Aven,*

he met a twenty-year-old painter, Emile Bernard, who brought him greetings from their mutual friend Van Gogh and showed him a few of his own studies. Gauguin was too vain to admit, in later years, to the enormous effect of these studies upon him. He was, after all, twice Bernard's age at the time, yet Bernard's pictures had determined, or at any rate greatly influenced, the direction he was next to take. In them, certain ideas, as yet only half-formed in Gauguin's mind, were not merely confirmed but shown to be valid in action. Bernard gave me documentary proof that he had 'been there first' : Gauguin was too conceited to admit this.

I saw a lot of Bernard. He received me in the wooden studio in his parents' little garden at Asnières where Van Gogh, too, had often called on him to talk painting.

H. P.: But didn't Bernard speak of Cézanne ? He was one of his first admirers.

F. J.: *Yes, and it was at Bernard's that I first saw one of that difficult master's landscapes. I must admit that it took me some time to understand his sorrowful, magnificent and, at that time, disconcerting genius. Towards 1892, Bernard wrote to me from Brittany and urged me to go, on his recommendation, and see his friend le père Tanguy, who was ill... Yes, that's right : Tanguy was in hospital when I first saw him. Then when he was back in his shop in the rue Clauzel I often went to see him with my dear friend Léon-Paul Fargue. There I really came to know Cézanne's work. We used to turn over the pictures by him, and by Van Gogh, that were stacked against the walls.*

H. P.: Do you remember exactly which pictures you saw at Tanguy's ?

F. J.: *Well now—there was a Van Gogh 'Berceuse', the big 'Arlésienne', a*

Bonnard: « Garden ». **Private coll. Paris. Jourdain was an early admirer of this Nabi painter. ▶**

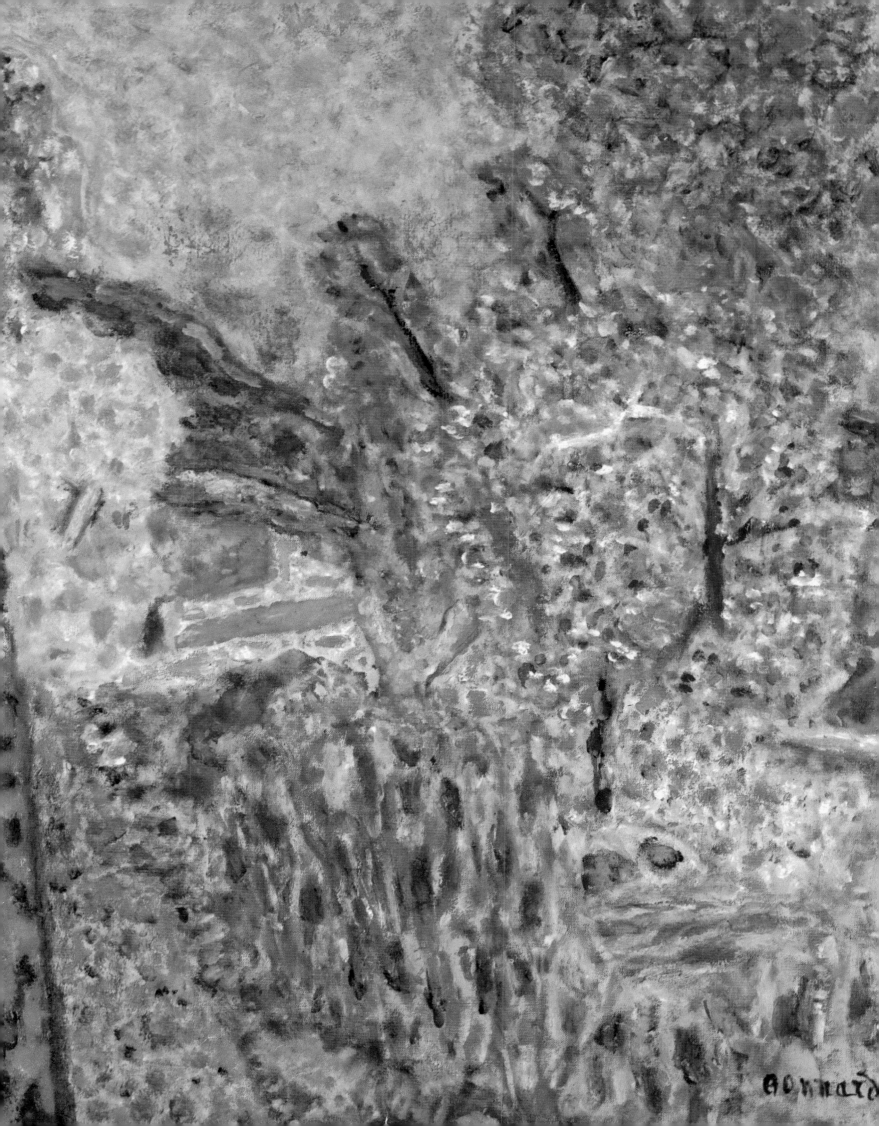

A Monet reproduced for the first time in color: « Les Nymphéas. » 39½″x79″. 1919. Private coll., Paris.

'Sunflowers', Tanguy's portrait, some still lives, a view of Arles through the trees, the 'Aliscamps', and some works of the Auvers period. The 'Daubigny's Garden' was hung on the wall. As to Cézanne, I remember especially a big landscape. One day, out of curiosity, I asked Tanguy how much it was. "It's something I'm very fond of", he said, "and I wouldn't sell it for less than 600 francs". And he blushed, as if he'd said "I want fifteen million for it". But, as I said, Cézanne's pictures were harder to understand than Van Gogh's, with their immediate appeal. To grasp the full extent of Cézanne's genius you had to make, as it were, an intellectual effort... Ah, Tanguy! What a saint he was! He was really touching. Goodness personified, goodness in the likeness of a color-grinder. He believed in his painters—"ces messieurs", as he called them. For Van Gogh he had a veritable cult, and it was of Van Gogh that we made him speak

most. *There were also pictures by Maurice Denis in the shop, and by Ibels, Bernard, and Gauguin—the 'Bonjour, Monsieur Gauguin'—a self-portrait, and a little 'Yellow Christ'...*

H. P.: I know that you did not meet Cézanne till much later. You and Charles Camoin went to see him at Aix.

F. J.: *Yes, and how moved we were!*

Cézanne had been for so long a man of mystery, and so many legends had sprung up about him, that I felt I was about to enter the presence of... I don't know how to explain it, but... of God Himself. It was quite supernatural.

H. P.: And were you disappointed?

F. J.: *Not at all. Cézanne made us extremely welcome. He said in his slyest*

way that "Impressionism's done for—it's all a joke!" but a few moments later he was singing the praises of "Pissarro the humble Colossus". It seemed to us that there was an element of contradiction in the master's words—for Pissarro was certainly an Impressionist. And when I ventured to ask Cézanne what advice he would give to a young painter he said "Let him copy his stove-pipe".

Le Père Tanguy

BY HENRI PERRUCHOT

*How a modest color-grinder's shop became one of the high places of impressionist
and post-impressionist painting*

All witnesses are agreed on the subject of *"le père Tanguy"*. He played a preponderant role in the dazzling renewal of French painting at the end of the 19th century. Just after he died Octave Mirbeau said of him that "the story of his humble and upright life is inseparable from the history of the Impressionist group... and when that history comes to be written, Tanguy will have his place in it". He couldn't have been more right. Maurice Denis once said that his little shop in the rue Clauzel was the "origin of the great gust of fresh air that blew new life into French art in and around the year 1890"; and Emile Bernard would have it that "the so-called Pont Aven school would be more accurately named the Rue Clauzel school".

Julien-François Tanguy was a Breton. He was born on June the 28th, 1825, half a dozen miles from Saint-Brieuc, in a village in the commune of Plédran, where his father was a weaver. The fifth child of a very poor, indeed almost penniless family, he went to Saint-Brieuc while still very young, and began life as a plasterer. In 1855, when he was thirty, he married a *charcutière*, abandoned his former trade, and helped his wife to market her ham and sausages. Whether he disliked being a pork-

butcher, or whether they just couldn't make a go of it, is not known: but in any case, in 1860, he and his wife, and the little daughter who had been born to them meanwhile, made off to Paris. There, Tanguy was employed by the Compagnie de l'Ouest until in 1865 he found work as a color-grinder with the firm of Edouard in the rue Clauzel, which at that time had a great reputation among artists. Soon after this he set up on his own, prepared his own colors, and hawked them himself in those parts of France which were becoming popular among open-air painters. So it was that he came to know Pissarro, Manet, Renoir, Monet, Cézanne—all of them then more or less unknown — at Barbizon, or Ecouen, or Argenteuil, or Sarcelles...

Unfortunately the war of 1870 interrupted all this and embroiled "Papa Tanguy" in a sequence of catastrophic adventures. What happened exactly is still a little obscure, but it's beyond question that at the time of the Commune Tanguy was one of the Fédérés. He was taken prisoner, sent to Satory, court-martialled and found guilty. He was sent to Brest, and there rotted until one of his fellow-Bretons, the academic painter Jobbé-Duval, who was a member of the Paris Conseil Municipal, managed to get him a pardon.

He was back in Paris in 1873, or thereabouts, and reverted to color-grinding. As the firm of Edouard had just left the rue Clauzel he seized the opportunity of opening a shop in that very street, at no. 14.

The painters whom Papa Tanguy had known before the war, and who at once gave him their custom, were at that time in the thick of the fight. Their first group exhibition was to open on the Boulevard des Capucines in the spring of 1874; and on that occasion an art critic, M. Louis Leroy, who saw himself as something of a humorist, gave them the name of "Impressionists" in the "Charivari"; and, as everyone knows, the name stuck. Papa Tanguy became the most fervent and loyal of the Impressionists' allies: as to just how this came about, a word of explanation is needed.

Papa Tanguy was a man of golden good nature. Heavy and dullish at first glance, he was in reality the most delicate, pure-minded and upright of men. He was easy-going almost to a fault: never did a painter appeal to him in vain for credit—and often this credit remained open indefinitely. Papa Tanguy was, in his own way, a stoic: "Anyone who spends more than fifty centimes a day is a blackguard" he liked to say, and the phrase fits the man in whom the kindness of an evangelist was allied to a natural sympathy for the revolutionary and the rebel.

For Tanguy had put himself on the side of the rebels ever since he had fought with the Fédérés and had a taste of prison life. The Impressionists, his friends, were making enemies on every hand; they must be fought for, tooth and nail. In his simple, tender-hearted way Tanguy thought that painting in

Le Père Tanguy. 92″×72″, circa 1887, Musée Rodin, Paris. Van Gogh left three portraits of Tanguy. This one is the most famous. It shows the elderly storekeeper wearing a Breton straw hat and backed by a number of Japanese prints.

Above : Van Gogh's Guinguette. *19¾″×33½″, Musée de l'Impressionisme, Paris. In 1886 or thereabouts Van Gogh painted the inner garden of a little restaurant in Montmartre which had been a favorite with painters since the beginning of Impressionism. It was at the corner of the rue Sainte Rustique and the rue des Saules and was then called "Le Franc Buveur". It still exists, but now bears the name of "A la Bonne Franquette" and draws its clientèle from the numerous tourists who visit* La Butte. *Opposite, Van Gogh's garden as it is to-day; page 19, the outside of the restaurant photographed when Van Gogh was alive.*

a high key was Revolution itself. Anyone who fought for the victory of Impressionism and stood up for "the men of our *School*" (he liked to linger on the word) was fighting for a radiant, high-keyed to-morrow. And besides—Tanguy liked Impressionist painting for itself, and detested the "tobacco-juice" tonality which the middle classes of his time had taken to their hearts.

Unendingly generous by nature, Tanguy liked to assemble "his" painters around his frugal table. Paints and canvas he gave them gladly, and in return would take a picture or two : and what pictures, after all ! No one else would look at them. Ribaldry and sarcasm met them on every side : the Pissarros, it seemed, were simply "palette-scrapings laid one after another on dirty canvas"; the Monets were painted "much as people touch up fountain-basins" and as for the Cézannes, they were best not talked of : it would be many years

before they were considered as anything but "painting as a drunken scavenger would see it" as someone remarked.

To get back some of his expenses—and, of course, to help his artists—Tanguy tried to sell some of the canvases which cluttered his shop in ever greater numbers ; but only rarely did he succeed. His pictures were pledges that none could redeem. His collection grew steadily bigger and bigger until the shop became a real little avant-

meanwhile from no. 14 to no. 9, by the way) was the only place in Paris where Cézannes could be seen.

"People went to Tanguy's as if to a museum", Emile Bernard tells us, "to see some studies by the unknown painter who lived at Aix... The unpretentious shop became, without knowing it, a Parisian legend. It was talked of in every studio. Members of the *Institut*, influential critics and writers who wanted to set everything to rights—all flocked there. Such was the unsettling effect of these canvases... the young people sensed that they were works of genius, their elders saw in them the madness of paradox, and the envious invoked the name of impotence".

Gauguin, Sérusier, Anquetin, Signac and Maurice Denis were among those who came to Papa Tanguy's shop to learn the lesson of Cézanne. (Later, as is well known, Cézanne, never the most conciliatory of men, was to accuse Gauguin of stealing from him his *petite sensation*.) But there were many other regular visitors, from Octave Mirbeau to Francis Jourdain and Léon-Paul Fargue, and from Toulouse-Lautrec to Dom Verkade and Jacques-Emile Blanche. It was also—and this is a remarkable fact—in Tanguy's window that in 1892 Ambroise Vollard saw a Cézanne for the first time. Nor, of course, must we forget Van Gogh who in 1886 and 1887 was a daily visitor to the shop. He had a profound admiration for Cézanne, and one day, to his great joy,

he lunched with the Master of Aix at Tanguy's. The two artists set forth their ideas on painting : at the end of the meal Van Gogh gave Cézanne one of his pictures and Cézanne, abrupt as ever, looked hard at it and said : "No, but honestly—that's a madman's painting".

Tanguy held Cézanne in the deepest and most respectful regard ; no less strong, for that matter, were his feelings for Van Gogh. And when, on returning from Provence in 1890, Van Gogh shot himself dead at Auvers-sur-Oise, Tanguy wept for him as if he had been his own son.

Octave Mirbeau once described a visit to Tanguy, not long after Van Gogh's death. "Ah, poor Vincent !", Tanguy lamented. "What a misfortune ! Monsieur Mirbeau ! What a misfortune ! What a great misfortune ! A genius like him ! And such a delightful fellow ! But wait—I'll show you some more of his masterpieces !" Papa Tanguy went off to fetch more Van Goghs from the back of his shop and came back with four or five in his arms and two in each hand. As he laid them lovingly against the backs of his chairs, shifting and turning them to get the best light, he went on groaning : "Poor Vincent ! Are those masterpieces ?—Or are they not ? And there are so many of them, so many... And they're so beautiful that when I look at them it gives me a pain here, in my breast... Why should a man like that die ? It's not right, it really

garde museum of contemporary art and a meeting-place for all those who supported the Impressionists and liked to know what was new in the world of art. It was Cézanne's work, above all, that they came to see. During the third Impressionist exhibition in 1877 Cézanne was attacked so violently, and suffered so deeply in consequence, that he decided that never again would he show his pictures in public. For nearly twenty years—until the famous exhibition organised by Vollard in 1895, which marked the beginnings of his great fame—he took no part in the activities of the art-world. And during all that time, or at any rate until Tanguy died in 1894, the shop in the rue Clauzel (moved

The catalogue of the Tanguy sale is here reproduced for the first time. The only known copy belongs to the successor of the auctioneer who held the sale on June 2nd 1894. The prices and the buyers' names are written in the margin. The picture by Cazin, a painter of landscapes and historical subjects who was much admired at the time for "the infectious melancholy of his twilights", went for twenty times as much as the Cézanne, bought by Vollard, which we reproduce above : Village (18⅛″ × 21″).

isn't... Poor Vincent... I'll bet you don't know his "Pot of Gladiolus" ? It's one of the last things he did. Marv—ellous, simply marv—ellous ! I must show it to you—when it came to flowers there was no one to touch him, no one. He had such a feeling for everything..." And Papa drew a circle in the air, as painters do, as if to single out some part of a painting for particular notice. "Just look at that sky ! And those trees ! Aren't they just right ? And the color ! And the movement, I ask you !"

From time to time some lover of painting would buy a picture from the shop in the rue Clauzel. But Papa Tanguy's business methods were not at all those of the dealer-speculator. For his Cézannes he had a fixed price : a hundred francs for a large canvas, forty for a

small one. The story is told of an enthusiast who asked the price of a Van Gogh : "Just a moment !", said Tanguy, and went and pored over his account-book. "That'll be 48 francs", he said, finally. "48 ? That's an odd figure—why not 50 ? Or 40 ?" "Well", said Tanguy, "48 francs is exactly what poor Van Gogh owed me when he died".

No, Papa Tanguy was not at all a speculator. "How he loved the pictures that he was obliged to sell !" Dom Verkade remembered. "Often he was in despair at seeing so fine a picture go out of his shop". And there was one picture that he would never consider selling : his own portrait by Van Gogh. (It is now in the Musée Rodin in Paris.) Vollard tells us that when anyone

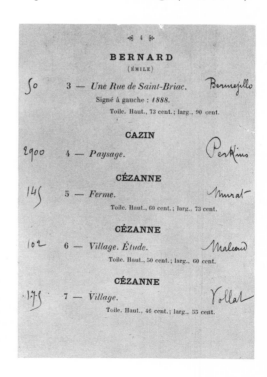

wanted to make a bid for it Tanguy would coldly ask a flat five hundred francs. This, at that time, was enough to put off any potential buyer at the start.

These idiosyncratic methods meant that Papa Tanguy never became rich —was never, indeed, even moderately well off. He remained to the day of his death frugal in the extreme and lived as sparingly as he possibly could. Yet fate had another hammer-blow in store for him : when he died, in 1894, it was of cancer of the stomach, and he had had to suffer appallingly. He had been taken to hospital, but when he sensed that the end was near he asked to be brought back to the rue Clauzel. "I want to die in my own home, with my wife beside me and my pictures all around". One evening he gave his wife his last instructions : "Life won't be easy for you when I'm not there. Our pictures are all we've got. You mustn't hesitate to sell them..." He was saying good-bye : the next morning, February 6th 1894, he died.

Madame Tanguy followed her husband's advice and made what money she could from the canvases which were still in the shop. The sale was held at the Hotel Drouot on June 2nd 1894. It brought in 14,621 francs—not a bad total, in itself, especially for people like the Tanguys who had been poor all their lives. (It was the equivalent of 2,500,000 francs today.) But in relation

This photograph of the "Franc Buveur" dates from the period at which Papa Tanguy's friends were regular customers there and belongs to the Bibliothèque Nationale, Paris.

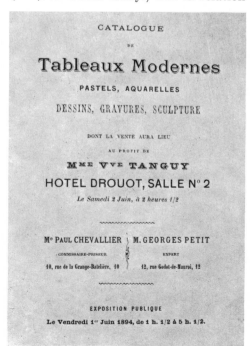

to the masterpieces which came under the hammer it was pitiably small. The only picture that got anything like a good price was a Monet, a view of Bordighera, which fetched 3000 francs. Six Cézannes (five went to Vollard and one to Victor Chocquet) went for 902 francs in all : their individual prices varied between 92 and 215 francs, and the auctioneer actually complimented Vollard on his 'recklessness' in bidding up to the latter figure ! The six Gauguins didn't average as much as 100 francs each. The Guillaumin went for between 80 and 160 apiece. Pissarro got up to more than 400, but a Seurat was knocked down for 50, and a Van Gogh for 30.

Papa Tanguy would have been deeply hurt, no doubt, to read of these prices. He had so longed to see his painters triumph—and that triumph, as it seemmed, lay still in the distant future. But it was nearer than those concerned then dared to think. Only a year later Vollard was to hold his Cézanne exhibition, and in 1899, at the Chocquet sale, the painting by Cézanne which Chocquet had bought at the Tanguy sale (it was the *Pont de Mennecy*) was to fetch 2200 francs. Thereafter the prices rose continually—and not of Cézanne only, but of all Papa Tanguy's painters.

He never got rich, Papa Tanguy, but he wrote a fine page in the history of French art.

Victor Chocquet, customs officer

BY HENRI PERRUCHOT

*A civil servant who sacrificed professional advancement to his passion for painting,
Chocquet was discerning enough to buy Cézannes and brave enough to stand up for them*

The first Impressionist group exhibition was held in 1874 and, as everyone
now knows, seemed only to amuse and
exasperate its visitors. In the following year four of the despised painters
— Renoir, Monet, Sisley and Berthe
Morisot — decided to put up their works
at the Hotel Drouot in the hope of
making a little money. The sale took
place on March 24th in circumstances
of unbelievable disorder. Each picture
was received with howls of indignation
as it was put on the stand. The room was
crowded, arguments broke out all over
the place, brawls threatened. The auctioneer had to ask for police protection
before the sale could run its course,
and in spite of the efforts of one or two
discerning enthusiasts like Caillebotte
and Théodore Duret, the sale was,
financially speaking, a complete fiasco.
The 73 pictures went for absurdly low
prices, and Albert Wolff, the 'Figaro'
critic, took the opportunity of saying
that "the impression left by the impressionists is that of a cat walking on
the keyboard of a piano or a monkey
playing with a color-box".

But the Impressionists did, at least,
win one new friend at the Hotel Drouot :
Victor Chocquet, an official in the
Customs & Excise department, who
collected in a small way and had a
passion for Delacroix. They had noticed
him at the sale as one of the few who
stood out against the howling mob—a
man no longer quite young, tall in
stature, with fine silver hair, a thin,

Césanne : The Little Bridge. 23¼″ × 28⅜″. *Once in Chocquet's collection, now in the Louvre.*

bony, almost ascetic face and eyes that burned with a fever of intensity in their hollow sockets. He had been vehement, though always perfectly polite, in their defence. Who could he be ?

Renoir found out next day, when a letter arrived, complimenting him on his pictures and asking if he would consent to paint a portrait of Madame Chocquet. It seemed that Chocquet had wanted to visit the group exhibition, but had been dissuaded by his friends ; and then, to his great joy, had just happened to drop in at the Hotel

Drouot. Renoir's pictures had reminded him a little of his revered Delacroix, of whose work he possessed a substantial collection.

Renoir and Chocquet liked one another at once. Chocquet was the personification of the true collector, who cares nothing for fashion or finance. He had not much to spend ; often he went without, and cut down on clothes and food, in order to buy pictures, he did not even possess a warm overcoat for the winter, but he had, in its place, what money cannot buy : Taste. He

only bought what he loved. Art for him was, in fact, more than a pleasure— it was a necessity—Life itself. Chocquet could have gone higher in the civil service, had he been willing to be posted to some frontier-station. But he had preferred to sacrifice his advancement, stay in Paris, and be free to ferret about among the antique dealers, the print-shops, and the bookstalls on the quays. What with his unfailing eye, his limitless patience and the imbecility of an age which held even Delacroix in low esteem, he had made quite an

21

Pissarro : Fog. 21¼″×25½″. 1874. Once in Chocquet's collection, now owned by Durand-Ruel

important collection in his apartment, which was in the Rue de Rivoli and looked on to the Tuileries gardens. Renoir was amazed by what he saw there : twenty paintings by Delacroix and a profusion of drawings and watercolors by the same master, Courbets, Manets, a Corot, furniture of the sixteenth century and the periods of Louis XIII, the Régence, Louis XV and XVI, a whole collection of old clocks, faiences from Nevers and Lorraine, porcelain from Sèvres, the Compagnie des Indes, Tournai, Chantilly, Saint-Cloud...

From the moment he met Chocquet, Renoir realised that here, if anywhere, was the man who would see the point of Cézanne. And so, one day, he took Chocquet along to Papa Tanguy's shop in the rue Clauzel. Cézanne was at that time the most despised of all the Impressionist group, but Renoir's intuition was proved right : Chocquet took to Cézanne's paintings from the start.

He picked out a *Baigneuses* and bought it at once. "How well that will look", he said, "between a Delacroix and a Courbet !" And he set off homewards in the highest spirits, with Renoir at his side. But when they got there he was suddenly seized with anxiety : perhaps his wife wouldn't like the picture ? "Look here, Renoir", he said. "Do me a favor : tell my wife that the Cézanne belongs to you and, when you go away, forget to take it with you. Then Marie will have time to get used to it before I confess to her that it's mine, after all".

The confession was not long delayed, for Chocquet was now longing to make Cézanne's acquaintance. Would Renoir invite him to call on the Chocquets? He did: and it was clear from the threshold that the two men were of one mind. "They tell me you like Delacroix", said Cézanne as he stepped in. "I adore Delacroix", said Chocquet. "Come and see what I have by him". In a few moments, portfolios were opened and drawers ransacked, and drawings and watercolors by Delacroix were spread everywhere—on tables and commodes, on the pink silk of the Louis XVI fauteuils, even on the floor. Chocquet and Cézanne darted about the room, examining, re-examining, shouting aloud with pleasure and admiration. Suddenly their feelings overcame them and they began to weep. A great friendship had begun.

Cézanne found in Chocquet what we now call "a moral support". Chocquet was alert to Cézanne's every intention and came to regard him as the greatest painter alive. Whenever painting was mentioned in his presence, three words rose instantly to his lips: "What about Cézanne?" Unluckily he did not often convert his friends. Vollard tells us, for instance, that one day Chocquet arrived at Renoir's house in radiant good humor. He had persuaded a mutual friend, one of the earliest patrons of the Impressionists, to accept a little Cézanne study as a present. "I don't ask you to hang it, of course". Chocquet had said. "I should think not!", said the great connoisseur, "What an example to set to my daughter, who is learning to draw!" "But, as a favor to me", Chocquet had gone on, "do look at it from time to time. Just put it in a drawer and take it out occasionally". Later, when Cézanne's prices were rising steeply, the amateur in question turned up the long-forgotten canvas and hurried off to sell it. "Ah", he said, rubbing his hands, "How happy that madman Chocquet would be if he could see how much it'll fetch!"

Chocquet soon came to know all the Impressionists, and naturally he stood by them when they appeared in public. During the exhibitions of 1876 and 1877, when the newspapers covered his friends

Manet: The pavement layers of the rue de Berne, *detail.* 25¹/₅″ × 31³/₅″. *1878. Formerly owned by Chocquet, now in the R.A. Butler collection, London.*

with derision and the public came only to jeer, Chocquet was always at hand. From morning till night he took his friends' part, arguing and cajoling in front of their canvases. Ironical and vehement by turns, insistent though always polite, he did all that he could to persuade those who turned away in rage or laughter that they were making a mistake. But it was mostly in vain, and he was taken, as a rule, for a well-mannered madman. The exhibition of

1877 was a particularly bitter experience for him, in that the picture most savagely attacked was his own portrait by Cézanne. One journalist called this "Billoir in chocolate" (Billoir was a murderer who had just been executed for cutting a woman in pieces). "If you happen to go to the show with a lady who is in an 'interesting condition'", the 'Charivari' wrote, "hurry past M. Cézanne's portrait. The brownshoe-leather face might frighten your

companion and give her 'expected' yellow fever in the womb''. Ribaldry and sarcasm never failed to greet the picture.

On other occasions Chocquet showed a fine turn of mischief in his friends' defence. Himself from Lille, he took a great delight, as Renoir tells us, in "putting the locals right about the reputation of Carolus-Duran, who was also born at Lille". "Carolûsse Dûran ?", he would say, to those who spoke of *The Lady with the Glove* and its author. "Carolûsse Dûran ? No, I've never heard him mentioned in Paris. Cézanne, Renoir, Monet—they're the people that everyone talks of. But this Carolûsse of yours,—no, really I think you're on the wrong track !"

It was not only in words that Chocquet defended the Impressionists. He also, of course, bought many of their pictures. Until he knew them, Delacroix was the mainstay of his collection. His holding covered every aspect of the master's work, and amounted to 23 canvases, 35 water-colors, and 24 drawings. He also had 3 Courbets, a Corot, several Manets and works by other painters—Tassaert among them. Among the Impressionists he had three particular favorites : Cézanne, whom he ranked first of them all, Renoir, and Monet.

Over the years he bought some 10 Monets, among them a *Haystack*, *View of Argenteuil*, and a *Cliff at Varangeville*. Among his 20 or so Renoirs were a replica of the *Moulin de la Galette* and a view of the *Grenouillère*. As for his Cézannes, they made a magnificent counter-balance to his Delacroix, alike in numbers (32 oil-paintings and three water-colors) and in quality. It's difficult to imagine a finer ensemble : views of Auvers-sur-Oise, the *Mur d'Enceinte*, the *Little Bridge*, the famous *Maison du Pendu*, some still lives, the *Mardi Gras*, a l'Estaque landscape, of which Cézanne had written that "It's like a playing card—red roofs on the blue sea".

Towards the end of his life Chocquet came into money, and moved from his

Manet : Monet in his studio. 31½" × 38⅝". *Chocquet bought several Manets.*

flat in the Rue de Rivoli to a little 18th century town-house in the Rue Monsigny. But, contrary to his expectations, he was not happier for the change. In fact he was bored and fell into melancholy. The house was darker than his old flat, and although there was more room for his collections they never got enough light. Chocquet also missed his marvellous view across the Tuileries gardens. And perhaps above all, as Georges Rivière suggests, "Chocquet got less fun out of his discoveries, now that he was rich".

After Chocquet and his wife had died his collections were put up to auction, on July 1st, 3rd and 4th, 1899, at the Galerie Georges Petit, Rue de Sèze. The Delacroix went for from 30 to 9500 francs ($15 to $4750, in present-day terms), the Corot for 290 francs ($145), one of the Courbets for 2750 francs ($1375), and Manet's *Paveurs de la rue de Berne* for 13,500 francs ($6750). A Monet *View of Argenteuil* fetched 11,500 francs ($5750), the Renoir *La Grenouillère* 20,000 francs ($10,000).

Among the Cézannes, the most sought-after was the *Maison du Pendu*, which Isaac de Camondo bought for 6200 francs ($3100) and the *Mardi Gras*, which fetched 4400 francs ($2200). Not all the Cézannes, by any means, fetched this kind of price. The cheapest went for 145 francs ($72.50, to-day). And yet the sale did show a marked all-over rise in Cézanne's prices. For instance the *Little Bridge*, which Chocquet had bought for 170 francs at the Tanguy sale five years earlier, was knocked down for 2200 francs. But not everyone who bid up the Cézannes did so from pure admiration. Camondo, for instance, said later to Vollard about his purchase of the *Maison du Pendu* : "Not everyone likes it, of course, as yet, but I'm covered —I've a handwritten letter from Claude Monet to say that it's bound to be famous in the end. I'll show you that letter one day,—it's kept pinned up behind the picture, just in case people think I was crazy to buy it".

Vollard may have 'touched up' this story, but at least it shows, indirectly, how sure was the taste and how exquisite the sensibility of that convinced collector, Victor Chocquet.

in the kitchen

Cooking had no secrets for Toulouse-Lautrec

By Henri Perruchot

Who would have thought, to see Lautrec the dwarf making his painful way along the street, that the most violent appetites often traversed his invalid frame ? Yet such was the case, and never more so than when the pleasures of the table were in question. Not merely did he have a fastidious palate : he was greedy—as greedy, he used to say, as a Bishop's tabby.

It ran in his family. All the Toulouse-Lautrecs took care to eat well. Game, poultry, foie gras, and truffles abounded in their kitchens, where every dish was carefully thought out in advance. Quantity *and* quality reigned there and the "Lautrec stomach" was legendary. This we know from Mary Tapié de Celeyran, a connection of the painter, who tells us also that Lautrec was soon given the family-nickname of "Henri the cook" on account of his prowess in the kitchen. Frying-pan and casserole were favorite playthings of his and he loved to stand in front of the stove and supervise the execution of a recipe—often a rather extravagant one, as we may judge from the "Steak à la Lautrec" which Mary Tapié de Celeyran describes: "Take three steaks, grill them one on top of another (above a fire of vine-shoots, of course), don't spare the pepper or the mustard, and serve only the one which will be done perfectly : the middle one".

Lautrec had an artist's approach towards cooking. He was as exact with the ingredients of a dish as with the ingredients of a picture. In the one, as in the other, every detail deserved the minutest attention : a grain of salt one way or the other could make or mar the success of a dish. Where food was concerned nothing pleased him but perfection : each forkful had to open out in the mouth, as he said, "like a pea-cock's tail". And his sensibility was such that he always had in his pocket a nutmeg and a diminutive grater with which to perfume the glass of port that he might chance to take in a café.

For he was, alas ! as fond of liquids as of solids. He drank, first, "too much", and then doubled and redoubled the dose, never tiring of the "new cocktail" on which he and his friends would get hopelessly drunk. In the end, as everyone knows, drink killed him, and for some time previously it had the effect of taking away all appetite for food. But Lautrec remained a glutton to the end : his friends noticed only that it took an ever more delicate flavor to tempt him to eat.

Cooking had no secrets for Lautrec. "He knew", as Vuillard said, "every speciality in every restaurant in Paris, and could always say what should be eaten where, and so forth..." When he invited his friends to a meal the display was one of amazing virtuosity : nothing was left to chance, and every dish had the wine that best suited it. When he travelled, his journey often took on the air of a gastronomical campaign. When going from Paris to Bordeaux, for instance, he would take his time and embark at Le Havre on a cargo-boat headed for Dakar. Maurice Joyant, who was one of his closest friends and no mean authority on food, would sometimes go with him ; and he remembers that they always had in their luggage some cases of vintage port and olive oil. Lautrec, a tremendous tyrant where his pleasures were concerned, would turn the stokehold into a kitchen and insisted that the ship should put in at such fishing-ports as offered especially good fish. "Homard à l'américaine" and "Bourride Bordelaise" were two specialities of his (his recipes for them are given below) that came off particularly well at sea.

He soon became famous for his culinary gifts, and it was not surprising that Georges Henri-Manuel of the Bibliothèque Mazarine should one day invite him to come to his apartment and prepare this very "Homard à l'américaine". But Lautrec was the most mischievous of men ; and Henri-Manuel, who was a bachelor and almost exaggeratedly careful of his apartment and its excellent old furniture, was appalled to find that Lautrec insisted on preparing the dish on a portable electric stove in the very middle of the drawing-room. Lautrec's cousin Gabriel Tapié de Celeyran was, as usual, with him, and he did his best to dissuade the master-craftsman from his unexpected project. But a sharp "Mind your own business, Charlotte !" was all he got for his pains.

Paul Leclercq, who was also present, tells us that "Henri-Manuel's anxieties were heightened by the fact that a lobster which is to be cooked à l'américaine has to be cut up alive. Sheets were spread over the more valuable pieces of furniture, and then Lautrec, in a long white apron that got in the way of his little legs, went to work with his casseroles and a spoon hardly smaller than himself. So beautifully did he do it that not a thing in the room was spoiled. Henri-Manuel breathed again, and we sat down to a lobster that I shall remember for the rest of my days".

Lautrec loved a joke. Once it was Alfred Edwards, the founder of the 'Matin', who fell foul of him in this way : I have the story from Count de Cercy d'Eville. who had it from Edwards himself,

Lautrec knew that Edwards loved to eat well and was always interested in any new dish. One day, when he met him in the street, he said "I've got a treat for you, Edwards,—unless you've already tasted kangaroo ?" "Why, no", said Edwards, "I didn't even know it could be got in Paris". Lautrec went into a pantomime of astonishment : "But, my dear chap, it's the only thing a man can eat nowadays ! And it tastes simply too marvellous for words !" Edwards' appetite was whetted and he gladly agreed to meet Lautrec at eight o'clock that evening at Weber's in the Rue Royale.

"I turned up at Weber's", Edwards went on, "and Lautrec insisted on my having a tumbler of gin and vermouth, half gin and half vermouth. "It wont, hurt you", he said. "The vermouth neutralises the gin. It's the indispensable aperitif if you're eating kangaroo". So we drank the two gin-and-vermouths— they'd have felled an ox, if there'd been one around—and then Lautrec pushed me into a cab and we went off to a rather nasty little restaurant in the Rue Helder, where Lautrec had taken a private room. He didn't waste words with the head-waiter—just ordered hors d'œuvre, salade oranaise and jambon de Bayonne, with a bottle of Meursault. Next two fillets of kangaroo, with a bottle of Chambertin, and then the *collia*... At that I interrupted him : *collia*, he told me, were cocks' testicles. "You eat them like green peas". "That's something else I've never had", I said. "My dear Edwards", said Lautrec, "you've got a lot to learn".

"Anyway, the meal began, and there was plenty of spice in our hors d'œuvres. Then came the fillets of kangaroo. "Imagine a Hungarian goulash covered thickly with Cayenne pepper—something almost inconceivably hot to the taste. Lautrec said it was all exactly right, and after he'd gone on about it for a quarter of an hour I began to believe him. The Chambertin was absolutely first-class, by the way... The kangaroo was served in a sauce with new potatoes, sliced carrots and tomatoes. Lautrec warmed more and more to his theme as he told me how the whole dish was planned to stand up to the heaviest possible spicing. "It's common physiological sense", he said, "spices are indispensable to the proper functioning of the brain", and kangaroo-meat, which is the ideal nourishment for the man of genius, is nothing but a means—but a *perfect* one, mark you —of introducing spices into the human organism".

It goes without saying that they drank a great deal. The Chambertin was followed by a Corton 1872. And then came the *collia*. "The cocks' testicles made good eating", Edwards remembered, "and were served in a tartare-type sauce. They reminded me oddly, as a matter of fact, of those little,

Cat sketched on a menu by Lautrec. 1897.

rather rubbery mushroom-heads with which the Basques embellish their omelettes"—. The rest of the meal—*entremets*, peaches, coffee and brandy—need not be followed in detail. "Thirsty ?", asked the mischievous Lautrec when the time came to go home. "Surely you can see that I've had too much already ?", Edwards replied. "I can't, actually", said Lautrec, "I've had too much myself".

Three days later Edwards received a call from Lautrec. "I've come", he said, "to ask you to be an honorary member of the committee of the Salon des Indépendants". "With pleasure, my dear fellow", said Edwards, "on condition that the banquet on varnishing day includes neither kangaroo nor *collia*". "But surely", said Lautrec, "you don't suppose that restaurateurs go to the Zoo for their victuals ?" "All I can say is," said Edwards, "that it's three days now since you treated me to kangaroo and *collia* and my mouth's still on fire".

Lautrec never batted an eyelid. "Kangaroo, my dear Edwards ? *Collia* ? I can't remember any such things".

"And he said it so naturally", said Edwards later, "that I really wondered if I wasn't going off my head".

This was not the only time that the wretched Edwards was the object of Lautrec's ingenious mischief. Once when he was suffering from eczematous arthritis and had to follow a strict diet, he was invited to dinner in Lautrec's studio, in the Rue Tourlaque. "I'd like to come", he said, "but I must keep strictly to my diet, and above all I must only drink water". Lautrec took careful note of all this, but when Edwards arrived for the meal he had two distinct surprises. One was that the girl who served at table was stark naked. The other was that although several carafes of water were on the table they all had goldfish in them. "I told you I could only drink water", said Edwards. "Yes", said Lautrec, "That's quite understood". "Then why all those fish ?" "Just to show you that there's no gin in the carafes", said the painter.

Lautrec once invited a group of his friends to a really prodigious luncheon —one at which he surpassed himself. When it was all over and he wanted to end on a note of even greater perfection he got up from the table and took his guests off to the Rue Frochot. There in the apartment of the Dihauts he showed them the famous Degas of Dihaut the bassoonist in the orchestra-pit of the Opéra. This he considered one of the greatest pictures ever painted.

"That's my dessert", he said.

A touching story, and a good one to end on : for was not 'Henri the cook' also Lautrec the painter ?

Bourride bordelaise

Take a large pan, make a roux blond *sauce and work into it some mixed herbs, parsley, watercress, fennel, minced lemon, bay, and thyme.*

Put in five pounds' weight of ordinary deep-sea fish, cut up but including the heads : black conger, coalfish, whiting, pelouse, red mullet, dab, flounder, lophius, *weever, gurnard, hake. Add salt, white pepper, saffron, cloves, red Cayenne pepper.*

Cover with water and let it boil till the flesh has quite "come away"; meanwhile you will have put in, cooked, and withdrawn, a particularly fine fish which you will have chosen to eat as a whole : a turbot, a sole, a dace, a brill, or a haddock.

When the bouillon has boiled low, throw in the following sauce, which you will meanwhile have prepared separately :

Take a marble mortar and pound in it five or six cloves of garlic, add salt, a yolk of egg, and, little by little, two or three tablespoons of oil; use the pestle continuously until you have, in the end, a kind of mayonnaise.

Allow the bouillon to go on simmering for a good quarter of an hour, strain, and pour it into a shallow dish on grilled croûtons. Serve boiling hot, with the chosen fish, which must be eaten with it, like the beef in a pot-au-feu.

Homard à l'américaine

Choose two fine lobsters fresh from the pot, cut them in half, cross-wise, while they are still alive, cut the shells again lengthways, break the claws and arrange the tails as elegantly as you can. Keep all the liquid.

Take a large shallow pan and put in it half a pound of butter, three or four spoonfuls of fine olive oil, two onions, and a large shallot (these last very finely minced) : make the whole white-hot but do not on any account allow the olive oil to boil.

When the oil and butter are the right heat, throw in the pieces of lobsters and cook for ten minutes.

This done, put the contents of the pan and the lobsters' liquid into a large casserole, cover with boiling water, add a glass of good brandy, half a glass of good white Bordeaux, a whole half-lemon, a large glassful of very thick tomato sauce, a large glassful of glace de viande, ordinary pepper, some red Cayenne pepper, and some salt.

Allow the whole to simmer for twenty to thirty minutes, take out the pieces of lobster and put them on a dish which has been made hot in readiness. Should you have plenty of lobsters, take the meat of the claws and tails for the best pieces, crush the shells and go on boiling them in the casserole.

Put the strained juices from the casserole into the shallow pan, and reduce still further to make the sauce. Bind with butter, a touch of flour, heighten the taste with red pepper, salt, and finely-chopped herbs, and pour the sauce on the pieces of lobster which are lying in the hot dish.

Ramereaux (Wood-Pigeon) aux olives

Take some young wood-pigeons, gut and clean them and stuff them with a force-meat made from beef, veal and sausage-meat, heightened with aromatic pepper, nutmeg, and sliced truffles. Truss them, brown them quickly in a pan, and then put too in a casserole : butter, lard, shallot, onion, and make a light roux sauce with flour ; add salt, pepper, a bouquet garni, put in the wood-pigeons and moisten with a good bouillon. Cover the casserole and let it simmer quietly for up to an hour. In the last twenty minutes add some stoned green olives (having taken care to un-salt them) and a glass of brandy. Braise thoroughly and strain.

Put the pigeons on a dish, surround them with the olives, and anoint them with the strained sauce, which should be rich (onctueuse).

THREE OF TOULOUSE-LAUTREC'S MOTHER'S RECIPES

Morue (Cod) à la biscaienne

Heat up, over a low fire and in a copper casserole, some sliced onions in good olive oil.

Above : *Menu for a dinner chez Palmyre. 1897. Opposite : Goose. Pen-and-ink. 1899.*

Take some un-salted cod, cut it into small pieces, and put it into the casserole with a glass of good white wine, a bouquet garni, some sliced tomatoes (or tomato sauce), saffron, as much ordinary and Cayenne pepper as you like (no salt), and a Madeira glass of good brandy. Set aflame, and then fry, some large pieces of cod, put them in an earthenware pan, and pour on top, through a strainer, the contents of the casserole.

Let the cod and its sauce simmer for five to ten minutes. Serve with fried croûtons which have been rubbed with garlic.

Bœuf à la Malromé

Take some beef (a piece of the buttock) and cut it into squares two fingers thick. Brown these pieces in fat. Make a roux sauce with onions, garlic, shallot, carrots and turnips and brown it. Then put the beef in an earthenware pan and take it to the fire. Add salt, pepper, and cloves of garlic and cover it with the excellent red Malromé Bordeaux wine. Put the lid on and simmer over a low fire for five to six hours. Then take the liquid, strain it, and bind it with nutmeg, and finely chopped parsley and pour it over the beef.

The same receipe will serve for deer, stag, and boarmeat.

Poule verte

Take a piece of ham, some lard, some sausage-meat, a piece of pork or veal, some bread-crumbs, and some parsley; chop the lot and add salt and pepper.

Scald a borecole (chou frisé), take the inside of it, chop it, and mix it in with the meat.

Mix the whole with two beaten eggs and half a glass of milk. Roll the forcemeat in some large cabbage-leaves and build it up in the shape of a galantine of chicken.

Tie it with string and cook in boiling water with some fat and some potatoes, as if it were cabbage-soup, for an hour and a half to two hours. Add salt and pepper (aromatic and ordinary).

Untie the 'poule verte' and serve surrounded with the potatoes.

The liquid makes a delicious soup.

Above : *Doctor G.T. de C. composing a sauce. Pen-and-ink. 1899.* Opposite page : *Woodcock. Water-color. 1880.*

Family album

BY ANNETTE VAILLANT

To the Natanson brothers the "Revue Blanche" owed much of its inspiration,
and the Nabis much of their success

My father, Louis Alfred Natanson—Alfred Athis was his pen-name—was born in Warsaw on August 15th 1873. "Russian Poland" is how my old family album describes it. Like many Poles —Mickiewicz among them—, my paternal grandfather was called Adam : Adam Natanson. Many of his cousins, fervent Polish patriots, were destined to expiate their patriotism in Siberia, but my grandfather preferred to live the life of a free man, and a French citizen, in France. But he cannot have born too great a grudge against the Russia of the Tsars, for he travelled as far as Odessa to fetch and bring back with him to Paris the young girl of sixteen, Annette, who was to become his wife.

When my father was five he and his elder brothers, Alexandre, Thadée and Léon, were taken back to Warsaw for a visit : he remembered especially how his grandfather took him to one of the windows in the Natanson family house and said "It was from here that I saw Napoleon !" The Warsaw Natansons were bankers. French was spoken at table and at the end of the meal they ate fruit—fresh oranges, among other things. At Christmas-time there was sometimes a great commotion as the servants called out "The chopkis ! The chopkis !" from floor to floor and the children were brought out of bed to see the marionette-show which had come to the house.

◄ *Vuillard :* Paris Gardens. *85″ × 60″. Detail. Musée de l'Art Moderne, Paris. Part of the decorations painted in 1894 for Alexandre Natanson's dining-room. There were in all ten panels. Vuillard took his subjects from the Tuileries gardens near his home. Like most of his decorations they were painted à la colle.*

The elder Natansons, parents of the founders of the "Revue Blanche" : Adam Natanson *in the center, his wife Annette (right), and to the left a cousin.*

My father and his brothers went to fashionable schools in Paris and grew up to be cultivated men of the world. My father did not look quite like a Frenchman, but his qualities, and above all his nice sense of proportion, were quintessentially French. Only his constant anxiety seemed to come to him from the distant past : unsure of himself where his talents were concerned, he would write and re-write his plays over and over again. When he was thirteen his mother died at Cannes, and his father, whom I hardly knew, lost all interest in life. I remember his house in the Rue Jouffroy. Number 85 it was,

with a black grille in front and latticed windows on the stairs. My father never allowed me to go near the pool in the garden. In the shadowy dining-room the finger-bowls were of dark blue crystal. Old Alphonse, with his chronic laryngitis, still served at table. He it was who, many years previously, had been the last to speak to Uncle Léon when he came home in evening dress in the early morning : an hour or two later Uncle Léon shot himself. He had been a good-looking young man of twenty-three. Marie Quinault the house-maid, hurrying to his room at the sound of the shot, had dropped the stopper out of the

"La Revue Blanche" was founded by the Natanson brothers (Alexandre, Thadée, and Alfred). During the last ten years of the century it had a great influence on French literature and art. Among the avant-garde artists whom it sponsored were Toulouse-Lautrec, Bonnard, Vuillard, Maurice Denis, K. X. Roussel, Vallotton. As Thadée Natanson said, the Nabis could as accurately be called the "Revue Blanche group". Bonnard made a series of color lithographs for the review, his poster for it of 1894 became famous. During the review's twelve years' existence (1891-1903) the painters met often with its contributors, writers like Jules Renard, Octave Mirbeau, Mallarmé, Tristan Bernard, Romain Coolus, Félix Fénéon, Apollinaire, Fagus and others.

The Natanson's wit, intelligence and flair made them for many years an indispensable part of the literary and artistic world of Paris. Lugné-Poe said that "No fashionable first night can possibly begin until the Natansons have been seen and greeted in their box".

◄Facing page : Thadée Natanson and his first wife, Misia (later Misia Sert): a photograph which shows the kind of décor in which Bonnard and Vuillard so often went to work. Thadée was remarkable for his insight into all that was new in art and literature. He wrote essays in his own review and, shortly before his death in 1951, books of invaluable memoirs: "Peints à leur tour", "Un Henri de Toulouse-Lautrec", "Le Bonnard que je propose"...

Vuillard : Vallotton and Misia at Ville-► neuve. 28½"×21". Private coll. Luxembourg. Vuillard recaptured exactly, in pictures such as this, the atmosphere which we re-discover in the Natansons' album.

Thadée married Misia Godebski when she was fifteen. In 1895, when Lautrec used her as the model for his "Revue Blanche" poster, she was regarded as the prettiest woman in Paris. (Yet when she asked him: "Why do you make women look so ugly ?", he replied "Because that's what they are, Madame"). In 1902 Misia left Thadée and married Alfred Edwards, director of 'Le Matin'. Her third husband was the painter José Maria Sert. She died in 1949 after reigning over Paris for half a century, leaving an autobiography which is not the most reliable of documents. ▼

Pages 28-29. Vuillard : Luncheon at Vil-► leneuve-sur-Yonne : Misia Natanson with her half-brother Cipa Godebski. (1897. 13"×21⅝". On cardboard. Private coll. U.S.A.) Lautrec painted a fine portrait of Cipa Godebski in 1896. Once when the two friends were both staying at Villeneuve they decided to collaborate on a book called "The Bachelor". They got no further than the opening sentence: "It is only in the country that one would really wish to be a bachelor again".

Alexander Natanson, in 1901, at the wheel of his first motor-car in the garden of the Natansons' house at Villeneuve-sur-Yonne. The passengers are his three daughters, and his wife Olga is standing in front of the car to the left. Alexandre was titular director of the "Revue Blanche". His extravagant tastes led him to take a house in the Avenue du Bois (now Avenue Foch), and later in the Champs Elysées. Toulouse-Lautrec often designed the invitations to his evening-parties, which were of exceptional brilliance.

Théâtre Libre were giving a new impetus to the theatre at that time ; Vuillard designed scenery and programs for the *Théâtre de l'Oeuvre*, and it was through him that my father met a young actress, Marthe Mellot, who had appeared as Aricie in *Phèdre*, Antonia in Edouard Dujardin's symbolist drama, and various characters in Ibsen. She was to become my mother.

But before long it was the *Revue Blanche* which came first in our thoughts. My grandfather had been persuaded by his sons to put money into it, and during its short life—1891 to 1903—it was the headquarters, so we thought, of all that mattered in litterature and art. When it came to an end we would look at the complete set of the magazine in its grey watered-silk binding and speak of *La Revue Blanche* as people speak of a dead queen or a great building that no longer exists. Even the youngest of us had some vivid recollection of it : my cousin Evelyne, for instance, remembered that when she went to the offices of the review in the Rue Laffitte Verlaine was there and wrote a sonnet for her.

Alexandre Natanson was the titular director, but his two brothers shared with him the moral and material responsibility for all that went on. My father, when still a schoolboy at the Lycée Condorcet, talked of nothing but the *Revue Blanche* with his friend Fernand Gregh and Robert Dreyfus, the

bottle of vinegar she was carrying. She always remembered my grandfather coming out of his study and calling out : "Steady now, Marie ! Don't go dropping things all over the place !" Marie had brought up my father, and I in my turn was initiated by her into the necessity of finishing my spinach. She liked to tell how once she had had to lay out every evening on each of the young gentlemen's beds the tail-coat, the white waistcoat, and the gardenia from Zagrodska's, the flower-shop further down the street. Once when I was ferreting about in my father's drawers I found a little revolver ; but 'Uncle Léon', for me, was not the owner of that revolver, but the handsome young man whose photograph I looked at every evening before going to sleep.

Vuillard's three large and incomparable decorations—one of them is now in the Musée de l'Art Moderne in Paris— were painted for my grandfather. At the end of his life he came to live with us in

the Boulevard Malesherbes, and the decorations came with him. Did he take spontaneously to this sort of painting, or did his sons prompt him ? Many people laughed at Thadée when he showed them his treasured Vuillards of humble sewing-women in their flannelette dressing-gowns. It was their friend Percheron—the son of Mélanie Percheron, the dressmaker—who took Thadée and his youngest brother to see Vuillard : just after 1890, I think. Vuillard became my father's closest friend and was with him by his death-bed.

Antoine and Lugné-Poe and the

Photograph taken at Villeneuve on September 10th 1898, the day of Mallarmé's funeral at the nearby cemetery of Samoreau. From left to right : Bonnard, with his back to the camera, Cipa Godebski, his wife Ida, Thadée, Misia, Renoir. Renoir was then 57 : Mallarmé's death was a great grief to him and he was one of the few who accompanied the coffin all the way from the poet's home to the cemetery.

Thadée, Vallotton, Romain Coolus and Cipa Godebski **playing chequers at Villeneuve.**

A few years later Aunt Misia would watch over the cradle in which I lay: she had herself sewn the lace and tied the ribbons for it. She was a magician, but a dangerous one, as quick to un-make as to make. She was pretty, but common-ish, in spite of her little Minerva's profile, and had not yet become the sumptuous, heavy-chinned matron that Lautrec perpetuated. Every young man fell a victim to her, for her wit and beauty and cunning were such that none could resist her. But she was as cruel as she was winning, and we never had an unclouded summer when she was at Villeneuve. Thadée, in the end, fled her presence. After my father died he came to live with us for a while; but it was Misia's name that was whispered with regret—yes, even in the servants' hall—so great was the spell of her wilful gaiety, her whims, her imperious hold upon life.

Paris. The visions flick past like snapshots and I see, for instance, Alphonse Allais as our guest: with his arm tenderly about his wife's shoulder and his attention somewhere out of the

Misia in the garden of "Les Relais".

intimate of Proust. Proust himself wrote for the *Revue* when he was still quite unknown, and other contributors were Seurat, Lautrec, Vuillard, Bonnard, Valéry and Gide. At the turn of the century it was the smart thing, as people say now, to contribute to the *Revue Blanche*, alongside of Jarry, Francis Jammes, Charles-Louis Philippe, and Claude Debussy. Mallarmé was prized highest of all.

During the summer months our friends would join us at *Les Relais*, our house at Villeneuve-sur-Yonne. Vuillard, for one, would immortalise our ephemeral cretonnes on any available scrap of cardboard: and as for my father's photographs of those days, I have so lived in, and with, them that they have become a part of my own life. Lautrec is there, chasing the wasps round the garden with his short stick and a cry of "Tally-ho!" Cipa Godebski, too—the model for some of Vuillard's best pictures, with his round felt hat on the back of his head. Félix Vallotton, K.X. Roussel and his wife Marie (Vuillard's sister), played *boules* with my uncle Thadée. Romain Coolus, his face as yet unmarked by life, was still the young man in the Albi portrait. Bonnard would ride up on his bicycle, steel pince-nez firmly in position and a look of delight in his short-sighted eyes. Misia, every-where and always: Uncle Thadée's wife, with one arm round her husband and the other round her father, old Godeb-ski, who had been a friend of Liszt. Once at the end of the day we formed a circle round the already ageing figure of Renoir: Mallarmé had just been buried.

window, somewhere in the distant future that was to come to an end the next day. Or it is Jules Renard's tiny, unpretentious flat in the Rue du Rocher: I can still smell the fresh polish and the clean linen, still see, the white porcelain swan on the green table-cloth. Or the Roussels at Etang-la-Ville on a Sunday, or Madame Vuillard spelling out a polka at the piano, in the Rue de Calais. Or the Léon Blums, when we acted *Le Petit Poucet* at their house in the Rue du Luxembourg. Madame Catulle Mendès, made up as heavily as the Empress of China, and the Bibescos, handsome enough for Olympus, arriving when I was already asleep in bed, and playing interminable poker games, much to my grandfather's exasperation. Mirbeau, at Cormeilles-en-Vexin, taking off his tweed jacket and playing billiards in his shirtsleeves. Edmond Sée, an old friend of my father's both from the Army and from the days of the *Revue Blanche*, spending a month at Fontainebleau with my father: and once Madame Philippe Berthelot coming to tea. She had been Armand Point's pre-Raphaelite model and we children were spellbound by the thick hair coiled over her ears and the Carthaginian jewellery. I remember, too, going with my father to Bernheim Jeune's in the Rue Richepance, and Félix Fénéon, a strange tall figure, half goat, half evangelist, showing us some Monets.

And then Ouistreham, on a bend of the river Orne, in Normandy. Vuillard's big picture shows Uncle Alexandre and Aunt Olga in front of the tennis court at Ranville, with the great cedar-tree, at the back, where the white balls went to ground. I was four or five when I went there: every morning my Aunt Olga would settle down with her needlework in the garden, and sometimes Uncle Alexandre would take Marcelle and me out driving in the phaeton. This was more fun than the new motor, with its

brass headlamps; but I was always a little afraid of my uncle's ironical smile and bursts of uncontrolled good spirits.

Vuillard : The Conversation. 14¼″×17¾″. 1897. Private collection. U.S.A. To the right is Marthe Mellot, the actress who married Alfred Natanson and became the mother of the author of this article. She is also seen in the photograph, opposite.

On his birthday my cousins would play him a fourhand piece and I recited a fable of Ratisbonne.

There were guests all the time: one day a lady, Madame Lucie Delarue-Mardrus, imitated the cries of animals. Her husband, Dr Mardrus, always called her the Almond Princess. He spoke oriental languages and from time to time would send my father his translations of the "Thousand and One Nights": these were always put away in a safe place and we were not allowed to see them. Sometimes a group of foreign cousins would come over from Cabourg, complete with parents, governesses, and starched nursemaids. We would take them hand in hand in their white sailor suits along the long green *allées* and when they went away, never to be seen again, they left us a little in love and pining for the Russia that we had never known.

Vuillard, Coolus and Tristan Bernard spent August with the Jos Hessels at their Chateau Rouge, a big house in the Louis XIII style, a mile or two from

Vuillard : Man with Pipe. Portrait of Cipa Godebski. 26½″×21″. *Oil on cardboard. Private collection Paris.*

Ranville. And later my little sister and I were taken holidaying with them. We saw many curious people with the Hessels: Marthe Brandès, the Garbo of her day, pale and trembling, her nostrils touched with carmine, Georges Carpentier, at the height of his career in the ring, with his little motor-car upholstered in flowered velvet, Ambroise Vollard, a hairy giant, prehistoric in bearing but far evolved in other respects, in a light beige suit.

Jos Hessel the picture-dealer rarely spoke. Vulture-eyed, hook-nosed, portly, soft-handed and short of stature, he was capable of a certain short-lived gaiety but was generally seen to founder in silence. Money was all he really thought of. Lucy, his wife, a gentle, warm, charitable and deeply human person, was Vuillard's faithful muse. Age enhanced her beauty. She was cousin-german to Tristan Bernard's second wife, the elegant, dazzling, widely-admired Marcelle.

Tristan and Marcelle were so completely a part of our everyday life that I cannot dismiss them in a few words. When a play by Tristan and my father, *Le Costaud des Epinettes*, was in rehearsal, we went to the balcony of the *Theatre du Vaudeville* to watch a Mid-Lent procession go by. Papa introduced us to Lantelme, the famous actress. Small as I was, I shall never forget her velvety eyes, her suede suit with its mink trimmings, and the brilliant effect

of the face and figure that were to succumb, as Misia had succumbed, to the horrible Edwards and his millions.

The Alexandre Natansons no longer lived in the Avenue du Bois, where they had had their famous cocktail-party, with invitations designed by Lautrec. There, too, Bonnard had painted my four cousins in green and white, with their dogs. But now they had moved to the Champs-Elysées. Balls were given in the long gallery where Vuillard's *Jardins de Paris* series was hung, and in the big drawing-room, beneath Lautrec's portrait of Oscar Wilde, with blue suit and yellow hair. My mother thought these balls altogether too luxurious. But then my mother would have rather lived on black broth and Evian water than owed anyone a penny. Her mother had been as irresponsible as she was pretty, and she herself had seen what it meant to be in debt and dunned.

Thadée's ingenuities had therefore little appeal for her. An aesthete, and naturally drawn to the most complicated way of solving any problem, Thadée

had a genius, though often an unhappy one, for business. His enthusiasm was irresistible, and when the spirit moved him he could persuade his brothers, his

Above, a photograph of Romain Coolus : *right, Lautrec's portrait of Coolus painted at Villeneuve-sur-Yonne. (Oil on cardboard. 21¾" × 13¾". 1889. Musée d'Albi.) Coolus was working on plays*

when Lautrec came up and dragged him over to his easel : "Sit down", he said, "and I'll do an El Greco of you". (Lautrec had just come back from Spain.) Coolus was a favorite of the artist's.

Bonnard : The four young ladies. 47¼″ × 52″. *Natanson collection Paris. This painting shows Alexandre Natanson's four daughters : Evelyn, Bolette, Georgette and Marcelle.*

Uncle Alexandre had tremendous style, Uncle Thadée was a spendthrift, but it was my father who was generous. He would sit on a sofa in his office and read Hans Andersen's stories aloud to me while Vuillard painted my portrait. The wooden chair was hard, and I had pins and needles in my legs, but I wasn't allowed to move. I liked Vuillard for the unstudied way he tied his tie and the warm-heartedness which came out in everything he said. Such was my respect for him that I never spoke to him familiarly, never called him anything but *Monsieur Vuillard.*

My father did not have his tea served in a glass, like Uncle Thadée, but sometimes, when bortsch was being prepared in the kitchen, my eye was caught by a basin full of bright violet liquid. My mother had travelled with my father to St Petersburg and the Caucasus, and had never quite lost, as he also had not, the flame of passion which had burnt high on that journey. My father was for a time the dramatic critic of Jaurès' *Humanité*, and he and my mother went to all the first nights ; after a late supper they would sleep until well on in the morning, while we left the house on tip-toe.

At the beginning of August, 1914, Uncle Thadée married his second wife, Reine. He took her off to Lyons, where to my mother's horror he became the efficient Director of an armament factory. My father went off to the war with

friends, even his housemaids—such was the effect of his quasi-royal good manners—to put money into the rashest of enterprises. He would consistently arrive half an hour late for luncheon : but no one knew half as well how to send flowers. Nor have I ever seen the equal of the enormous pigskin cigar-case which he had bought in Vienna. He had an ogre's appetite and ordered himself the most gigantic meals at Larue's. What would Mallarmé have said— Mallarmé whose special treat for his disciples was a glass of sugared water ? Uncle Thadée sent out to Houbigant's for the scent, *L'Idéal*, which he used on his unpredictable Charvet handkerchiefs.

My father was much simpler in his habits. The same ties, the same white duck-suits came out every summer. He thought more of others than of himself.

► *Félix Fénéon and his wife at Villeneuve. The enigmatic Fénéon was the Revue's editorial secretary. Dismissed from the War Ministry on account of his relations with the anarchist movement, he employed Thadée Natanson as his lawyer. Employed by Thadée in his turn, he remained with the Revue for the rest of its existence, and then joined "Le Matin", to which he contributed a series of three-line news items which were famous in their time. From 1906 he was in charge of modern pictures at the Galerie Bernheim Frères. He was one of Seurat's earliest admirers and exerted an immense, though discreet, influence on art and letters. He died in 1944.*

a new book in his knapsack : Proust's *A la Recherche du Temps perdu*, vol. 1. And when the war was nearly over, at Easter 1918, we went to stay with Uncle Thadée near Lyons. Bonnard, as young as ever, and as ready to laugh and be amazed, was painting his first portrait of Reine. Later Reine went to Vernon and began her stormy friendship with Madame Bonnard, a strange little person with bright lettuce-green eyes. Reine was a beautiful woman, but for all her gazelle-like eyes she had not a kind heart. Much as she loved Thadée, she was the cause of his losing all his oldest friends. She hated his first wife, quite naturally, though she had never met her, and sometimes in spite of ourselves she made us wish that Misia, with all her charm and her engaging duplicities, were still the mistress of the house. Yet she didn't lack character : and during the occupation of 1939-1944 she could be seen walking slowly and proudly in the Champ de Mars, arm-in-arm with her husband—an old man, by then, with the big yellow star that meant "Jew" on his sleeve. Thadée, silent, pale as marble, looked like Michaelangelo's Moses. But in his retirement he had taken up the pen again, and his memoirs give a vivid and authentic picture of Lautrec and the Nabis.

Just after the war of 1914-18, my father found that, thanks to Thadée, he had lost all his money. When I came

Left to right : Misia and Thadée Natanson ; Cipa and Cyprien Godebski the sculptor, (father of Misia and Cipa) ; and Romain Coolus at "Les Relais".

back from my honeymoon the little Renoirs that I had loved so much were gone from our walls. But I never heard

◄ *A game of* boules *in the garden of "Les Relais": From left to right : Marthe Mellot, Madame Roussel, Vuillard, Coolus, K.X. Roussel, Cipa Godebski, Vallotton.*

my father complain or show the slightest bitterness. He joined the Galerie Druet, a gallery which painters loved for its cordial atmosphere. In 1935 Alexandre fell ill, and I was at the other end of Europe when his magnificent existence, with its extremes of euphoria and melancholy, came suddenly to an end.

I have never got used to the fact that all these people are no longer with us. Not for me are they buried deep in the earth, with a faithful gardener to bring fuchsias and chrysanthemums at the appropriate moment of the year. It is

they, not I, who are still on earth, as it seems to me—so insistently do they come to life when I think of them.

Alfred Natanson, the father of the author of this article, wrote for the Revue Blanche *under the name of Alfred Athis. He took all the photographs which illustrate this article : none has been published before.*

43

The Bonnard Affair

BY HENRI PERRUCHOT

The legal tangle dividing Bonnard's heirs points up the problem
of an artist's rights over his own works

The drawings ornamenting this article are chosen from those which Bonnard made for Octave Mirbeau's account of a motoring trip "The 628-E8" in 1908.

Nothing could be more curious, or in its way more painful, than the "Bonnard affair". It is, moreover, a matter in which every French artist is intimately concerned ; for what is at stake is not merely the inheritance of a great painter, but the position of all painters, great and small, in relation to French law.

Let us first establish the facts :

Bonnard was born on October 3rd 1867, and he was 26 when, in 1893, he met a young woman who called herself Marthe de Melliny and was then working as an artists' model. Marthe de Melliny remained with Bonnard for the rest of her life, and we have a shrewd portrait of her in Thadée Natanson's *Le Bonnard que je Propose.* "She was like a bird", he tells us, "with a bird's startled look, its love of water and passion for splashing about, and its bright plumage and incorporeal tread. She was even bird-footed, in her high slender heels, but her speech was more cackle than song, and at that was often hoarse and indistinct. Slightly built, and invalidish by conviction, as much as by necessity, she was for fifty years the despair of her doctors but managed, none the less, to flout their gloomy forebodings. She was Bonnard's most constant model — often without knowing it, for he had no need to ask her to pose and many of his finest pictures grew out of some

trivial incident in their shared life. They were always very simply installed, and as they were both very shy they said hardly anything when other people were there ; but it was clear that each found in the other a much-needed support".

Who was Marthe de Melliny, and where did she come from ? Bonnard didn't really know, and, as it seems, didn't really care. Whatever she told him must have owed a good deal to her ready imagination. It was, in any case, quite untrue that her name was Marthe de Melliny. Her real name was Maria Boursin. It was also untrue that she had no relations still living.

It may be that she told him these things under the impression that theirs would not be a lasting attachment. But, as it turned out, the union was anything but ephemeral. Year followed year, and she did nothing to undeceive him. In 1909, after sixteen years of living together, Bonnard still did not know who she really was ; and in the will which he drew up in that year she appears as Marthe de Melliny.

Time passed, and in 1925, after the liaison had lasted more than thirty years, Pierre Bonnard married Maria Boursin. She had then no alternative but to give her real name ; but she stuck to her untruth and told the registrar that she had lost her father and mother, although in point of fact her mother was still alive.

This photograph, one of the last taken of Bonnard, shows him at Le Cannet at the end of 1944.

On January 23rd 1942, Madame Bonnard died. She left no will. Bonnard knew nothing of the law, in such matters, and in any case it would never have occurred to him that his wife might be, in her own right, a woman of property. He therefore sat tight and did nothing.

Nine months later, Authority caught up with him. Bonnard, greatly surprised, consulted a lawyer. What could they possibly want of him? And it was then that he found that, contrary to all he had supposed, his wife did, after all, have "something to leave". There had, of course, been no question of either dowry or marriage settlement. But she was none the less possessed,

in law, of half their joint estate. As Madame Bonnard had 'no relations living' Bonnard was, of course, the sole beneficiary. But even so, certain formalities had to be gone through, as a consequence of her having left no will. Seals were placed on Bonnard's studio, and a complete inventory would have to be taken. A technical irregularity had occurred, and Bonnard, at the age of seventy-five, was obliged to provide a surety and, in general, to go through an elaborate procedure which was altogether too much for him. He simply couldn't see why he should have to pay duty on his own pictures. Surely, he thought, something could be done about it?

It was as this point that a friend of his took pity on his distresses and gave him a piece of rather curious advice — nothing less than that he should forge a will in his own favor. Who would be harmed by it? Nobody. Bonnard, who was innocence itself, saw nothing wrong with the idea, wrote out the will in his own hand, and sent it in. Authority was appeased, Bonnard went on with his work, and nothing more was heard of the affair until after he himself died on January 23rd 1947.

Bonnard had had a brother and a sister, and their respective children — one of whom is Charles Terrasse, the curator of the Palais de Fontainebleau — were his heirs. It seemed as if all would run perfectly smoothly.

But not so! As often in the history of art, a great painter's work was to be the subject, after his death, of strenuous and envenomed controversy.

Bonnard left behind him a very considerable collection of his own work. The several hundred items constituted, in fact, a great fortune. It was at this point that Bonnard's counsellor-confidant, who alone knew the history of the forged will, decided to see if there were not, on Madame Bonnard's side, relations entitled to a share in the large estate. Researches into Maria Boursin's family tree soon revealed that there were, in effect, other claimants: the 'demoiselles Bowers', nieces of Madame Bonnard. Bonnard's own relatives were told the story of the forged will and agreed, in consideration of it, to offer the demoiselles Bowers half of the joint estate of Monsieur and Madame Pierre Bonnard. No agreement was reached, however, because the parties differed irreconcilably on the question of what constituted the joint estate. This is the heart of the matter, and one which concerns every painter or sculptor now subject to French law.

This, briefly, is the point at issue: in the Bonnards' view, the joint estate is restricted to those canvases which, at the date of Madame Bonnard's death,

had been completed and made known — offered for sale, i. e., or otherwise put before the public by Bonnard himself. All other canvases then in his studios were to be held as his own personal property; they were work, that is to say, on which he had not said his last word, and he was free either to finish or to destroy them, as he pleased.

This did not suit the demoiselles Bowers at all. *All* the canvases in Bonnard's studio belonged, they said, to the joint estate, irrespective of whether or not they were finished. The mere fact that they were there at all made them irrevocably a part of the joint estate. And they went further: Bonnard had been guilty of fraud, they said, in forging his wife's will, and he (and therefore his heirs) should forfeit the whole estate.

The resulting legal proceedings have been both lengthy and complicated. The Bowerses began by bringing an action against the heirs of Bonnard under penal law — accusing Bonnard of forgery, perjury, and receiving and concealing stolen goods. In September 1952 this indictment was rejected by the examining magistrate at Grasse, and his judgment was later upheld by the Aix court of appeal and the Supreme Court of Appeal.

The Bowerses had better luck when they turned to civil law. The Tribunal de la Seine held that Bonnard, acting in full cognisance of the illegality of what he was doing, had appropriated to himself pictures which were not legally his. The entire contents of the studio were declared part of the joint estate, and the plaintiffs were awarded everything that had been in that studio at the time of Madame Bonnard's death.

Notice of appeal was given, of course, and before long the judgment was

Pierre Bonnard: Woman leaving her bath. 48"× 44". *Private coll., Paris.*

Vuillard: Sketch for a portrait of Bonnard. $45^3/_5'' \times 57^1/_5''$. *1925. Petit Palais Paris.*

over-ruled. The Paris court of appeal considered that Bonnard, who had no idea of the Bowerses' existence, could not have intended to do them out of their inheritance. Nor had either he or his heirs attempted to use the faked will to this end. The court of appeal therefore decreed that the joint estate should be divided equally between the two families, and that only those canvases which were 'sufficiently' completed and 'sufficiently' able to command a 'Bonnard price' should be included in the joint estate. The choice was to be made by experts appointed for the purpose.

This judgment satisfied nobody. Two further appeals were lodged, one by the demoiselles Bowers, the other by Bonnard's own heirs. The upshot of those appeals will be of the greatest importance to all artists.

Let us now, therefore, take a general view of the issues at stake. What are an artist's rights, where his own work is concerned ? Everyone knows that the 'joint estate' consists of all possessions that are acquired during the marriage in question, with the exception of certain strictly personal possessions — family relics, professional equipment, etc... Where one of the parties concerned is an artist, a musician, or a writer, his or her works belong in law to the joint estate.

Should the marriage be dissolved, the other partner or his heirs are entitled to half the joint estate. This division, simple enough in the case of ordinary possessions, becomes altogether more difficult when an artist's life-work is in question. The division may, in fact, handicap him for the rest of his life and make it impossible for him to develop as he would otherwise have done. He no longer has that absolute control of his work which the law assures him in all other contexts, and it becomes possible for it to be put on the market in ways, or at a time, which do not at all suit him. That is why efforts are being made to restrict the harmful effects of these dis-possessions.

Initially the law decreed that the joint estate included unpublished as well as published work. But the Appeal Court has ruled that, where writers and musicians are concerned, the 'joint estate' laws apply only to work published during, or before, the marriage. Any literary or musical work which is still in manuscript at the time when the marriage is dissolved remains the property of the writer or musician concerned. This ruling has not hitherto been held to apply to painters or sculptors, but it is difficult to see why they too should not benefit by it. Manuscripts and unpublished novels or symphonies have, after all, their counterpart in the sketches, notes, adumbrations and abandoned canvases which are to be found in every painter's studio.

The Paris court of appeal tried to establish a distinction between pictures which were 'more or less' finished and

pictures which remained in the sketch-stage. This would be difficult to apply in practice. Where the artist is not present to make the distinction himself, no firm criterion can be laid down. The concept of 'adequate market value", for instance, is not easily defined. In referring the decision to a panel of experts, the Court took what is, on the surface, a sensible line. But in practice it means that the artist is no longer master in his own studio, as Rouault, for instance, was not long ago declared to be master. The 'experts'' judgment is to over-rule the judgment of the artist himself. Not he, but the experts, are to say whether this or that canvas is 'finished'. They, not he, will decide whether it is to be put up for sale — against, it may well be, his own wishes.

In thinking over the Bonnard affair we do well to forget the peculiar characteristics of the case — and, in particular, we must forget that Bonnard is now dead, and try to envisage a case in which a *living* artist sees his work divided into two halves and has no control over what happens to one canvas in every two. If the Paris court of appeal's ruling were to be applied in such a case, the following might happen :

A well-known painter of high quality is involved in divorce proceedings at a time when his pictures are fetching high prices. His wife has the right to have his studio sealed and locked, his canvases put in sequestration, and a choice made among them by a group of experts. The artist will simply have to keep quiet or — as happened not long ago — die of despair. Any protests he may make will be ignored. The experts alone will decide which of his canvases are fit for sale...

A disquieting vision : and one which makes us hope that painters and sculptors may soon be accorded the right now enjoyed by writers and composers — that of disposing of their own work as they themselves think best.

Ideas of Georges Rouault

BY JEAN GRENIER

To base his entire art on "one glance from a broken-down acrobat" has been the challenge accepted by the old master since 1903

A great artist like Rouault cannot be summed up in a few words. He has loved beauty under too many forms, in his long life, and sought the Ideal in too many of its manifestations. Yet two things have remained constant: his temperament, which is that of a man who never strays far from the earth: and his idealism, which will not allow that earth to be sundered from heaven. He has been an artisan, a disciple, a believer, and a rebel, while remaining at the same time a man preoccupied with justice, a prophet, a painter who will make no compromises in his art, and the poet of the pure in heart.

Since the end of the war he has lived in a light and airy apartment which looks on to one of the great railway stations of Paris. (The winter he spends mostly in the south of France.) His drawing-room is full of old Breton furniture belonging to Madame Rouault, and there is also a portrait of her by Lehmann, who was a friend of Rouault himself. Both he and his wife are of Breton origin and at one time they summered in St Malo, in a house that stood on the ramparts and looked out to sea.

At 86, Rouault's mind remains perfectly clear although he has to take care of his health. With his working clothes, at home, he wears a round white bonnet, like a surgeon's, and walks with a rubber-tipped stick. His eyes are pale grey, his lips long and firm, his

Georges Rouault, in 1955, on one of his excursions to the Parc de Sceaux.

nose straight. You might take him for an elderly craftsman from the Faubourg St Antoine,—more especially when he talks of Degas, Renoir and Jacques Maritain. There's great integrity in the way he speaks of others, and one remembers how, some nine years ago, he burnt 315 of his canvases in front of an officer of the law, rather than see them put on the market. His conduct at that time was a comfort and an example to all artists.

Rouault was born in Paris, in the working-class quarter of Belleville, on the very day—May 27th 1871—that the troops from Versailles overran Belleville, winkled out the *communards*, and shot a great many of them in the nearby cemetery of Père Lachaise. All the Rouaults were craftsmen. His father came from Montfort in Brittany and was an *ébéniste* whose particular job was with Pleyel's, the piano-makers. His aunts painted fans and porcelain. His maternal grandfather admired Manet, unlike most of his

left an ineffaceable impression upon him and was to become his master for life.

This influence came out in many ways. At first, for instance, Rouault took even his subjects from Moreau. Putting in for the Prix de Rome, he did a *Samson at the Mill,* a *Jesus among the Doctors,* a *Deposition.* Independent as he was by nature, Rouault did not strain after originality, but accepted a continuity of tradition which goes far beyond mere 'alikeness'.

Moreau was a '*grand bourgeois*', a professor, a Member of the Institute. All those things bound him to the official art of the period, but he was alert enough to see it for what it was and courageous enough to speak out against it. Anxious as he was to see Rouault follow a line of his own, he none the less wanted him to go in for the Prix de Rome. Official recognition was very important, at that time. At his last attempt Rouault submitted a *Dead Christ.* "Christ's foot is too big" said Bonnat. "All the more reason to send him to Rome", said Moreau. "Don't fob him off with a second prize. Let it be Rome or nothing. He's a boy who likes to exert himself and tackle something new, and even if he

Samson at the Mill. 57½″×45″. The earliest known painting by Georges Rouault, this was executed in 1893 as part of an unsuccessful entry for the Prix de Rome. At the time young Rouault was working under Gustave Moreau, having entered the Beaux-Arts in Paris in 1891. It is now in the County Museum, Los Angeles.

contemporaries, and indeed all the Rouaults were people of individual habits and individual taste. Rouault's father, for instance, was a Catholic, like most Bretons, but he was also an anarchist by temperament, and sided with his compatriot Lamennais against the Pope. Young Rouault went, therefore, to a Protestant school.

Rouault once wrote under a photograph of himself at the age of seven : "Not at all precocious. A round strong head and bulging brow, blue eyes, fair hair. Midway between reality and dreamland, most often... Will be more venturesome in his work than in life, but the two will be inseparable in success or— who knows ? certainly not he—failure".

One day, when Rouault had been severely punished at school, his father, thinking the punishment altogether too heavy for the crime, took him away and apprenticed him to a glass-maker. Rouault became a glass-painter, learnt to restore stained-glass, and had a hand in the windows that Hirsch was making for Saint-Séverin. Then he went to study under Gustave Moreau, at the Ecole des Beaux Arts, after a term or two at the Ecole des Arts Décoratifs. Moreau

Rouault, aged seven. He later wrote beneath the photograph with typical lucidity : "Not at all precocious. A round strong head and bulging brow, blue eyes, fair hair". By the age of fourteen Rouault was working in a glass-painter's studio.

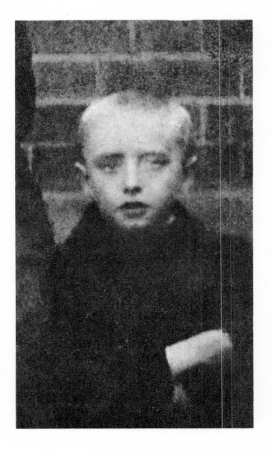

just sends us landscapes it'll still have been worth while''. But the prize went to one of Bonnat's own pupils.

Moreau's manner was rather of a stimulating colleague than that of a professor, and his friendship with Rouault does honor to both. They had, after all, little in common, since the one was a learned member of the upper middle class, no enemy of the academic tradition in drawing, and as impassive in art as in life, while the other was working-class in origin, a craftsman by education, and as violent in his feelings as in the manner of their expression.

Yet there is something in the gorgeous color and brilliant *mise-en-scène* of Rouault's paintings that calls Moreau to mind, just as the cut of Rouault's figures reminds us that his first master was a painter of stained-glass. But Rouault's debt to Moreau is, above all, a moral one. "Moreau taught us", he says, "to discipline ourselves without relying on pre-conceived method. He gave us a taste for the element in life that is heightened and rare and yet means as much to us as the most

Lithographed portrait of Gustave Moreau, by Rouault, 1926.

Portrait of the artist by himself. *Watercolor. Rouault collection.*

palpable realities. He taught us to respect those who can look within themselves..." Rouault remembers Moreau saying: "Look at Nature and the old masters, for they alone can help you bring it off... Send me packing from time to time—me and all the moderns!"

Rouault was thirty before he really learned to "look within himself". He had already looked to Forain, Daumier and Lautrec for his themes—clowns, judges, prostitutes—but he had not yet found the inspiration peculiar to himself that was to give these themes an

Gustave Moreau's pupils. In the foreground is Georges Rouault (1); Henri Matisse, above left (2), and Albert Marquet, behind Rouault (3), also worked at the time under Moreau in the Ecole des Beaux-Arts.

original and profoundly religious flavor. In 1903, when he was 32, the world was suddenly changed for him

Bella Matribus Detestata, *a plate from* Miserere. *This book was carried out as a commission from Vollard, between 1922-1927, but it was only published in 1947.*

and, in his own words, "I saw what I had seen before, but the form of it, and the harmony, were new". He was shaken to the roots of his being. A letter which he wrote to Schuré, and which Mademoiselle Isabelle Rouault has kindly communicated to us, gives a first-hand account of this capital event in his evolution :

"One day I noticed how, when a beautiful day turns to evening, the first star shines out in the sky. It moved me deeply—I don't know why—and it marked the beginnings of poetry in my life. A gypsy caravan halted at the side of the road, **a** weary old horse nibbling stunted grasses, an old clown patching his costume—the *contrast*, in fact, between the brilliance and scintillation of laughter and the intense sadness of life itself... That was how it began. Then I enlarged it all. I saw quite clearly that the clown was myself, us, all of us, almost... The gaudy spangled dress was what life gives us. We all wear a spangled dress of some sort, but

Rouault and his daughter Isabelle going through the plates from Miserere. *She has worked closely with her father for many years and acts as his secretary.*

if someone catches us with the spangles off, as I caught that old clown, oh! the infinite pity of it! I have made

Etching in colors for The Circus of the Shooting Star, *published by Vollard in 1938. Rouault illustrated a book by Vollard "The Reincarnations of Père Ubu".*

the mistake, (if it is a mistake—certainly it causes me suffering beyond description) of never allowing people to keep their spangles on. King or emperor, it's all the same. I want to see through to his soul, and the more the world thinks

of him, the more I fear for that soul..."

This letter contains the key to Rouault's work. As he himself said later : "Anyone who bases his entire art on one glance from a broken-down acrobat must be crazed with pride—or entirely humble, if that's the purpose he was made for"

At that period Rouault met Huysmans and Léon Bloy. Bloy had a decisive influence on him. Temperamentally they were made for one another, with their hatred of half-measures, love of outrageous statement, and shared conviction that if you want to get to Heaven it is better to pass through a thousand ordeals than lead the irreproachable, flavorless life of the 'right-thinking person'. Hypocrisy of any kind, and religious hypocrisy above all, was anathema to them. Rouault was bowled over by Bloy's *La Femme Pauvre*. As Bloy noted in his diary for March 16th 1904, "That book has struck him to the heart, wounded him for ever. I tremble to think of the unhappy man's punishment" And, just as Bloy inherited from Baudelaire his loathing of the bourgeois and preference for evil, as opposed to mediocrity, so Rouault inherits much from Goya and Daumier.

Rouault enjoys a day with his grandchildren. Here he is in the Parc de Sceaux, between his daughter Agnes (Mme Yves Le Dantec), and his grandson Olivier, who has hoisted his cousin Bernard on his shoulders.

But anger, with him, is a pretext for pity:

"If it be true that everything has to be paid for—strength, beauty, grace, and faith in You, Lord Jesus—and paid at a high price, then I should prefer, if You think me worthy, to pay with my own flesh—do you hear me, Shylock ? Pay with my own flesh rather than take my pleasure as you take yours. And as for you, my dear contemporaries, you will never get me to adopt the terrible fake-seriousness that afflicts the marionettes of the political world when they put their hands on their hearts and talk of Progress and the Future..."

Rouault ranks high among the artist-pamphleteers, and the higher because he speaks always as one prompted from Above. Bloy, too, spoke as one sent to save the world, and he and Rouault should have been close friends. If they were not, it was partly because Bloy only really enjoyed academic painting. "Atrocious, vengeful caricatures" was the best he could say of Rouault's mature works ; and after visiting the Salon des Indépendants in 1907 he wrote and said : "I've got just two things to say to you, and two only : One : you're attracted by nothing but what is ugly. You have an obsession with ugliness. Two : if you were a man of prayer, a man of obedience, you couldn't paint those horrible pictures. A Rouault with depth in him would get the shivers at the sight of them".

The same might, of course, have been said to Bloy himself by an uncomprehending friend. Certain 'good Catholics' have always reproached Bloy and Rouault alike for speaking of the angels in the language of the Devil. But there was no bridging the misunderstanding between them when Bloy called Cézanne a 'bungler' and a 'man who didn't know how to finish a picture'. He would never admit, above all, that Rouault was, like himself, a Gothic artist, a Bernanos or a Ghelderode born out of time. As Rouault has written in his 'Souvenirs Intimes' : "Some people linked our two names, so that I became, willy-nilly, the 'Léon Bloy of painting'. It's usually a mistake to try to establish such parallels. There may be a shared point of view, but it's too easy, and too misleading, to compare artists who happen to practise two quite dissimilar arts".

The Beautiful and the Good can take, as we all know, many different forms, and it may even be that the ideals which an artist holds most dear can find expression only in their opposite. Such is the case with Rouault: his prostitutes, judges and clowns are the counter-balance of his purity, humility, and gravity. They bring these virtues before us, just as a shadow makes us newly aware of the light. His subjects are horrifying certainly, but it is the horror of vice, the horror of hypocrisy, the horror of human nature defiled, that Rouault lays before us. His rage is directed not against human beings, but against the monsters which have forced their way into them.

Those monsters he intends to drive out, as a cauteriser drives out poison. Even his technique shows this: whereas in 1903 it was made up of delicate gradations, it became a matter of abrupt contrast. Brown vanished from his palette, and in its place came reds that merged now into violet, now into orange. The color became aggressive, the forms provocative, and always there was black, an abundance of black.

Ghastly, terrible as are his cathedral-gargoyle prostitutes, they are not as terrible as some of his judges. Tartuffe and Sade dispute for dominance in these horrible men as they violate Christ's injunction: "Judge not, that ye be

The Chinaman. *Oil. 25⅝″×19¾″. 1938. Farra coll.*

not judged!" Pathetic, too, are the clowns as they resign themselves to suffer that others may be amused.

The art of Rouault's maturity is truly religious, Christian, *catholic*, in fact, in as much as it is universal and embraces every aspect of Man's redemption by God incarnate. But until 1903, as Venturi has remarked, it was 'church art' in the sense that it was religious only in so far as its subjects were taken from religion. Maritain, as we know, wrote his "Art et Scolastique" with Rouault in mind, and no one has evoked Rouault the man more vividly than Raissa Maritain in her "Grandes Amitiés," for Rouault, when he lived at Versailles, dined every week with his friends the Maritains. He would arrive with a great deal on his mind and unload it at once, without preliminaries, and with no thought for 'general conversation'. Like many artists, great and small, he never really lost sight of himself. Nor need this be egoism, if an artist has begun to encompass the whole universe in his own person. His pockets were full of papers covered with illegible scrawls —new poems of his own composition which he would proceed to read aloud. These poems have never been printed

Christ Mocked. *Oil. 35⅝″×28⅝″. 1930-39.*

in full : punctuation and grammar are erratic, repetitions and inversions the rule. In subject, Rouault's poems are either satiric (aimed at the ferocity of judges, the hypocrisy of the bourgeois, the presumption of art critics) or idyllic (ancient legend, it may be, or a landscape in which inland water plays a great role—canals, springs, rivers...). The Holy Family may be found in these poems in the guise of everyday neighbors—much as they appear in certain writings of the German mystics— and Raissa Maritain is near the mark when she says that Rouault's poems have the character half of popular songs, half of "a relaxed Villon".

Rouault has always imposed upon himself where his painting is concerned. Never will he say what it is he is working on, never will he allow anyone to visit his studio. Even his private address remains a secret. He is perfectly disinterested, and he has never written, any more than he has painted, "to make a name". When he was poor and had a family to keep, he protested indignantly when a priest advised him to "paint something that will sell easily..." His paintings at that time were dark in color, and bitter and violent in inspiration.

During the inter-war period, 1918-38, he worked in his studio for Ambroise

tions du Père Ubu. Between 1917 and 1927 he was preparing the great series of large copper plates for his *Miserere* (these finally appeared only after the death of the dealer, in 1947). Rouault devoted himself with passion to this activity, cutting himself off from everything else. He worked the plates himself, using every possible instrument and discovering new techniques of his own such as adding acid with large brushstrokes. Then he turned back to painting, celebrating his return with an even greater richness and brilliance and variety of color. All this was made clear at the Petit Palais in 1938 ; Vollard lent twenty canvases to the

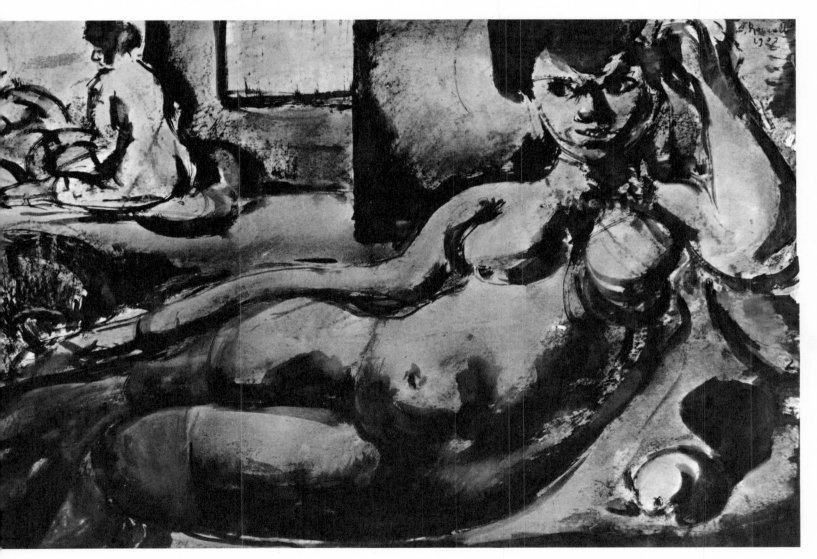

Odalisque. *Watercolor, 25¼″×38⅝″. 1907. Bangerter coll., Montreux.*

Rouault's written work does not enhance his glory as an artist, but it does help us to know and define him better. It's very profusion is in sharp contrast to the extreme reserve which

Vollard, the famous dealer, and showed nothing. For Vollard he undertook a whole series of engravings to illustrate books published by the dealer. Among these were *Le Cirque* and *Les Réincarna-*

exhibition. The retrospective exhibition of 1957 revealed a further fifteen canvases from this period ; lent by Rouault himself, they included *The Dwarf, The Last Romantic*, some portraits, *The Travelling Circus*, and *The Peasants*. The new intensity of color had the effect, Venturi said, of making the light "seem to come from within the picture itself. Even when the tones

the forms and underline their expression. Rouault had never ceased to be an artisan. On the contrary, he sought out new forms of craftsmanship in the knowledge that they would nourish and

musicians transpose." And, side by side with these transpositions, his art passes from paroxysm to serenity. His Christ becomes the Christ of the Resurrection rather than the Christ of the Passion.

Late Autumn No. 1. 29⅝″×41½″. *1948-52.*

are dark, they shine out with a color which is within them: that is what makes these pictures unique in the history of art. Rembrandt, Daumier, Cézanne—all would admit that there is something new in Rouault's color: phosphorescence".

After the war of 1914-18 Rouault also applied himself to the problems of ceramics. These reminded him of his old skill as a glass-painter—the use of lead, in particular—and even in his paintings one can discern the heavy lead-like strokes which at once outline

strengthen his painting. He went back, in short, to the tradition which Colbert had broken when he founded an Academy exclusively for the 'fine arts'.

Rouault could have moved towards decoration, and from decoration towards abstraction. But he feared that in doing so he would, as he puts it, 'dry up'. Equally well he could have become a 'realist' in the narrow sense of the word; but there again he feared that the dignity of his art would suffer. "Our task is not to rival Nature, or to imitate her exactly, but to transpose, as

The byzantine character of his art becomes accentuated. Majesty predominates, in place of pathos. Landscape, and even still life, plays a part in his subject-matter, and there is a new limpidity in the atmosphere. As he says himself: "When I first went to Moreau I knew nothing of *la matière picturale*. But when he saw my first clum-

Onesimus. *Oil.* 15″×9⅛″. *1952. The ▶ color is thickly applied. The frame, heavily painted by Rouault himself, is an integral part of the picture. Rouault coll.*

sy efforts he raised his arms high in the air and said "Ah, you at least love the stuff of painting! I wish you joy of it!" It was as if my doctor had said "You've cancer of the stomach and there's no hope for you at all. But at least we can stop you suffering too much..." And I shouldn't have wanted to be cured".

Our epoch has so often abused the concept of *Matière* that one must distinguish between paint that is flung down anyhow on the canvas and the substance of color itself, which needs a certain weight behind it, just as flesh needs muscle and bone. *Matière* of this second kind has a spiritual quality, as we see in those pictures of Rembrandt where the painter has made the light rebound from the richly-worked paint. Generosity is a virtue, as Aristotle said : but, as he also said, you can't be generous if you've nothing to give.

Another constant element in Rouault's work, and one which has never had its due of recognition, is joy. Yet Rouault is, in his way, a joyful painter. It comes out most, of course, in his latest pictures, where the solemn quiet, the unforced assurance, are clear for all to see. Rouault himself says : "A painter of joy! Well, and why not? I've always been so happy to paint, crazy to paint, forgetful at such times of even the cruellest grief. The critics never noticed it, because my subjects were tragic. But surely joy can be elsewhere than in the subject!" And on another occasion, writing of Renoir, he said "He understood what a great joy resides, for a painter, in letting the eye move across water, flesh, flowers and fruit... I envy those who can do it without second thoughts, like children born under a favoring star..."

But who to-day has no second thoughts? Rouault was quite right. And between the joy of the Resurrection and the joy of an unthinking life in the sun, a great gulf is fixed.

Still-life. *Oil* 13¼"×18½". *1953. This picture, one of the artist's rare still-lifes, belongs to Rouault himself and has never before been reproduced in color.*

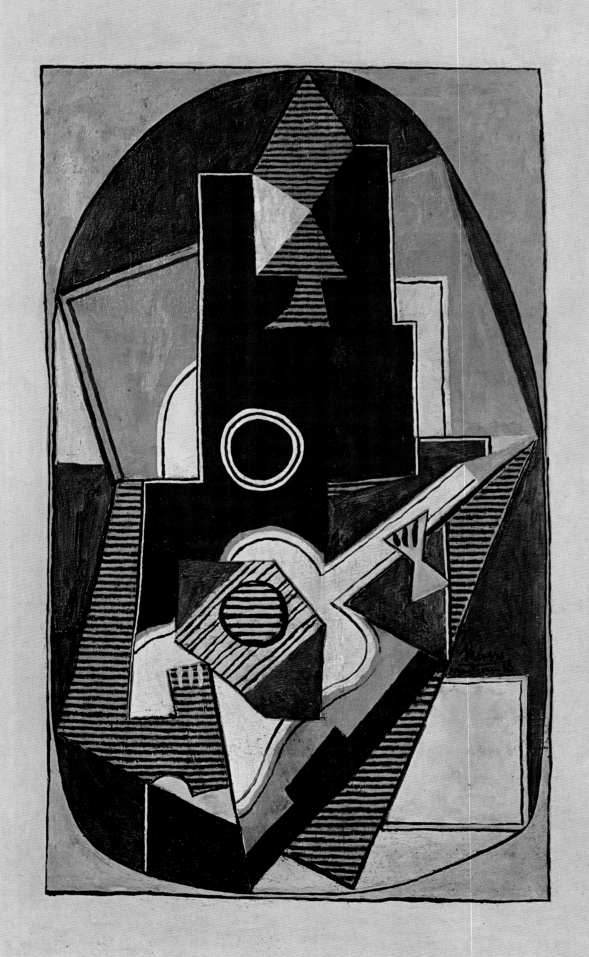

The Apollinaire Collection

BY GEORGES LIMBOUR

A Paris apartment still houses the paintings and objects gathered by the great poet who championed the Cubists and the Fauves

The house where a poet has lived and died is often turned into a museum. The floors are waxed, the objects dusted and "arranged", and it is the most difficult thing in the world for the visitor to experience something that genuinely relates to the poet himself. A legend has already grown up around the Paris apartment on the Boulevard Saint Germain in which Guillaume Apollinaire died ; but few of those who remember the address have ever got farther than the door. They know that the poet is supposed to have heard the crowd shouting "Guillaume à mort !" ("Death to Kaiser Wilhelm !") as Apollinaire lay dying on November 11th 1918 ; but hardly anyone, save the poet's widow, has seen the inside of the apartment since he died. Order was restored there ; part of his collection of paintings was moved elsewhere, as we shall see, but the majority of his belongings were left where they were.

The time has come to knock on the door and call to mind not only the poet himself, and the women he loved, but also the paintings which were the other ruling passion of his existence. Not all such things escape the passage of time, and we can hope to recover only a part of the rich original complex of Apollinaire's affections.

What is most moving and, it may be, most suggestive to the imagination

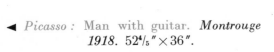

◄ *Picasso :* Man with guitar. *Montrouge 1918. 52⁴/₅″×36″.*

Dufy : The Bathers. *Inscribed "to M. Guillaume Apollinaire". 21¹/₅″×25³/₅″. One of Dufy's few fauve figure-subjects.*

about the apartment at no. 202 Boulevard Saint Germain is that although Apollinaire, a natural vagabond, was not often physically present there, yet it was haunted by his spirit. This was especially the case during the first years of the 1914/18 war, when he himself led a desperate life in the trenches.

It's a remarkable fact that not until he had passed the age of 25 did Apollinaire have a 'home of his own'. His childhood was spent piecemeal in Rome, Nice and Monaco, and until 1907 he

lived—if we are to except for the moment his stay in the Rhineland—with his mother, the tyrannical Madame Kostrowicka, whose irregular habits had at any rate the advantage that she was rarely at home in the evenings. This it was, perhaps, which gave Apollinaire a liking for noctambular café life. (It was in a café near the Gare Saint Lazare, where he was waiting for the last train that would take him home to his mother in Le Vésinet, that Apollinaire was introduced to Picasso by Max Jacob.) It would seem that Apollinaire was considerably in

The apartment at no. 202 Boulevard Saint Germain, Paris, which was Apollinaire's from 1912 to 1918, has remained just as it was at that time. Pictures and drawings by Dufy, Picasso, Vlaminck, Marie Laurencin and Derain still hang on the walls (he was close to the avant-garde painters of the day and wrote prefaces for many exhibition catalogues). Here we see his room with, above the bed, a 'portrait-document' by Marie Laurencin (see p. 66). On the chimney-piece is a sculpture by Brancusi.

awe of his mother and would have been glad to move out to a quiet lodging of his own. Such, at any rate, is the implication of the poem called "The Cat" which forms part of his "Bestiary" (1911). In it he dreams of having in his house "a woman in her right mind, a cat to move among my books, and at every season the friends without whom I cannot exist".

These were modest desires, but Apollinaire realised them only in part. The cat, at least, he came to acquire, only to have it assassinated on the staircase of no. 202 Boulevard Saint Germain by that same Dr Delarue-Mardrus who had made such an exemplary translation of Apollinaire's favorite "Thousand and One Nights". (André Rouveyre describes the incident in his 'Souvenirs'.)

Apollinaire was to have many and various lodgings. In September 1911

he even spent a few days in the Santé prison in Paris, where he was committed on suspicion (groundless, it need hardly be said) of being implicated in the theft from the Louvre of the "Mona Lisa". When he came to the Boulevard Saint Germain from Auteuil, his beloved 'Marie' came with him. He was sorry to leave Auteuil for, despite its outward respectability, it had been the scene of what he called his *grandes tristesses*. Max Jacob, a great prophet and reader of horoscopes, had foretold that certain sadnesses would come his way, and it was with heavy foreboding that Apollinaire took up residence on the Boulevard. His apartment was on the fourth floor, under the rooftops, and the staircase which led to it was narrow and lit by a single lantern which the poet himself had installed. The apartment gave on to a little terrace with a view

of innumerable chimney-pots. These chimney-pots disquieted Apollinaire by

André Derain: Joy. One side of the vase made by Derain from a shell-case. The other side is entitled Sadness.

their habit of turning in the wind. Evil spirits, he considered them, and for a year or so he avoided the little terrace on their account. The apartment was too small, in any case, and the kitchen long and narrow, like a corridor. For this reason he preferred to work elsewhere—in cafés, for preference, and above all in the nearby Flore. The Ile Saint-Louis would have suited him best of all, and he often went off to Madame Louise Faure-Favier's apartment at the very end of the Ile. There he had his armchair, his window, and, what was more, his own room. When he was editing the "Soirées de Paris" he occasionally invited his friends home for a 'session of work', but these 'sessions' were few and far between. Apollinaire was a devoted friend and detested to be alone. For this reason he often had living with him in his apartment a bizarre character called "The Baron" who served him as secretary and general handyman, polished his furniture and did his marketing in shining yellow gloves. The Baron also cooked for him. Opinions differ so widely that it is difficult for us to tell whether Apollinaire, who loved eating and soon became very stout, was a good cook and a man of fastidious taste in such matters, or whether he was just a glutton who didn't care what he shovelled into his mouth. But on the whole it seems more likely that he was a man of true discernement where food was

Picasso : Apollinaire seated in uniform. *Drawing.*

Picasso : Watercolor painted on card-board on which can be read the words "Galeries Lafayette, Paris". Negro period.

concerned. Such, at any rate, is the implication of the poems in which this man of great appetite celebrates the pleasures of the five senses—smell and taste not least.

From the feasts to which he sometimes invited his friends two things remain : the *pot-au-feu* and the big earthenware coffee-pot, both decorated by Picasso. (On the coffee-pot

we see the poet himself, smoking his pipe.)

The apartment soon filled up—partly with things brought from Auteuil, and partly with new acquisitions : above all, with specimens of Negro art. Apollinaire loved all that was novel and new ("You have lived long enough with the Greeks and the Romans") and he was one of the first to realise the importance of primitive art and to form a small collection of it. Vlaminck is said to have been the first to discover the beauties of Negro statuary. He was

Marie Laurencin : Portrait-Document. *1909. Apollinaire in the centre. Behind him, the Pont Mirabeau. On his right an angel crowned with fruit, then Picasso's friend Fernande Olivier, and Gertrude Stein, one of the cubists' earliest supporters. On his left are Picasso, an unidentified friend of the group, Cremnitz the poet, and seated, Marie Laurencin (once the poet's mistress).*

soon followed by Picasso and Derain, and all three had an influence upon Apollinaire, who somehow combined his new passion with the love of Catholicism which had been part of his nature since childhood. (He once wrote of how he went home to sleep "among the fetishes of Guinea and Oceania, the Christs of another faith and another belief, the inferior Christs who speak for unformulated hopes...")

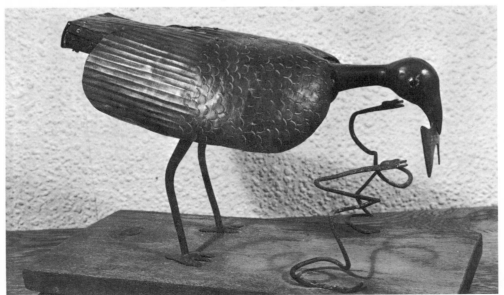

For the most part these fetishes are still there, enthroned above his furniture and his shelves of books. The most famous and mysterious of them is the bird from Benin which inspired the nickname given to Picasso in Apollinaire's "Poète Assassiné". Apollinaire loved to give his friends nicknames and

Benin Bird. This mysterious object inspired Apollinaire's nickname for Picasso.

Picasso : Head of a Woman. *Oil. Barcelona. 1903. 14″×10⁴/₅″.*

he chose, for preference, strange names whose music delighted him. These came to haunt him—each speaking, as it seemed, for some ancient myth. The Benin bird, the Phœnix dying and reborn, the Pihi bird which has only one wing and flies everywhere in couples, the Palace of Rosemonde...

Pictures came crowding in as fast as books, either because he bought them for almost nothing, or because his painter-friends gave them to him in acknowledgment of the prophetic articles in which he sang their praises. Apollinaire's articles did a great deal to spread the fame of the new movement in painting. (And the fame of Apollinaire, of course.) His poetical adventures are intimately linked with the pictorial adventures of his friends, and he was as much inspired by them as they were by him. In 1912, before coming to the Boulevard Saint Germain, he had lived for a while with Robert Delaunay. They walked endlessly about Paris, and shared the same admiration for the Eiffel Tower and the exploits of the first aviators. (Cf. Delaunay's "Hommage to Louis Blériot".) Apollinaire's "simultaneism" in poetry had its counterpart in painting, and Delaunay's 1912 exhibition included a picture called "Simultaneous Windows". Apollinaire's preface to the catalogue featured his famous poem "The Windows". He also found the name of Orphism which was then given to Delaunay's lyrical use of color, and a year later Apollinaire baptised the dynamic abstractionism of Larionov and Nathalie Goncharova "Rayonnisme".

Apollinaire's poems were traditional in form, and he admired Maeterlinck and the symbolists ; but in painting he sought out the creators of a new aesthetic, and these in their turn drove him to seek new rhythms in his poetry. The cubist portraits of Apollinaire by Picasso, Metzinger and others took hold of his features and imprinted on them the seal of the modern movement ; and his mind likewise became permeated with the spirit of modernity. He had the honor of presenting to the public the great exhibitions of the day—those of Matisse, Braque, Picasso, Léger, Derain, and others. (See his "Cubist Painters",

Picasso : Portrait of Jean Moréas.

1913.) He admired—even if, at first, with an ironical inflection—the Douanier Rousseau, whose "Muse Inspiring the Poet" (1909) shows him with Marie Laurençin, and who had painted for him his "Pont Mirabeau". Many of the Douanier's works were bought by close friends of Apollinaire, such as the Baronne d'Oettingen and her brother, Serge Férat. All that was new interested Apollinaire, whether it was the early work of Chirico or the experiments of the futurists.

It is probable that Apollinaire had more than one ephemeral love-affair in the apartment on the Boulevard

Picasso: Apollinaire as coffee-pot. Watercolor and gouache. C. 1905. 8³/₅″×12″.

Saint Germain—deep as was the chagrin that persuaded him to move there—but when the war came, and he found himself at Nice in the winter of 1914-15, he fell in love with a pretty woman, who at first resisted him. It was a bad time for the poet, for the newspapers no longer printed his articles and he was very short of money. Lou (that was her name) was well born : the blood of Saint-Louis ran in her veins. Apollinaire, though still a Pole, joined the French Army and was soon in barracks in Nîmes. Lou relented, joined him in Nîmes, and became his mistress. It was

as it seemed, in his hand again. On the other hand, what would his mother say ? A disturbing question : and then she had brought her dogs with her... In the end Apollinaire's mother looked after the dogs, and from then until the end of 1916 the poet wrote to Lou almost every day. Often he spoke of the apartment. The 220 letters remain unpublished and we cannot, therefore, speak of what is in them. Suffice it to say that they show how deeply Apollinaire cared for his apartment, and how absolutely it symbolised for him the haven of peace and contentment in

Chirico : Premonitory portrait of Apollinaire. *1914. 32⁴/₅″ × 26²/₅″.*

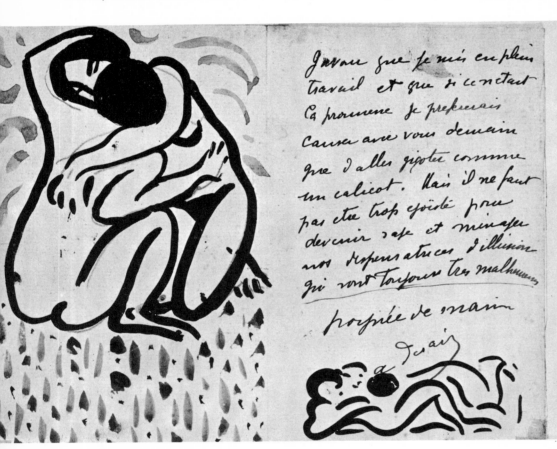

Letter in watercolor from Derain to Apollinaire.

a curious affair—sensual, perhaps, rather than tender, and Lou was a person of impulse who did not remain for long in love with Apollinaire. But when he was in the trenches, and she was bored with provincial life, she took it into her head to come up to Paris and live in no. 202 where the key was still, after all, under the mat. And so there she soon was, an idol among idols, and Apollinaire was delighted to think of her being there,—under his roof and,

which he would one day recover from the torments of war and get on with his work.

The letters portray, too, a man whose dangerous way of life—and, for all his expansiveness, there was much that he kept back from his comrades in the trenches—made him ever more dependent upon letters. The letters for which he waited were not Lou's only ; for he was corresponding at the same period with a young girl called Madeleine whom he had met in a train in 1915 on the way from Nice to Nîmes. He wanted to marry her and hoped that after the war he would at last have, at no. 202, a "woman in her right mind", and children in place of a cat. This was never to be, alas ! for the chimney-pots were to bring him the bad luck that he dreaded.

On March 17th, 1916, he was wounded in the head by a shellburst. Trepanned, he was taken first to the Val de Grâce in Paris, and then to the Italian Hospital on the Quai d'Orsay. In August 1916 he reappeared, his head bandaged, in

Marie Laurencin : Portrait of Fernande Olivier. *Inscribed (top right) "Madame Pickaçoh". Watercolor. 1910. 8³/₅″ × 7″.*

the cafés of Saint Germain des Prés and Montparnasse. A great banquet was held in his honor. He forgot Madeleine and Lou and began to take a new delight in life. His "Mamelles de Tirésias" was performed on the stage, he lectured on the new movement in art, and he organised exhibitions of Irène Lagut and Leopold Survage. Survage brought him back to his old theories about rhythm, color and 'painting in movement'. He shared the opinions of Marcel Duchamp and Picabia, and his collection was enriched with a number of pictures by both these artists.

On May 2nd 1918 he married Jacqueline Kolb, whom he called Ruby—the "Jolie Rousse" of his "Calligrammes". As he had very little money he decided to write a novel whose success would rival that of Pierre Benoit's "Kœnigsmark". It was to be called "The White Lady of Hohenzollern", and would deal with the fatal lady of legend who vouchsafes herself only to those dynasties which are destined to disappear.

In November 1918 he caught influenza and took to his bed in the 'pigeons' loft'. Ruby read aloud to him each morning a serial novel by Louise Faure-Favier which was appearing in "L'Œuvre". Set in the year 2000, it described the adventures of a descendant of Apollinaire's and portrayed him as looking back with nostalgia to the poet's own day. This delighted Apollinaire, who was himself both a prophet and a devotee of the past. But after

Apollinaire's books and papers have not been touched since he died. Negro sculptures, curiosities of one sort and another, and Picasso watercolors ornament his shelves.

Brancusi : Head. *Stone.*

a very few days he could hear the serial no longer...

Apollinaire lies now in his last lodging, in the Père Lachaise cemetery. People rarely move house when once they arrive there, but Apollinaire's restless nature would have been amused to note that in 1920, when the concession bought by his mother ran out, he was moved to a concession bought by his widow. A last vagabondage ! Meanwhile his widow had carefully tidied the pigeons' loft and taken down

to his house near Amboise such pictures as could not be hung in Paris. There remain at no. 202, over and above the pictures which we reproduce here, many papers, documents, pictures and illustrated books—among them the Maeterlinck for which Marie Laurencin made illustrations. The most touching souvenirs are perhaps the helmet with a hole in it which Apollinaire had on at the time he was wounded, the uniforms he wore during the war, the walking-sticks whose handles he carved while in the trenches, and the aluminium rings which he engraved himself.

The International

DADA

BY MICHEL SEUPHOR

Not everything illustrated here was well received at the time; but Dada's witty and resolute "No to everything!" has been one of the sources of contemporary art

Academic art is death. When art tends towards the academic, it should be killed off. Life is what matters, and anything at all can be art—or anti-art—provided it has the free insolence, the provocative youth, of life itself. "Everything that an artist spits out is art", said Kurt Schwitters. And when we look at Dada it does seem as if its exponents did, in fact, create works of art even though their activity was one long deliberate "spitting-out" of traditional art. When Picabia scrawled across a huge white board "Sh.. on anyone who looks at this" his categorical contempt does not suffice to create "beauty" or a work of art. Yet this white board, once put in a frame, became a unique object, a document put on exhibition, a collector's piece, and therefore a work of art and a thing of beauty. And as time puts it more and more in perspective we see that Dada, by rejecting art, created a completely gratuitous form of art, an art of pure nonconformity to all accepted canons. This gratuitousness was, in fact, Art itself: this pure non-conformity was true Art. The Dadaists were incapable of not making art. The act of rejecting everything was not an act of denial but a declaration of high standards. "Dada was not a joke", said Arp, and Robert Motherwell, the American painter and publicist who edited "Dada, Painters and Poets", in New York in 1951, says quite rightly that the famous "Bottle-dryer" to which Marcel Duchamp put his name in 1916 may now be considered

more beautiful, in the strict sense, than most of the sculpture that was being made in the world at that date.

Raoul Hausmann: Collage. 1919.

The Dada epoch could be said to begin with that gesture of Marcel Duchamp's. For Dada was in the air before it exploded. If the air had not been, as it were, on Dada's side there would probably never have been an explosion. Similarly Alfred Jarry, Christian Morgenstern, Arthur Cravan, Erik Satie and Guillaume Apollinaire were, in certain of their aspects, authentic Dadaists before Dada itself was founded in Zurich in 1916.

"Dada was never anything but a protest", Tzara said later. But what a protest! Every contract was broken, every value thrown on the dust-heap in the interests of something new and fresh: an art that would not toe the line, an art that had nothing to do with fashion or speculation. Kandinsky had called for an art of free self-expression: Dada converted this into an "-ism," a sort of precept, but a precept which had the the ingenuity to laugh at itself.

The original Zurich explosion was set off by a group of people whose very diversity had much to do with it: Hugo Ball, Marcel Janco, Emmy Hennings, Hans Arp, Tristan Tzara and Richard Huelsenbeck. A little later they were joined by Walter Serner, Hans Richter, and Viking Eggeling. "Tzara and I," Janco writes, "were friends from before the war. We had worked together, in Roumania, on our first avant-garde review, "Simbolul." His pseudonym was Samiro, his name S. Rosenstok. We met again in Zurich just before the war broke out. I was studying at the Polytechnic School of Architecture and he was reading philosophy at the University. The war made me penniless and I began to make some sort of a living by singing French, English and Roumanian folksongs in the night-clubs of Zurich. My brother played the piano for me. One night when I was hunting for work in one of the narrow streets of the old city I met the fantastically elongated and asymmetrical figure of Hugo Ball.

All poetry, all thought was 'an open book' to Ball, who was then running a cabaret. When he found that I was a painter, had friends among the cubists and futurists, and knew other poets and artists in Zurich, he pressed me to join with him in founding a literary cabaret in the city. The next day I spoke to Arp and Tzara and got them to come in with us. Tzara saw at once what could be made of it. Arp did all he could to help. We called it the Cabaret Voltaire. Every evening our group grew larger. Poets and prose-men declaimed their work, the walls were brilliant with pictures and manifestoes, the room rang with sonatas played on the piano by Ball, and to the sound of Negro or Javanese music we danced in masks painted by me. Or, "he concludes, in a letter to myself, "we read aloud, simultaneously, four poems in four different languages."

Arp, too, fills in some details : "In June 1915 my brother François and I left Paris to rejoin my mother in Zurich. There I met Otto and Adya van Rees and in November I had an exhibition with them at Tanner's. Shortly afterwards I found, in the Otenbachgasse, a German bookseller called Hack. He was very ill, and a morphia-addict. He knew Ball, and must have told him about me, for Ball wrote to me, care of Hack's bookshop, and asked me to help with his new cabaret. At the corner of the Spiegelgasse and the Niederdorfstrasse there was a restaurant (it still exists) kept by a Dutchman, Oom Jan. It was there that we all met—Ball, Emmy Hennings, Tzara, the two Janco brothers and myself. Ball had worked in Munich as a theatrical producer. He'd produced, among other things, Kandinsky's *Der gelbe Klang*. When war broke out he volunteered for the German Army but quickly got sick of it and took refuge in Switzerland. His friend Emmy Hennings was with him, and to make a living he worked in the cabarets as accompanist to jugglers, acrobats, and singers. Emmy Hennings had had quite a success in the literary cabarets of Munich and to keep themselves more or less alive they decided to found a cabaret of that sort in Zurich. They'd got just the right place—a largish room in the Brasserie Meierei in the Spiegelgasse, just next to Oom Jan's restaurant. That's how the Cabaret Voltaire was founded, and it gave its name to our first publication, which appeared a month or two later. We often met, too, at Laban's famous dancing-school. Sophie Taeuber was trained there. Tzara and the others went to watch Mary Wigman's unaccompanied dancing.

The tumultuous evenings at the Cabaret Voltaire have often been described. The Zurich papers gave them plenty of

Hans Arp : The Glove. *Collage.*

ExcuRsIons & visiTES DADA

DADA

UN CULTE NOUVEAU :

1ÈRE Église VISITE :

Saint Julien le Pauvre

PROCHAINES VISITES :
Musée du Louvre
Buttes Chaumont
Gare Saint-Lazare
Mont du Petit Cadenas
Canal de l'Ourcq
etc.

JEUDI 14 AVRIL A 3 h.
RENDEZ-VOUS DANS LE JARDIN DE L'ÉGLISE
Rue Saint Julien le Pauvre — (Métro Saint-Michel et Cité)

COURSES PÉDESTRES DANS LE JARDIN

Les dadaïstes de passage à Paris voulant remédier à l'incompétence
de guides et de cicerones suspects, ont décidé d'entreprendre une
série de visites à des endroits choisis, en particulier à ceux qui n'ont
vraiment pas de raison d'exister. — C'est à tort qu'on insiste sur le
pittoresque (Lycée Janson de Sailly), l'intérêt historique (Mont
Blanc) et la valeur sentimentale (la Morgue). — La partie n'est pas
perdue mais il faut agir vite. — Prendre part à cette première visite
c'est se rendre compte du progrès humain, des destructions possibles
et de la nécessité de poursuivre notre action que vous tiendrez à
encourager par tous les moyens.

EN BAS LE BAS   EN HAUT LE HAUT

Sous la conduite de : Gabrielle BUFFET, Louis ARAGON, ARP,
André BRETON, Paul ELUARD, Th. FRAENKEL, J. HUSSAR, Benjamin
PÉRET, Francis PICABIA, Georges RIBEMONT-DESSAIGNES, Jacques
RIGAUT, Philippe SOUPAULT, Tristan TZARA.

(Le piano a été mis très gentiment à notre disposition par la maison Gavault.)

publicity and the room seems to have been full almost from the start. Young people and sober seniors sat side by side. People laughed, shouted, protested, began bawling in unison; in the end everyone took part in the tumult. Ball and Tzara were the Masters of Ceremonies, but Janco put all his energies into the making of masks and disguises of every kind and Sophie Taeuber, the only Swiss member of the group, organized dances in which she herself always appeared masked, for fear of being recognised and dismissed from the School of Applied Arts in which she was then teaching. Emmy Hennings says that the embroideries and tapestries which she executed after designs by Arp or herself were 'the finest ornament of the Dada exhibitions'! There were French evenings, Russian evenings, German evenings, Roumanian evenings. As Tzara says "Every evening Beauty or the Absurd took charge of our visitors, —none was spared—and the wind blew at gale force. Conscience after conscience was knocked sideways—it was like an avalanche—vitality and thoughtful silence, wisdom and madness were side by side, and none knew where the frontier lay. Slowly the girls slipped away and the family man was consumed with secret bitterness. A word was born, none knew quite how: "Dadadada." On the walls were pictures by Arp, van Rees, Picasso, Eggeling, Janco, Segal, Slodky, Nadelman, and futurist poems by Marinetti, Cangiullo and Buzzi. *Sous les ponts de Paris* was sung in chorus. Then an immense vat was brought in, and somebody hidden inside read aloud Arp's latest poem. Hugo Ball followed, with his famous poem-without-words *Gadji beri bimba*. He wore leggings of shiny blue cardboard that came up to his waist, and a red and gold collar that he could cause to rise and fall like a pair of wings. "With these sound-poems,"

From left to right: Arp, Tzara and Max Ernst, in 1920.

1. *Mme Janco, Arp, Janco, Zurich, 1916.* 2. *André Breton and Théodore Fraenkel in Adrienne Monnier's bookshop, Paris, 1917.* 3. *Man Ray, New York, 1918, at the time of his first meetings with Marcel Duchamp.* 4. *Walter Serner, Switzerland, 1917.*

he explains in his *La Fuite hors du Temps*, "language was abandoned. Journalism had killed it off. Our task was to withdraw into the deep alchemy of the individual word and even to abandon that word, thus reserving for poetry its most sacred domain." Tzara, between two

strange vaudeville acts, would 'explain' the new art or declaim a manifesto. 'Cubist' or Negro dances would follow, in which each participant carried a big drum on his head and beat it continually, and poems for four, or later for seven, voices were recited. "The most

important things," Tzara wrote in his journal, "are the masks and the revolver-effects. Bravo! And boum, boum!" And Emmy Hennings adds: "The Dadaists welcomed masks of any kind, even if they were not really suited to the person in question. But the mask

◄ *Announcement of a Dadaist manifestation in Paris, 1920.*

was indispensable and served as an underground refuge for people whose disconcertedness would otherwise have been too evident. For there was a lot of despair, in Dadaism, along with the un-dissipated strength of youth.''

The Cabaret Voltaire had opened on February 8th, 1916. Huelsenbeck arrived on February 26th. Aged twenty-four, he proved a powerful German reinforcement, particularly welcome to Tzara, who was then only twenty, and at once a 'simultaneous poem' in German, English and French, was composed by Huelsenbeck, Tzara and Janco. It was declaimed from the stage on March 31st with musical interludes by Janco (whistle), Tzara (castanets) and Huelsenbeck (big drum). In June the *Cabaret Voltaire* booklet was published, with contributions by Ball, Tzara, Apollinaire, Emmy Hennings, Huelsenbeck, Kandinsky, Marinetti, Cangiullo and Cendrars, and illustrations by Janco, Arp, Picasso, van Rees, Modigliani (a portrait of Arp), Slodky and Oppenheimer.

Max Ernst : Fatagaga. *Collage. 1920.*
▼

On July 14th there was a ''grand Dada evening'' in the Zunfthaus zur Waag. The prospectus announced : music, dances, *théorie,* manifesto, poetry, paintings, costumes and masks. The tumult was prodigious, fighting broke out, the police intervened. Huelsenbeck, with a huge bass drum and little bells attached to his left foot, held his own with a howling mob of two hundred people. Dada triumphant ! Books came out at the

Relâche by Picabia and Erik Satie, performed by the Swedish Ballet in 1924.

same period : *La première aventure céleste de Monsieur Antipyrine* by Tzara, and *Phantastische Gebete* by Huelsenbeck. A Dada exhibition was held at the Galerie Corray in the Bahnhofstrasse, all the Dadaists taking part. Tzara gave three lectures there. And on March 17th 1917 a Galerie Dada was opened under the direction of Ball and Tzara. Another soirée given on the 23rd ended in a wild dance of some four hundred people.

But the biggest demonstration was held on April 9th 1919 in the Salle Kaufleuten. Eggeling spoke on abstract art and *Male Fever*, a simultaneous poem by Tzara, was recited by at least twenty persons. Suzanne Perrotet played piano-music by Satie, and Arp presented fragments of the *Wolkenpumpe*. Between a thousand and fifteen hundred people were present and the evening ended in a general fist-fight. "When we

finally managed to get out we were completely exhausted," says Hans Richter, "and we set out to find Tzara. And there he was, calm and unhurt, sitting peacefully in the restaurant opposite, counting the takings. Dada had never seen so much money." Dada triumphant again !

Meanwhile Tzara was giving more and more lectures—even in the Kunsthaus itself—on abstract art and modern

UNE BONNE NOUVELLE

CHER AMI,

VOUS ÊTES INVITÉ AU VERNISSAGE
DE L'EXPOSITION MAN RAY (CHARMANT
GARÇON) QUI AURA LIEU LE 3 DÉCEMBRE
1921 DE 2 H. 1/2 à 7 H. 1/2

A LA LIBRAIRIE SIX

5, AVENUE LOWENDALL - PARIS VII°

SOUS LA PRÉSIDENCE
DU MOUVEMENT DADA

ni fleurs
ni couronnes
ni parapluies
ni sacrements
ni cathédrales
ni tapis
ni paravents
ni système métrique
ni espagnols
ni calendrier
ni rose
ni bar
ni incendie
ni bonbons

N'OUBLIEZ PAS

Invitation-card to a Man Ray exhibition, December 1921.

Above, Man Ray : Metronome. *1923.*

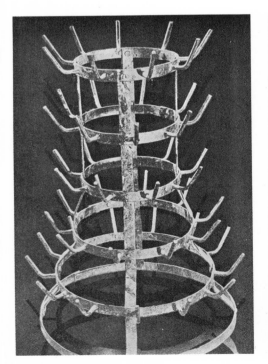

art in general, and the review *Dada* published three numbers (July 1917, December 1917, December 1918). The third number included among other things Tzara's second manifesto, which may be considered as a true 'point of departure' and the intellectual climax of the movement. A double number, 4-5, appeared in May 1919 under the title *Dada Anthology* : contributors were Picabia, Cocteau, Radiguet, Gabrielle Buffet, Pierre Albert-Birot and the future surrealists André Breton, Louis Aragon and Philippe Soupault. The Zurich Dadaists also contributed, and there was a long text by Walter Serner, *Letzte Lockerung*, and the first fragments of Arp's poem *Die Wolkenpumpe*. Arp was thirty-two in 1919 and seems to have been, after Ball, the oldest of the group : in this poem he achieved a mastery of the German language which he was to equal, often enough, but never to surpass.

Extreme left, Marcel Duchamp : Bottle-Dryer. *Readymade, 1914. Next, Man Ray :* Legend. *Painting in oils. 51⅝″ × 35⅞″. 1916. Man Ray collection, Paris.*

of 1919, Tzara went to Paris, where the way had been smoothed for Dada by the review *Littérature*, founded in March 1917 and directed by Breton, Soupault and Aragon.

Once again it was Duchamp who had a great influence—alike by the fresh and unexpected play of his imagination, his

Still from Entr'acte *film by René Clair on a scenario by Picabia, with music by Satie. 1924.*

When Huelsenbeck and Richter went back to Berlin Picabia took their place. He brought with him all the elements of pre-Dada New York : the 'ready-mades' of Duchamp and Man Ray, his own 'useless machines' (*La fille née sans mère*), issues of the reviews 291 and 391, the *Mona Lisa* with Duchamp's amendments, and above all his own tranquil, combative, radical spirit of demolition.

Pre-Dada New York would seem to have had its origins in the current of irrationalism which began with the Armory Show of 1913. At this, Duchamp's famous *Nude descending a staircase* caused a tremendous scandal. Katherine S. Dreier declares that in two weeks 80 000 horrified persons filed past in front of this immensely important picture. In this *Nude*—which is not a Nude at all, of course—cubism and futurism met, and the resulting unique picture remains one of the key-works of twentieth-century art. It was not till two years later, though, that Alfred Stieglitz, the organiser of the Armory Show, founded the 291 group and review. (The number was that of Stie-

glitz's gallery on Fifth Avenue.) The main contributors were Picabia, who was in New York in 1913 and 1915, Marius de Zayas, Agnes Ernst Meyer, Katharine Rhoades and Duchamp, who had just arrived from Paris. In 1916 Man Ray appeared on the scene with his very personal abstract paintings and the compound objects which paralleled Duchamp's ready-mades : the bicycle wheel and the famous *Fountain*, a urinal in porcelain which Duchamp sent to the Salon des Indépendants under the name of R. Mutt (a pseudonym he used later was Rose Sélavy). But in 1916 the seemingly-ubiquitous Picabia turned up in Barcelona and there founded 391 which he continued, the same year, in New York with Duchamp and Walter Arensberg, who became one of the world's greatest modern-art collectors. In 1917 Picabia was in Lausanne, and from there he rejoined the Zurich group. Arp has described how moved he and Tzara were to meet "the emissary of the American Dadaists." The emissary had a genius for dismantling alarm-clocks and re-assembling them in unexpected forms. It was with Picabia that, at the end

perfect unorthodoxy, and his radical detachment. But we must not forget Arthur Cravan, whose little review *Maintenant* had pursued its refreshing career since 1914, or the enigmatic Jacques Vaché, who had such a great influence on Breton and his friends during the war-years. All had prepared the way for Dada in Paris.

The arrival of Tzara and Picabia acted like an electric charge. At the first Dada matinée, held on February 5th 1920 at the Salon des Indépendants, the speakers could hardly make themselves heard. On May 26th the Grand Dada Festival at the Salle Gaveau featured Picabia, Tzara, Breton, Dermée, Soupault, Eluard, Ribemont-Dessaignes and Aragon. The program announced that "all the Dadas will have their hair waved on the stage." Also promised were : Dada's sex, a painless fist-fight (Dermée), the interloper-navel (music by Ribemont-Dessaignes), and Monsieur

Marcel Duchamp.

78

Antipyrine's second adventure (Tzara). The confusion was indescribable and volley after volley of fresh eggs greeted the performers. These were, in fact, duplicates of the Zurich meetings, with the difference that only French was spoken. At the same time Picabia published *Cannibale*, a sequel to 391, Eluard published *Proverbe*, Tzara *Dadaphone*, Dermée *Z*, and *Littérature* had a number with twenty-three Dada manifestoes.

On January 12th 1921 the entire group published a witty and penetrating manifesto : *Dada soulève tout*. Perhaps the completest and most significant of all such manifestoes, it made it clear that Dada 'said yes and no to all things,' that the Holy Virgin was an early

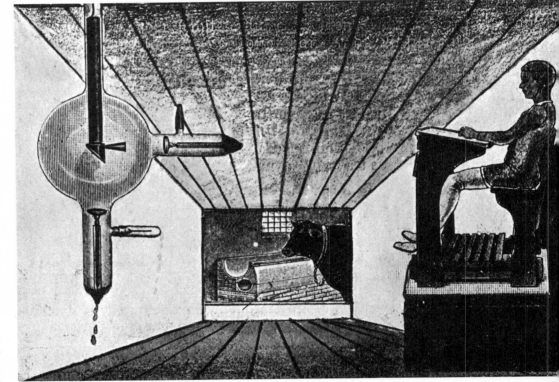

Max Ernst : Young people learn Dada. *Collage. 1920. Private coll.*

Dadaist, that Dada was never right, and that Dada is a form of bitterness that laughs at all that has been achieved, consecrated, and forgotten. Dada was the flower of anarchical dandysm, and its scent was intoxicating.

And then, slowly, the movement disintegrated. Internal quarrels accelerated its decay, but in June 1922 the Galerie Montaigne put on Tzara's *Cœur à Gaz* and organised an international Dada exhibition. In the album-catalogue the Parisian group, complete save for Breton and Dermée, may be found for the last time. Meanwhile Arp and Ernst had joined the group, and so had Peret, Duchamp and Man Ray who had just arrived from New York and was showing his photograms at the Galerie Six.

But an envenomed quarrel broke out over the imposing project of the Congress

of Paris. The plan was to hold an international enquiry, in Paris, into the new situation of literature and the arts. But as one palaver led to another so many differences of opinion were revealed, and so many enmities laid bare, that in the end the Congress was never held. Soon Tzara and Breton were to be completely estranged, and Breton's Surrealist Manifesto of 1924 was to mark the end of Dada. But the game was still being played out in Germany where, in 1918, Huelsenbeck had published the *Almanach Dada* in Berlin and founded the Dada Club, with Raoul Hausmann, George Grosz, John Heartfield, Walter Mehring, Jurg Baader and Hannah Höch. Jurg Baader liked to call himself "superdada" : he was a man of about

fifty who, in November 1918, had been brave enough to get up in the pulpit of a church in Berlin and deliver a sermon on "Dada, the saviour of the world". He also distributed among the constituent Assembly in Weimar a tract called *Grüne Leiche* (Green Corpse), got up as a supplement to an imaginary newspaper. It said among other things that "the president of the terrestrial globe rides the white horse Dada" and that, if the elections came out the right way, Baader would himself bring order, peace, liberty and bread to Germany.

It was at the same time that Hausmann the *dadasophe* composed his well-known photo-montages and the phonetic poems which had a certain influence on Schwitters. But the powerful spokesman of Dada in Berlin was still Huelsenbeck. He brought out manifesto after manifesto and became the first historian of the movement. Berlin Dada was above all anti-expressionist, and, even more than its counterpart in Zurich, it was anti-militarist, and, in politics, very far to the left. "Dada is the Germanic form of Bolshevism", Huelsenbeck wrote in *Forward Dada!* (1920), and he made a violent attack on the over-literary Dada of Paris. The great thing, he said, was always to remember that "the world is completely senseless"— a precept not so very different, as it happened, from the last Paris manifesto, which had said : "There's Humanity—and the imbecilities which have kept it happy up to its present advanced age".

In 1919 Max Ernst was in Cologne. He'd just got out of the army, was sick to death of the war, and longed to hear of all that was new in art. He fell in with other friends who likewise had come back from the war and didn't know quite what to do with themselves. All were predisposed to violence of some sort and, when they heard about Dada and what had happened at Zurich and in New York, they decided to do the same. "Our chief object", Ernst said later, "was to show how completely we were out of joint with all that had led to the war, and all that the war had brought to us". So Ernst wrote to Arp, whom he knew to have been closely connected with the Zurich group, and Arp later came to Cologne to join him. In his luggage were the drawings by Picabia and himself which were to enrich the Cologne Dada exhibitions.

Ernst had known Arp in Cologne just before the war. Arp, five years his senior, was then twenty-seven. "He made a great impression on me, Ernst

Kurt Schwitters : On blue. 6″×5″. 1921. Private coll. Paris. Schwitters collected those insignificant objects which greet an attentive observer as he walks along the street. The resulting collages now seem to us to have rare plastic qualities.

Arp : Mural for the "Aubette" cinema in Strasbourg. The décor of this cinema, now destroyed, was by Theo van Doesburg.

writes, and we had wonderful times together. Already we'd begun to envisage automatic painting and drawing. I remember us saying, in fact, that the only way to paint was with one's eyes shut, or quite automatically".

The foremost 'local product' of Cologne Dada would seem to have been Johannes Baargeld. Under this pseudonym, which means roughly "hard cash", was hidden the son of a local banker. When this banker saw his son turning away from communism and becoming a Dadaist instead he was so relieved that he set him up in a magnificent studio and gave him a handsome subsidy. And Baargeld made full use of it. (He died a few years later while mountain-climbing in the Tyrol.) The Cologne Dada held an exhibition in and around a municipal wash-room (there was a statue of Hindenburg, covered with nails and daubed with red paint : passers-by were allowed to take away the exhibits if they liked), and another in the wash-room of a restaurant. On one occasion Max Ernst was nearly killed in a brawl. The local Dada review, *Die Schammade* included contributions from Dadaists in Paris and Berlin. Ernst was congratulated by Breton and a show of his work was held at the Sans Pareil in Paris while he was still in Cologne. During this same period Arp and Ernst collaborated in a series of curious collages which foreshadow surrealism and were called *fatagaga (fabrication de tableaux garantis gazométriques)*. Cologne Dada had one immensely sensational exhibition which had to be closed by the police ; and then, when Arp left for Paris in 1920 and Ernst followed him two years later, it came to an end.

79

Francis Picabia : Udnie. 119 ″×119 ″. 1913. Museum of Modern Art, Paris.

But Dada was not dead in Germany. Schwitters kept it going by himself in Hanover, with his review *Merz*, his Merz-pictures, and the Merz-building which occupied two stories in his house, his unforgettable poems, and the innumerable permutations of his extraordinary nature. He gave collage a sculptural thickness which it had never had before.

A one-man flea-market, he took on what the rest of the world rejected and transposed it, with love and an unfailing eye, into a world of his own making. An old nail, a tramway ticket, a piece of scrap metal, changed climate and dimension at his touch and acquired a soul. With a humility all his own, Schwitters proves that art is neither something that can be learnt, nor yet something that is innate : it's something that *deserves itself*.

Schwitters laughed at the Berlin political Dada and called it Hülsen-dadaismus, or Husk-Dadaism, as contrasted with his own Kerndadaismus, or Kernel-Dadaism.

The Dada explosion was touched off by urgent intellectual pressure. That is why it 'caught on' everywhere, and almost at the same time—in America, Switzerland, Germany, Holland, Belgium, Paris. The time was ripe for the radical rejection of all received ideas. "Never say 'Art, Art'", I wrote in 1925, "Just yawn and lift your upper lip a little—it'll have the same result, but louder". The Dadaist says to art : "If you're what people say you are, you disgust me. If you can be free— show us.'" Thanks to this ultimatum we took a great step forward. Our meditations of the mystery of art were considerably enriched. We now know that art can be reduced to zero and yet still exist. It's then, in fact, that real art begins. The *reductio ad absurdum* provides an excellent point of departure. It's from nothing that everything must come. Art must daily go back to nothing in order to (re) begin again. Nothing is more revolutionary, more scandalous, than birth. The revolt, the lofty protest of Dada has built a new barricade against pedantry : within it— and we can't say this often—we can create freely, even if all history is against us.

Dada destroyed nothing and liberated much. It is in the wake of its great wave that we are living, and it is on that foundation of rough clamor and arrogant stuttering that modern art is being built and goes on with its conquests. It's quite understandable that Arp and Huelsenbeck should have protested when people said that Dada was a joke and a fraud. Jokes there were, certainly, but history has turned them into sources of strength, and on that strength we draw daily.

Arthur Cravan, who disappeared mysteriously in Mexico in 1918, is one of the legendary figures of Dadaism. From 1912 to 1915 he ran the review "Maintenant" which was already Dadaist in tone. His aggressive humor, near-duel with Apollinaire, dazzling article on the Salon des Indépendants in 1914 and prowess as a sportsman had all made his name famous in one way or another. In April 1916, he fought the world heavy-weight champion Jack Johnson in Madrid. To the left is an advertisement for that fight.

JACK JOHNSON = ARTHUR CRAVAN

Finalizará el espectáculo con el sensacional encuentro entre el campeón del mundo

Jack Johnson
Negro de 110 kilos
y el campeón europeo

Arthur Cravan
Blanco de 105 kilos

En este match se disputará una bolsa de **50.000** ptas. para el vencedor.

Véanse programas

PRECIOS (incluidos los impuestos)
SOMBRA Y SOL Y SOMBRA: Palco sin entradas, 20 pesetas.–Silla de ring 1.ª fila con entrada, 35 ptas.–Silla de ring 2.ª fila con entrada, 28 ptas.–Silla de ring 3.ª y 4.ª filas con entrada, 15 ptas.–Sillas de ring 5.ª, 6.ª, 7.ª y 8.ª filas con entrada, 12 ptas.–Barrera con entrada, 10 ptas.–Contrabarrera con entrada, 6,50 ptas.–Salón delantera de Palco con entrada, 8 ptas.–Silón tendido de Presidencia

BAUHAUS

BY WILL GROHMANN

*The famous school where Klee, Kandinsky, Walter Gropius and Marcel Breuer taught,
has still a great influence on the look of everyday life*

The Bauhaus, as a place where art and the applied arts were taught, came to an end in 1933. Yet it is still talked of : and that this should be so is the more remarkable if we remember that it existed for fourteen years only, and that during that time it was taken to pieces and put together again.

The "Building House", as it was literally called, was opened in 1919 at Weimar. Its organisers hoped to create "a guild of artisans which would ignore the wall of classconsciousness which elsewhere separates the artisan from the artist". The inaugural manifesto says, in fact, that "we must desire, imagine, and work together for that institution of the future in which architecture, sculpture and painting will combine in harmony. That institution will tower into the skies of the future as the crystalline emblem of our new faith in what is to come, and million upon million of workmen will contribute to it ".

It was Walter Gropius, its first director, who conceived the idea of the Bauhaus. This young architect was thirty-five when, in 1918, he took up his duties, but he was known in architectural circles for two buildings which he had designed before the war—the Fagus shoe-last factory in Hanover (1911), and

Above the title:

Ludwig Hirschfeld-Mack : experiments with the properties of white and black.

Under the title:

Experiments in optical illusion devised by P. Toliner. The effect of a third dimension is achieved by the use of two-dimensional elements : circles and parts of circles.

Opposite, and on p. 83:

Ludwig Hirschfeld-Mack tried out the different properties of white and black. He found that white, aggressive, centrifugal and dynamic comes forward from the picture-plane, while black is passive.

the machinery pavilion at the *Werkbund* exhibition of 1914. He surrounded himself with colleagues whom he considered to be his equals alike as creative artists and as constructive critics. Most of the Bauhaus teachers were, in fact, remarkable artists in their own right. Paul Klee taught in Weimar from January 1920 onwards; in June 1922 he was joined by Kandinsky, the founder of the Blue Rider group. Lyonel Feininger, who had shown with the Blue Rider group at the famous *Sturm* autumn salon in 1913, taught at the Bauhaus from 1919 onwards. The other teachers came from a variety of artistic milieux. There were, for instance, Oskar Schlemmer, the German painter, Laszlo Moholy-Nagy, the Hungarian whom Gropius met in 1923 and at once invited to the Bauhaus, Johannes Itten, George Muche, Gerhard Marcks the sculptor, and Adolf Meyer the architect.

The first years of the Bauhaus were marked by violent conflicts and controversies between the professors and their students; but Gropius, whose one interest was to get at the truth, was not a man to mind being contradicted. He had the instincts of a gentleman and,

with these, a marked flair for teaching and administration. The director of an institute like the Bauhaus cannot afford to lose his temper over trifles; nor, for that matter, should he be timid in his relations with leading politicians and captains of industry. His position demands an ardent but always flexible approach to day-to-day problems; and the desire to do as well as possible,

The last Bauhaus seal, designed in 1922 by Oskar Schlemmer.

rather than just to 'get by', may involve him in a great deal of stopping and starting. It was only when Gropius resigned from the Bauhaus, after ten years' onerous activity, and went back to private architectural practice, that people realised how vital a role he had played.

The Bauhaus was subject to continual attack. The élite were on its side, of course, but they were only a tiny minority and when a reactionary Government closed the Bauhaus in 1924 it was in vain that protests were received from the foremost artists and men of leaning of the day. Later it emigrated to Dessau: and there in 1932 it was closed for the second time when the Nazis got control of the town council. The teachers and students of the Bauhaus dispersed in all directions, bearing with them a message which, as it turned out, was particularly welcome in the USA.

What was it that so enraged the Philistines? The fact that neither men nor ideas, in the Bauhaus, conformed to pattern: that the teachers were an interna-

tional, free-thinking, anti-academic and generally disrespectful group of men. There were altogether too many talents in the Bauhaus: what could be going on, people thought, in all those clever heads? Doubtless they were plotting to destroy the 'spiritual heritage' of the nation, mocking at its traditions and undermining its morale. What is new is always assumed to be immoral in Germany: that's why it was so easy, in 1933, to slander men like Gropius, Kandinsky, Klee and Schlemmer.

Yet the idea of the Bauhaus had long been in the air. Already in 1907 Hermann Muthesius' *Deutsche Werkbund* had advocated a hand-made approach to industry and attempted to secure the mass-production of artists 'and artisans' designs. Immediately after the war, too, the *Arbeitsrat für Kunst* had been founded with much the same objects as the Bauhaus: the reform of art-schools, revival of craftsmanship in education, synthesis of the arts, and a close watch on excessive individualism... The members of this commission included such people as Erich Heckel, Karl Schmidt-Rottluf, Lyonel Feininger, Gerhard Marcks, Hans Peelzig, Wilhelm Valentiner, Paul Cassirer and, of course, Gropius himself. But Gropius already had his program in his pocket; he knew what he wanted, even if he didn't know who would be his colleagues in the Bauhaus. He was just back from the war and nothing seemed to him impossible. The years immediately after the war of 1914-1918 were a period of intense excitement and unbounded hopes in Germany. Utopias sprang up by the dozen, and Gropius seemed at first to be offering exactly what everyone was looking for; but later the reactionaries who had taken the brunt of the defeat

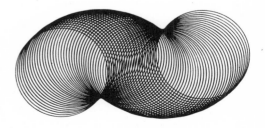

Study in optical illusion by P. Toliner.

Moholy-Nagy : Mobile and sculpture in glass and metal. ▲

Josef Albers : Table in light and dark oak. 1923. ▶

W. Menzel: fresco in the mural-painting classroom, Weimar. ▼

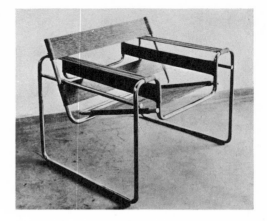

Marcel Breuer, director of the furniture-workshop, was the inventor of metal-tube furniture. Above, the first chair to be completed in this new material (1925).

regrouped themselves and regained the upper hand.

Gropius laid most emphasis on the elaboration of a functional architecture within which all the arts could unite to

serve the needs of industry and technical advancement. "The Bauhaus", said the initial manifesto, "means to restore the old harmony between all forms of art-activity, and between the respective disciplines of art and craftsmanship ; and it hopes to unite all the arts in a new conception of what building means. Our final, if still distant, aim is to create the unified work of art, the Great Work, in which all distinction between monumental art and decorative art will have disappeared". There were not, in a real sense, any teachers or students in the Bauhaus. There were masters and apprentices. Nor were there artists whose speciality was applied art or fine art. There were creators who complemented one

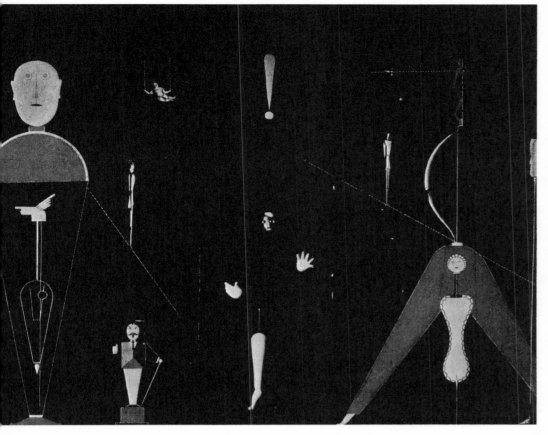

student was responsible to two masters —an artist and an artisan. Kandinsky, Klee, Marcks, Feiniger and Schlemmer were true "form masters"—Kandinsky for mural painting, Klee for glass-painting, Moholy-Nagy for metal-work, Marcks for ceramics. Muche taught the art of the textile, Feininger taught typography, Schlemmer taught sculpture and, later, theatrical design.

It was only when the Bauhaus moved to Dessau that Klee and Kandinsky had a painting-class. It was also possible at Dessau for a single master to be in charge of the artisanal side of the work, because there were graduate students on hand to combine formal with artisanal duties. The Dessau workshops were veritable research-bureaux in which 'stan-

another in the service of a collective ideal. The medieval conception of the workshop came back to life in the Bauhaus, and the traditional distinction between fine art and applied art no longer existed.

Art cannot be learnt, Gropius said ; but what can be learnt are the skills of the hand, and what can be acquired is knowledge. Genius, likewise, cannot be

taught in schools, but every creative artist is the better for having had a craftsman's training. If the artist who has been trained at the Bauhaus cannot make a living with his art he can always fall back on his craft. It's more difficult, in fact, to create a first-class chair than a tenth-rate picture—and a great deal more useful.

The Bauhaus course began with a preliminary session on the teaching of relevant forms and the use of materials. In his second year the apprentice took a course in practical craftsmanship, and learnt to work with stone, wood, metal, textiles, glass, or color. During this time he was never allowed to lose sight of the formal problems involved. Finally, before leaving the Bauhaus with his diploma, he took a course in architecture.

While the Bauhaus was at Weimar the courses proceeded simultaneously on the formal and the practical plane. Each

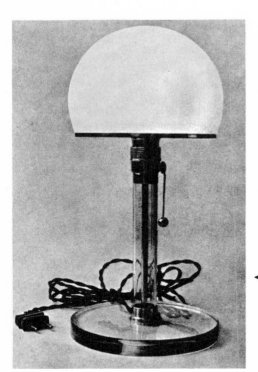

◄ *Lamp devised by Jucker and Wagenfeld. The wire is threaded through the glass base. Shade of opaline glass. c. 1924.*

Cotton wall-hanging, vivid in color, with ▶ 'contemporary' motifs.

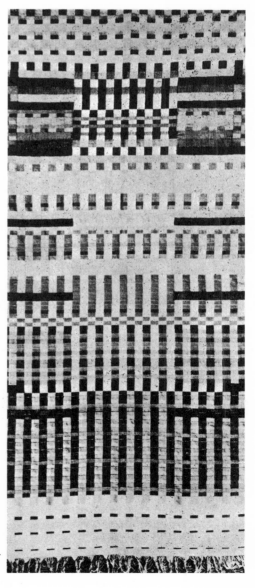

dard models' were devised for mass production. Preoccupied as they were with the technical side of work, they none the less never forgot that the aesthetics of form were also important. Many elements in modern living were first thought up at Dessau and its influence is especially strong in the design of metal furniture, household china, lamps, and textiles. The international public had its first opportunity of judging this when, in 1920, the *Société des artistes-décorateurs* held its exhibition in Paris, Gropius was in charge of the German

Bottom, left:

Herbert Bayer: Project for luminous exhibition-sign. The revolving sphere is covered with electric lamps, when lit they form differently-colored letters.

Lever right:

Herbert Bayer: Newspaper kiosk. Narrow-based, with an angular, multi-colored superstructure for the display of posters.

One of the 'double-houses' built by Gropius in 1925 at Dessau for the Bauhaus professors. This, one of seven faculty houses, belonged to Kandinsky and Klee.

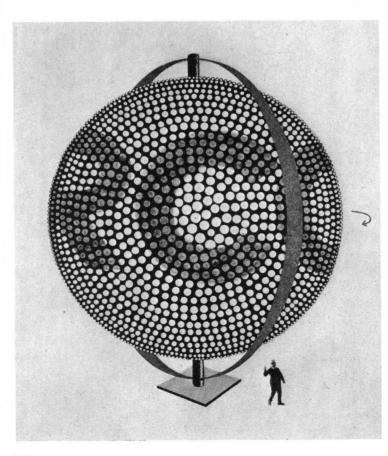

Georg Muche : Project for a building in reinforced concrete. 1924.

hand experience of the Bauhaus at work (or at play, for that matter) will forget the spirit of affectionate enthusiasm which reigned there and somehow enabled even the least gifted of the participants to surpass himself. The teachers expected nothing but the best and taught their pupils to do the same. Failure was condemned without indulgence, and success acclaimed as it deserved. Jealousy was unknown, and in its place reigned a keen sense of emulation. This intense seriousness spilled over into playtime : every party, for instance, had its theme—"metal", for example or "black and white"—and it was a point of honor that everything, music included, should be done by and in the Bauhaus. The students' jazz-band, the Bauhäusler, was one of the most famous in Germany and in great demand elsewhere. These outside dates helped the players to pay their Bauhaus fees, and they also got a percentage whenever their models or designs were sold to manufacturers. The Bauhaus at Dessau was able partly to pay for itself : in addition the local industrialists were glad to collaborate with its members—it was in this way, for instance, that the Bauhaus wall-papers brought it more and more money each year.

Anyone who looks through the "Bauhaus Books" which were published un-

Herbert Bayer : Poster for group-exhibition. 1923.

section. All the activities of the Bauhaus were admirably represented : paintings, engravings, stage designs, photographs. Germany was shown to have been the first country in the world to take a serious interest in the aesthetics of industry and create forms that were both useful and beautiful. Functionalism had been widely criticised : but at last it was proved that it had not, as people thought, impoverished life. On the contrary : both technically and economically it had led to great advances, and where the imagination was concerned it has acted as an indispensable regulator.

It's miraculous that for ten years— 1918-28—so many men of talent should have worked and lived together in perfect harmony. No one who had first-

Walter Gropius : The Bauhaus, Dessau, from the north-west. 1925-1926.

87

der Moholy-Nagy's editorship will be struck by the number of Bauhaus designs which quickly made their way. If art galleries, institutes and private firms were able to have Bauhaus furniture. There was also a great demand for lamps ment, became a factory and went into commercial production.

Herbert Bayer, the typographical expert, devised a new set of characters and adopted the lower-case alphabet in which the Bauhaus publications were printed.

The Bauhaus professors: from l. to r.: Josef Albers, Mimerk Schoper, Georg Muche, Moholy-Nagy, Herbert Bayer, Joost Schmidt, Walter Gropius, Marcel Breuer, Wassily Kandinsky, Paul Klee, Lyonel Feininger, Gunt Stölzl and Oskar Schlemmer.

these endure, it is because they were conceived with a total disregard for current fashion. Even the word 'fashion' was outlawed at the Bauhaus ; people hated the sound of it, and even the word 'style' was none too popular. Gropius disliked the phrase 'Bauhaus style', for he considered that contemporary style was not a thing to be created, but something that arose automatically when forms were adapted to contemporary needs after a preliminary scientific enquiry. 'Personal style' had no place in the Bauhaus, and although it was usually possible for them to identify the originators of any particular design they were more interested to discover what that design had in common with its neighbors.

Marcel Breuer was in charge, from 1925 onwards, of the furniture-workshops. The technique of the chair was what most interested him and he was the originator, for instance, of steel-tube seating. His Bauhaus stool created a furore in Germany. He and his students worked in complete harmony with the manufacturers, and in this way many

designed in the metal workshops under the direction of Mohoy-Nagy and Marianne Brandt. Anni Albers' weavers' shop, which began as a place of experi-

Paul Klee : The room of the ghosts with tall door. *Watercolor. 1925. 18¾″ × 11½″. Davidson Taylor collection, New York.*

The theatre had always played a part in the life of the Bauhaus, and Oskar Schlemmer was just the man to improvise performances in which light, color, form, space and movement all played a part. It was he who directed the Theatre Workshop till his departure in 1929, and he, too, who was in charge of Bauhaus festivities. His *Triadisches Ballett,* in which the dancers wore abstract costumes and moved like marionettes, had an international success and was put on in many cities. For lack of money it proved impossible to pursue his concept of purely mechanical stage-scenery to its conclusion, but something of it may be seen in Kandinsky's designs for Mussorgsky's "Pictures from an Exhibition".

The Bauhaus attached great importance to contacts with the world outside and the intellectual and artistic leaders of other nations. Klee in particular wished the students to be in touch with all that was going on. The role of the 'Friends of the Bauhaus' was not limited to emergency financial assistance ; it was mainly, in fact, to widen the students' horizons that men like Chagall, Einstein, Edwin Fischer, Schönberg and Kokoschka became members of the group.

The Bauhaus buildings were in themselves a remarkable achievement, and especially so at Dessau, where Gropius had been invited by the Mayor, Dr Hesse, to build his Institute anew. In 1925 he was responsible for the new building, which had four stories, was made of ferro-concrete, and was one of the finest architectural inventions of the decade. Beneath its terraced roofs were classrooms, workshops, and twenty-eight apartments for students. All the interior decoration was provided from the Bauhaus' own workshop, and the furniture was made to Breuer's metal-tube designs.

Paul Klee : The Equilibrist. *Watercolor.* ▶ *1923. 19⅛″ × 12⅝″. Berne Museum, Klee foundation.*

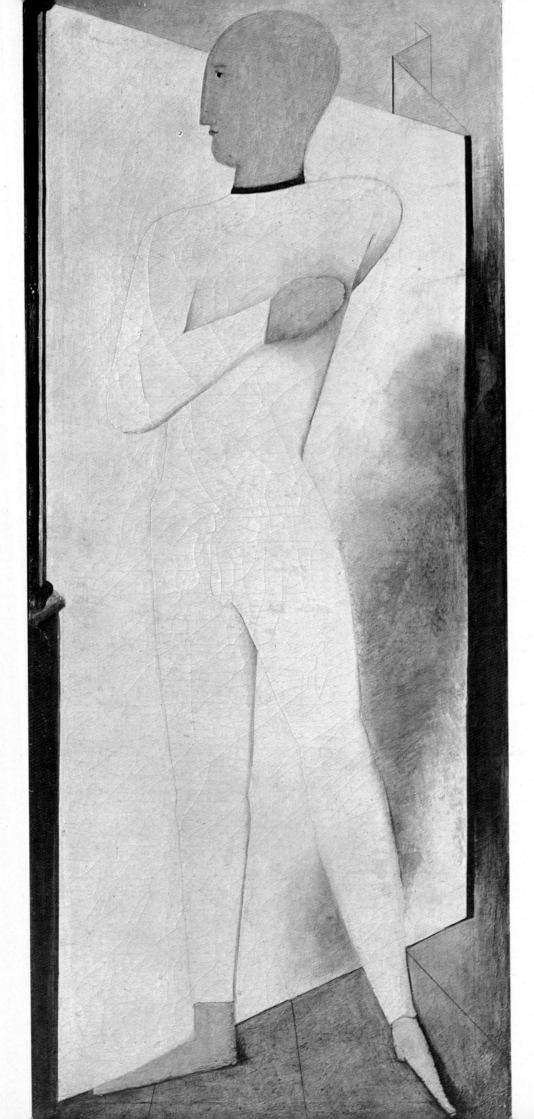

Fifteen hundred people came to the opening of the new Bauhaus in 1926.

Gropius also built seven houses for his associates. These became prototypes of "Bauhaus living", in which many an academic figure was to find, for the first time, a house expressly adapted to his needs. Relations between the members of the Bauhaus were all the closer, now that they lived so near to one another, and political differences or difficulties did little to impair them.

Gropius also built, at Dessau-Törten, a "workers' city" of 316 houses. This was erected with standard sections and partly furnished from the Bauhaus workshops.

At Dessau, both Kandinsky and Klee had a painting class and, at the same time, an art-teaching course. It was in connection with these activities that Klee published his "Pedagogical Sketchbook" in 1925 and Kandinsky his "Point and Line on the Plan" in 1926. Klee's lectures have recently been published in full, but Kandinsky's, unfortunately, remain widely dispersed. It's clear, in any case, that what was taught at the Bauhaus, in matters of art, was analogous to the teaching of harmony in colleges of music.

Germany could well be proud of the Bauhaus, but it was soon swept away when National Socialism came to power, and there remained only the memory of an institution unique in its time, in which the teachers were great artists as well as pedagogues, and where the atmosphere was such that everyone had a place of his own and could play his full part. The Bauhaus, in short, was a place where art, science, technique, intuition and inspired research were each enriched by the presence of the others.

The Bauhaus closed for good in 1933, and its most important members left Germany. But a certain proportion of its graduates stayed on there and kept the sprit of the Institute alive. Max Bill's "Senior School of Form" at Ulm is one of the most recent of its reverberations ; and in Berlin alone there are now

Oskar Schlemmer : The Dancer. 1923. 70″ × 28¹/₅″. Staatsgalerie, Stuttgart.

eighteen "Old Bauhaus men", architects for the most part, whose influence grows greater every year.

But it is in America that the Bauhaus has made itself most deeply felt, both through the direct action of former Bauhaus members and the influence of the art forms once created there. Certainly the impact of industrial design as it was originally conceived in Germany has marked many products of American daily living. American abstract art owes much to its German forbears. The American skyline has adopted and adapted concepts born in Weimar and Dessau.

Gropius went to the United States in

Wassily Kandinsky : Composition 308 modified. *Oil. 1925.*

Wassily Kandinsky : Wood engraving in colors. *1922.*

1937, and from 1938 onwards he directed the Department of Architecture at Harvard. Moholy-Nagy wanted to revive the "Bauhaus spirit" and from 1937 until his death in 1946 he directed the "New Bauhaus" which he founded in Chicago. This institution still carries on under the name of "The Institute of Design". He had continued his spatial experiments with plexiglass sculptures and through his paintings. The year after his death his "New Vision" was published, condensing his artistic experi-

Sculpture Workshop under Oskar Schlemmer's direction. Weimar, 1923.

riences and credos. Lyonel Feininger left Germany for New York in 1937, and went on painting there until his recent death. Marcel Breuer taught architecture at Harvard, and now has an office in New York, although he is in demand all over the world and is, with the French architect Bernard Zehrfuss and the Italian Pier-Luigi Nervi, responsible for the new Unesco building in Paris. He is designing the new American embassy at The Hague and has recently completed a large department store in Rotterdam.

Gropius himself, now rising seventy-five, gives "swimming and riding" as his recreations in "Who's Who", and on recent visits to Europe has left his mark upon yet another generation of architects and architectural students. In London, for instance, not long ago, he was entertained at the Royal Institute of British Architects and received one of the greatest ovations ever heard within the chaste walls of that institution. The tribute was to the man, as much as to that man's ideas, and it was difficult to know which of the two had lasted the better.

DE STIJL

BY MICHEL SEUPHOR

The "De Stijl" group, headed by Mondrian, made its influence felt in every department of modern art

Walter Gropius: Façade detail of an eleven-storied house built in 1930. The title reproduces lettering used on the magazine cover of the first De Stijl publication.

If Theo van Doesburg's nose had been less long the look of the world would not have been changed. But van Doesburg had the nose of a pointer and the look of the world *has* been changed. Yet the very keenness of that nose was a function of the illness of an elderly teacher in the village of Winterswijk, in eastern Holland—for history needs trivial pretexts before it can be set in motion. Sometimes I think that it could be reduced to a series of equations in which human relations are the numbers. For human relations are the stuff—and the drama—of history. Accident calls

them into being, passion gives them strength, habit and indifference slacken and finally destroy them.

The ailing teacher of Winterswijk had sent for his son who, for the previous two and a half years, had been in Paris. This was Piet Mondrian. He had just finished, in his studio near the Gare Montparnasse, several masterpieces as yet unknown to the world. It was July 1914. War broke out when Mondrian was in Holland and his road back to Paris was encumbered with armies on the march. For nearly five years Mondrian was cut off from Paris and from his series of now-famous pictures (since bought by Dutch or American museums). He had painted these after making contact with cubism, but they go beyond the laws of cubism proper and attain to pure abstraction. Mondrian's abstraction was a flexible, sensitive affair : as early as 1913 and 1914 the canvas is dominated by vertical and horizontal lines and painted, in nearly every case, in the primary colors. These canvases are the advance-guard of what he will later describe as 'neoplasticism', The years in Paris had wrought a complete change in Mondrian, and he was no longer quite at home in Holland, where ill-fortune kept him a prisoner. He went, none the less, in search of certain familiar places. As soon as his father seemed a little better—he died the following year at the age of seventy-six—Mondrian went to Domburg, where he had been used to stay for most of every summer, then to Scheveningen, and finally to Laren, where he stayed on until 1919. From Laren it was only a short journey to Amsterdam, and from 1915 he took part in a group-exhibition. It was the accident that history needed. Van Doesburg, the art critic of one of the local papers, wrote an intelligent appraisal of Mondrian's work. Mondrian wrote to thank him, they met, they became

friends, and a collaboration began which was to last for ten years.

The two men were very different : upbringing, experience, character—all would have seemed to keep them apart, but in fact they complemented one another. I knew both of them very well : and the fact that I was a close friend of the one and sometimes had colossal wrangles with the other will not affect my objectivity. But let Bruno Zevi speak : "There's no doubt that if we compare Mondrian's work with van Doesburg's the difference in class leaps to the eye. In Doesburg's case the experience is rapid, even feverish, and the artist brings his ideas at once to the boil with the object of proving a point. He is out to formulate a plastic language which cuts out figuration altogether and goes beyond cubism. Mondrian, on the other hand, has the extreme, ineffable patience of the artist who is searching for a perfection beyond all words. Van Doesburg is a painter-critic, a prospector for new means of expression, and his temperament, though a most interesting one, is essentially that of a *demonstrator*. Mondrian is a poet". (Poetica dell' architettura neoplastica, Milan, 1953).

Van Doesburg (his real name was C.E.M. Kupper) was born at Utrecht in 1883. His father, a German born in Bonn and later naturalised as a Dutchman, divorced when his son was two years old and emigrated to Russia. His mother, who was of Swiss origin though born at Rotterdam, re-married : and her son later took his step-father's name. Doesburg also wrote poems and essays under the pseudonyms of Aldo Camini and I. K. Bonset. He had, it would seem, an arduous upringing. Turbulent and ill-tempered as a child, he at first wanted to be an actor, went to the Conservatoire, gave it up, took to painting, left home for good in a moment of wildness, wrote poems, fables

Unpublished photograph of Piet Mondrian (l.) taken at St. Germain-en-Laye near Paris in 1925. With him, Monsieur and Madame Georges Vantongerloo.

and articles, and kept himself going by copying the pictures in the Rijksmuseum. In 1908 he had a show at The Hague, in 1912 he wrote on Asiatic art and the 'modern movement', and in 1913 he published a book of poems. Meanwhile he married, divorced, and married again. A few years later, he once again divorced and married a third time. At the time when he met Mondrian his record seemed to be that of a critic and a publicist. The list of his published articles—he printed it himself in *De Stijl* in 1922—is an impressive one. There seems to have been nothing that van Doesburg, a latter-day Pico della Mirandola, would not take on.

Mondrian's past was quite different. Born at Amersfoort, not far from Utrecht, in 1872, he came of an old Dutch family from The Hague. His father, the teacher, was a strictly orthodox Calvinist, and Mondrian's boyhood, alike at Amersfoort and later at Winterswijk, was quiet and studious. He soon overcame any initial resistance that there may have been to his being a painter, and thenceforward he was given every encouragement both by his father and by an uncle, Fritz Mondrian, who was a professional painter and lived in The Hague. He qualified for two diplomas which entitled him to become an art-teacher, but preferred to go on studying and, being tenacious and strong of will, he managed to get himself admitted to the Academy of Amsterdam. There he studied for five years. He was an assiduous and exemplary student, who thought of nothing but how to learn more and improve his work. Like van Doesburg, he sometimes eked out his income by making copies of museum-pictures, but unlike van Doesburg he did not disperse his energies : he painted a lot and talked hardly at all. But he was interested in comparative religions,

ancient philosophy and, above all, in theosophy. For many years he was a member of the Dutch Theosophical Society and in 1916, at the height of his neo-plastic researches, a portrait of Madame Blavatsky was still pinned on to the wall of his studio at Laren. He never married.

By 1915 a good deal had already been written about him in Holland. Much had been seen of his work (he had shown twice at the Indépendants, by the way, and been singled out by Apollinaire) and his pictures had passed through several distinct phases. It's difficult, indeed, to see what these have in common, unless it be that, as in the case of Van Gogh, there were to be found side by side energy and meditation, the search for symbols and a furious desire to paint. As far as symbols were concerned,

Mondrian thought he had found what he wanted in Paris by pursuing the cubist experiment to its logical conclusion in horizontal-vertical rhythms and the free manipulation of a flat surface with no thought of figuration.

At forty-four, then, Mondrian thought he had achieved the final aim of his career. But in reality he was on the threshold of a new experiment. At Blaricum, a village near Laren, he met the theosophical writer M.H.J. Schœnmakers and the painter Bart van der Leck. Both were to influence him profoundly, the first by what he had written on the subject of a rational mysticism, and the second by his researches in the domain of pure color and painting *en aplats*. For years, as can be seen from his notebooks for 1909-1914, he had been following up these ideas, and now

Van Doesburg : Counter-composition. 1924. Municipal Museum, Amsterdam.

Van der Leck : Composition, 1918. Kröller-Müller Museum, Otterloo.

Van Doesburg : Ceramic Square. 1917. Coll. A. Bartos, New York.

they were becoming every day clearer and more exact. When he pondered, as he did constantly, he pondered pen in hand. But when van Doesburg spoke of founding a review, he disapproved. The time was not ripe, he thought. But van Doesburg insisted. Scruple and reticence were things that never troubled van Doesburg: for him, as for all men of action, it was not a question of waiting for the hour to strike, but of advancing the clock-hand himself.

So it was that the first number of "De Stijl" ("Style") came out in October 1917. And at once the cards were on the table: it was Mondrian whose writings set the tone for the paper and made the deepest impression. For three or four years he contributed a steady flow of essays and manifestoes which showed that, if "the time was not ripe", Mondrian at any rate was just ready to give of his best.

who, in an article dated 1922, gave his associate the title of 'father of the movement'—had with them the painter van der Leck, whose collaboration was limited to the first number of the magazine, Vilmos Huszar, who lived at Voorburg, near The Hague, and shortly afterwards the painter and sculptor Georges Vantongerloo, who while serving in the Belgian Army had been carried over into Holland by the accidents of war. Nor should we forget Antonie Kok, the poet, who was a great friend of van Doesburg, and the architects Wils, Oud, van't Hof and, from 1918 onwards, Rietveld. They all had in common the idea that a work of art must be the product of a shared attitude of mind. It should represent the integration of many kinds of discipline, and it should be introduced into everyday life—above all in architecture, which was henceforth to be regarded a syntesis of the plastic

Facade of the "De Unie" café, *built at Rotterdam by Jacobus Johannes Pieter Oud in 1922. Now destroyed.*

too static. Vantongerloo was loyal to neo-plastic theory in his sculptures (see page 98) and in his paintings till 1937, though in painting he quite often used complementary colors. Later he came to tread a very different road and ended up by painting cosmogonies of a kind, made up of curved lines, many-colored dots and cloud-passages. The only one of the original group of painters who remained to the last unswervingly attached to the basic ideas of "De Stijl" was Mondrian (see pages 96 and 99).

"There was never a 'team'", Vantongerloo said to me later, "and the proof of it is that I only met Mondrian in 1920 and van der Leck in 1935. Van Doesburg kept his contributors apart and printed what he liked". That may be so: but the fact remains that van Doesburg, the mainspring of the whole business, brought out the magazine at

The "Schröder house" *built at Utrecht by Rietveld in 1924.*

Van Doesburg's articles are those of a theorist who has kept abreast of the modern movement in all its forms; incisive in tone, they are not always quite free from sectarian intolerance. "Nothing is more dangerous than fantasy", he wrote: "fantasy should be kept where it belongs: in the café-chantant. Only that which has been deeply worked, that which has been mortified, has any importance". This lofty outlook did not, however, prevent him from letting fly at the canons of neo-plasticism and abandoning the movement altogether, in 1924, to found his own "elementarism". But to go back to the foundation of "De Stijl": van Doesburg and Mondrian—it was Mondrian

arts. The basic principles could be put in a few words: horizontal-vertical lines, no curves, no diagonals, and the three primary colors, with no mixing or adulteration. Red, green and blue could, however, have as neighbors the three non-colors: white, grey and black.

Only in a few isolated pictures painted in 1917 was van der Leck true to these austere principles (see page 93); Huszar returned to the use of the diagonal towards 1922; two years later van Doesburg went so far as to make the diagonal his battle-cry, having decided that the horizontal-vertical principle was

Chair designed by Rietveld in 1917. *Municipal Museum, Amsterdam.*

Interior of the cinema "L'Aubette", in Strasbourg, decorated by van Doesburg in 1928. His decorations have since disappeared.

regular intervals and maintained among his contributors that coherence of ideas and affinity of intentions which are, whether we like it or not, the mark of a group or a movement.

In the domain of architecture the achievements of "De Stijl" were : the façade of a café in Rotterdam, now destroyed, by Oud, 1922, (opposite), a temporary house, also by Oud, with polychrome elements, 1923, and a villa in Utrecht by Rietveld, 1924, (see page 94). This last is usually considered the architectural masterpiece of the neo-plastic movement. Rietveld also

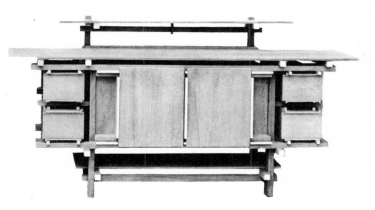

Cupboard by Rietveld. *1919. Municipal Museum, Amsterdam.*

designed a complete set of furniture on the same principles; these, remarkable rather than practical, are now museum-pieces (see pages 94, 95). From 1922 onwards van Doesburg, in collaboration with his young disciple Cor van Eesteren, made a great many sketches and projects for houses and villas; delightful as these are to look at, and often as they were on show, not one of them, to my knowledge, was ever erected. Later, the architectural principles of neo-plasticism were put to tremendously effective use by Mies van der Rohe.

Another matter, and an important one, that must be settled here is the exact nature of van Doesburg's relations with the Weimar Bauhaus. In April 1921, accompanied by the pretty and very young woman who was his third wife, van Doesburg left on a propaganda-tour of Europe. For the first time in

Sketch for a country house, van Doesburg and van Eesteren, 1923.

his life he got outside the slightly confined and very bourgeois atmosphere of Holland, where a new idea finds few, if any, supporters. The change of air had an instantaneous effect upon the thirty-eight-year-old adolescent. He was as if intoxicated; and he arrived at the Bauhaus with the presumptions of a conqueror, a man who walks in by right and takes over. The basic principles were good, he thought (they too were looking for a synthesis of the arts) but they were applied in too eclectic, and above all in too timid, a fashion. There must be reforms, wholesale reforms, and a complete break with expressionism. From the first day, from the first hour, the battle was on. Professors grumbled or kept silent, students were divided in their loyalties: most yielded, however,

for there was a strange dynamism in the hyperborean visitor who brushed every obstacle aside and in the clear ideas that not even van Doesburg's appalling German could obscure.

There's no way of knowing for certain whether van Doesburg was officially invited to teach at the Bauhaus. Walter Gropius, who was then its Director, says "No". Madame van Doesburg says "Yes". Be that as it may, I remember clearly that van Doesburg styled himself "Professor at the Bauhaus" in the years that followed, and I also remember that at one time "De Stijl" was printed at Weimar. Quite certainly, in any case, the wolf got into the sheepfold, stayed there for several months, and made himself thoroughly at home. He gave a course of lectures, independently of the Bauhaus, on private premises, and his ascendancy was all the greater for the fact that the 'official' professors had declared the lectures 'out of bounds' to Bauhaus students. Moments of high drama ensued: and calm was not restored until, in 1922, van Doesburg went off, with Kurt Schwitters as his partner, for a "Dada tour" in Holland.

Meanwhile in 1919 Mondrian had gone back to Paris, and in 1920 he published his "Néo-Plasticisme", under the auspices of Léonce Rosenberg's Galerie l'Effort Moderne in the rue de la Baume. In 1923 this same gallery invited van Doesburg to organise a 'De Stijl' exhibition, and in this way the two friends were re-united in Paris. Paris did not, however, take kindly to neo-plasticism —perhaps because its spokesman mismanaged his campaign, perhaps because its manifestoes were written in very poor French. The exhibition had, in any case, almost no effect and Mondrian,

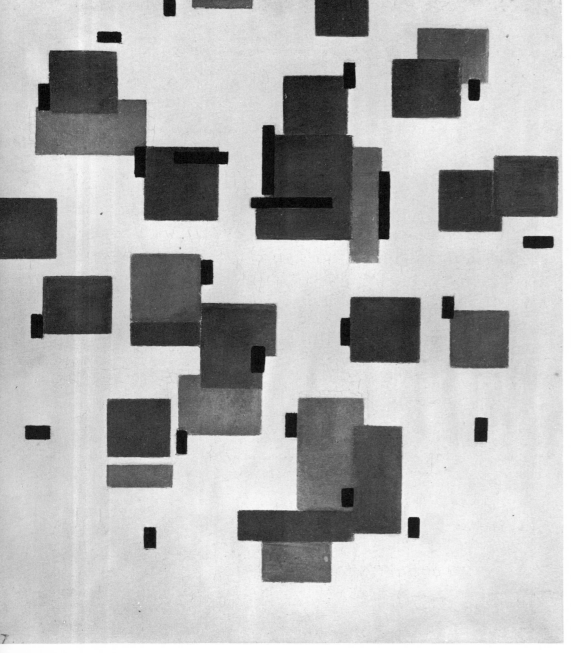

Mondrian. Composition *1917.* 19¾" × 17⅛". *Kröller-Müller Museum, Otterloo.*

tradition, and he never made any secret of his admiration for Mondrian. And the right angle is, after all, "De Stijl" in essence. The founders of the group did not, of course, invent the right angle, but they saw it as nobody had seen it before. They annexed, as it were, an already-existing truth and made of it a universal symbol: the verticality of man upright above the horizontality of the earth. In all things there is a dualism, a tension that produces equilibrium: and this is made visible in the horizontal-vertical sign—man & woman, mind & nature, night & day. To this sign—the sign of the cross, but of a cross handed back to life by the asymetry which decomposes and re-composes it—all things must be brought back, and all things reduced. The neo-plasticians saw it as a universal synthesis and the foundation of all rational structures. "The goal of nature is Man",

lute—a branch of metaphysics, in fact. And there's an element of truth in this. Mondrian himself, when writing of it said that neo-plasticism was the only way yet devised of revealing the universal strength that is in all things. Neo-plasticism, he wrote, is "identical with that which in the past was revealed under the name of divinity, and which is indispensable to us poor human beings if we are to live and achieve equilibrium". Mondrian's writings—and this will be properly acknowledged one day—show that he, like those other harbingers of abstract art, Kandinsky and Malevich, was a great moralist.

Mondrian stopped writing for "De Stijl" when van Doesburg renounced the horizontal-vertical principle and published his 'elementarist' manifesto. This manifesto was put into practice in 1929, when van Doesburg decorated a cinema auditorium in the 'Aubette'

who sold nothing, was near to dispair, while van Doesburg spoke with contempt of the "dead city" where nothing could be done. And yet it was on the outskirts of Paris, at Meudon, that van Doesburg was to have his house built, only a year or two later!

In Germany, on the other hand, the ideas of the neo-plasticists were taking root. Gropius, so far from bearing van Doesburg any grudge, included in his famous series of "Bauhaus Books" a book of Mondrian's ("Neue Gestaltung", 1925) and one of van Doesburg's (Grundbegriffe der neuen gestaltenden Kunst", 1926). And Gropius showed himself the most brilliant of "De Stijl" 's disciples when he built the new Bauhaus buildings at Dessau: these were finished in 1925.

About this same time, Le Corbusier also showed himself receptive to "De Stijl". Many of his essays, and in particular his dithyrambs about the right angle, are in the purest neo-plastic

The interior of Mondrian's Paris studio, 1925.

said van Doesburg, "and the goal of Man is—style". Everything that exists carries its own style within it; and that style, visible to all who contemplate it with a quiet mind, is summed up in the right angle. Whatever is created out of that contemplation will console and never weary, for its simplicity is a mark not of poverty of spirit, but of reserve. Inessentials have been cast aside. It has often been said that pure neo-plasticism, as Mondrian conceived it, consists in painting the abso-

The front page of an early number of the magazine "De Stijl", which appeared for the first time in October 1917.

in Strasbourg. (Sophie Taueber and Jean Arp also had a hand in the building.) Unluckily the cinema, which was undoubtedly van Doesburg's masterpiece, has since disappeared (see page 95). Photographs show us how far it was from Mondrian and the original principles of 'De Stijl': the decorations are not integrated into the architecture, but tend rather, with a certain arrogance, to destroy it. Van Doesburg has, in fact, broken across the horizontal-vertical rhythm of the walls with a powerful diagonal thrust.

In March 1931 van Doesburg died suddenly at Davos. Mondrian, who was eleven years the older of the two, lived

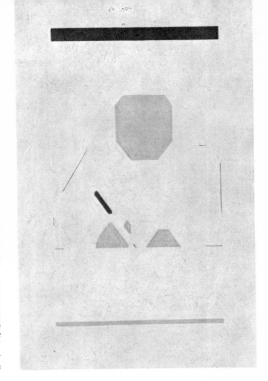

for another thirteen years. By the time he died in New York in February 1944 he had acquired a certain discreet celebrity, and some part of this he undoubtedly owed to the ideas which, originally put about by Doesburg in the Bauhaus, had gradually made their way throughout central Europe and thence all over the world.

The whole story stems, therefore, from the meeting of two exceptional and diametrically dissimilar men. On the one side an extreme prudence, a tendency to ponder long and carefully; on the other an extraversion that knew no restraint. A thunderbolt that troubled the topmost snows!

But "De Stijl" did not come to an end with its two great protagonists—nor even with its earliest adherents. In architecture, and in urbanism, its reverberations can be felt all around us.

Many painters and sculptors—in America, France, Switzerland, Holland—have recently turned back to neo-plasticism, even though the climate of art is often hostile to it and inclined rather to the violences of neo-expressionism. Its principles are engraved deep in the texture of our century and it is impossible that they should not be heeded again. In America, apart from Mies van der Rohe, many architects—Philip Johnson, Saarinen, Charles Eames, Skidmore and others—are impregnated with the ideas of "De Stijl", and their work has been acclaimed all over the world.

But the most beautiful monuments that "De Stijl" has given us are still the paintings of Mondrian—the tranquil power of those painted between 1926 and 1932, and the renewed lyricism of the final period, the famous New York "Boogie-Woogies". These works have

Van der Leck. The Writer. *1923. 35½″ × 21¼″. Kröller-Müller Museum, Otterloo.*

been seen in many European and American museums, and at the Venice Biennale of 1956. It is in them and through them that something is happening: a new spirit is amongst us for ever. Did I not say that the face of the world had been changed? So it has, a little—for those who look on the right side of things!

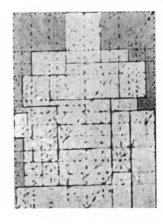

Georges Vantongerloo: Plastic II. *1919. To the right are photographs which show how the sculptor approached his final result: above, the point of departure: below, a sketch-plan of the volume-relations which make possible the definite work of art.*

Mondrian: Picture-poem. *1928. Gouache and Indian ink, entirely from the artist's own hand. 24¾″ × 19¾″. Coll. Seuphor, Paris.* ►

T
E
X
T
U
E
L

îlot physique Seuphor sous l'aile de Mondrian
sous les drapeaux sérieux du Néo-Plasticisme
battant le pavillon très pur

échappée belle de l'art
enfin mesure d'hygiène
ralliez-vous tous au pavillon du grand secours
du grand sérieux quand nous serons mieux éclai-
et disparaisse la flore sous le regard néo[très]
et cessent les éboulements

l'îlot physique sort des cavernes
il ose construire dans le clair
il lève la tête
où il n'y a que le grand bleu
et le grand gris et le grand blanc
et le grand noir et le soleil tout feu
suivi des synonymes bonheur sagesse connais-
et de la joie... [sance
qu'il ne faut pas confondre encore

mais il fallait y penser si j'ose dire
être déjà et non choisir et choisir bien quand-même
mais il fallait prendre contact
marcher longtemps et sous le juste signe

M.Seuphor

16 mai 1928

P.M

André Breton's collection

BY ALAIN JOUFFROY

The founder of surrealism lives surrounded by pictures and objects which evoke a lifetime of experiment and exploration

One evening in August 1947, when I happened to have the room next to André Breton's at the Grand Hôtel d'Angleterre, Huelgoat (Finistère), he showed me some rock crystals that he had picked up while exploring an abandoned mine-shaft. This was my first personal contact with him. He told me at length about his long stay in the U.S.A., where he went during the war as a refugee, about the Hopi Indians, with whom he had spent three months, and about Haitian voodoo and the agates that he had found on the Canadian sea-board. Later he invited me to call on him, in Paris.

André Breton has lived since 1921 in an apartment in the Rue Fontaine, not far from the Place Blanche, which constitutes in itself a kind of Museum of the Marvellous. It's an ensemble of South Sea masks, Hopi dolls, surrealist paintings, and paintings by 'modern primitives' in which the element of the strange, the rare and the unknown comes uppermost. André Breton's visitors are surrounded, in fact, by a powerful, captious, unique and magical presence. If there is anywhere an 'ideal museum' of surrealism it is in Breton's studio in the Rue Fontaine. Yet his collection is unlike any other. Taste and sensibility have played their part in it, of course, but it also reflects those imperious intellectual preoccupations which have enabled Breton to create a new poetical climate and, in so doing, to leave his mark upon our time.

It was in adolescence that Breton first became interested in painting. The first beginnings of a revolution in aesthetics may, in fact, be traced to the walk which he took every Sunday, with his parents, from the Gare de

l'Est, in Paris, to the Madeleine. The only point of excitement, for young Breton, was the Galerie Bernheim, then run by Félix Fénéon, which lay on the unvarying route. André Breton begged, Sunday by Sunday, for a brief halt in front of the windows where paintings by Bonnard, Vuillard and Matisse were on view. Matisse was his favorite, and it is possible that he liked him all the more because of the rage and horror which Matisse inspired in his parents.

When he was seventeen (in 1913-14, that is to say) he kept up with one section of the modern movement by reading the *Soirées de Paris*, of which Apollinaire was director. Each number had photographic reproductions of work by one of the avant-garde : Picasso, Matisse, Rousseau, Picabia, Braque, Derain. The importance of this review, in where Breton's development is concerned, can hardly be over-estimated. It taught him, for instance, the lessons of futurism— Apollinaire's articles introduced him to Chirico. And in the last number of 1914 Marius de Zayas' caricatures even foreshadowed the Dada movement. Breton's own post-war review *Littérature*, to a certain extent followed through with the work of emancipation which Apollinaire had initiated in his *Soirées de Paris*.

André Breton knew Derain personally. Between 1910 and 1914 he was completely fascinated by the way his work was developing ; and one of the pictures which most excited him was Derain's *Portrait of Chevalier X...* This had been reproduced in the *Soirées de Paris*, and it represented a man sitting down and reading a newspaper with, in the foreground, a half-open curtain. What hypnotised Breton was that Derain had pasted a real newspaper on

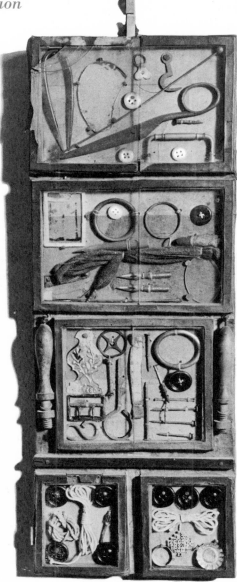

Object constructed by a lunatic, and bought at an exhibition of work by invalid artists in 1929.

to the canvas. This admixture of conventional and unconventional ingredients fired Breton's imagination, and he determined to explore it to the limit of its possibilities.

To the left, Duchamp's Portrait of Washington *(1943). Centre: Chirico's famous* The Child's Brain *(1914). Right: the* Head *which Picasso gave Breton on June 11th 1940. Above the paintings are two transformation masks from British Columbia. The long thin objects are totems from British Columbia. In the foreground, to the right, an ancestor-statue from New Ireland.*

Cubist analysis had pulverised the "thing seen". The futurists, in their attempts to represent that same thing in movement, had spread it out fanwise and then reduced it to a play of forms in which it disappeared as if in a whirlwind. Elsewhere Chirico had introduced a dreamlike and enigmatic element, and Chagall a sense of pictorial metaphor. Breton thought that somewhere in all this effervescence painting was preparing for itself that triumph of the imagination which had been adumbrated by Redon, Gauguin and Gustave Moreau. Cubism and futurism had given realism a beating, but they had not destroyed it : the "thing seen" was still the normal point of departure. Breton wrote of this stage in modern art that "the old subjects, drawn from the

world outside, have gone, as it was inevitable they should. But the new subject, the subject from the world within us, has yet to be discovered". Poetry and painting had to be reconciled to one another, and painting to be freed from its servile, purely descriptive station. Imagination and the dream were its true province, and somehow or other it must be made free of them.

Its enfranchisement was long delayed. Breton's own interest, at the end of the war, was centred on the 'displaced genius' of Soutine and Modigliani and, from 1918 to 1921, the ancient excitements of cubism and futurism seemed to have no successors. Breton lost heart, and spent hour after hour walking aimlessly about the streets or day-

dreaming on a bench in the Place du Chatelet. One morning in 1919 he happened, not far from the Closerie des Lilas, on the lonely, down-at-heel and authentically visionary figure of Modigliani. Lautréamont's poems had just come out in Breton's review *Littéra-ture* : and never, Breton says, has anyone spoken of them more brilliantly than Modigliani that morning. But Breton's Modigliani and his two Soutines did not hold their place in his collection for long ; in 1926 he traded them both for a totem from Oceania.

The "Chirico monument", as Breton called it, came tumbling to the ground

Breton has always been deeply interested ▶ *in masks and the collection of Eskimo masks shown opposite hangs above his bed.*

102

in 1918: thenceforward the painter of arcades, jointed figures and metaphysical interiors sent Paul Guillaume, his dealer, nothing but inferior copies of Raphael. Breton transferred his interest to Max Ernst, who was still living in Cologne. Ernst's collages set the tone for the surrealist movement, even though surrealist painting, properly so called, did not emerge till later.

When Breton married, in 1920, Derain gave him a painting as a wedding present, and Breton later bought several Derains—among them the famous *Portrait of Iturrino*. Later he got rid of them all—not because he didn't like them, but because he needed other things more. Certain 'works of art' speak to the observer's intelligence, others to his sensibility, and Breton's collection is drawn from the first of these two classes. Everything in it has, in his eyes, an *exemplary* quality: and the collection as a whole reflects his ideas, rather than his sensibility, and responds to the demands of intelligence rather than to those of taste.

Up till 1924, the year of the first Surrealist Manifesto, and even immediately after its publication, even Breton's close friends did not quite believe in the possibility of surrealist painting. Dadaism was still influential, and its systematic negations and love of scandal for its own sake had made people question the whole validity of "painting".

It was in 1924 that André Masson told Breton of a young Spaniard called Miro whose pictures were worth seeing. Breton was delighted by the sponta-neity, the simplicity, the naivety and the extreme freedom with which Miro invented the forms which, at that date, constituted a new poetical alphabet. In paintings such as *The Farm, The Hunter, The Trap,* and *Harlequin's Carnival* Miro was creating an original picture-language, in which a ship (in

Above left, a 'medianimic' painting by Joseph Crépin. Right: King Solomon 1st of Brittany, *a gouache by Charles Filiger, considered by Breton to be Gauguin's master.*

The Hunter, for instance) is represented by a cone, the horizon by an eye, and a tree by a circle and a leaf. Miro's forms owed nothing to cubism or futurism and were entirely free from the tyranny of 'external reality'. He alone was the arbiter of what should or should not be on the canvas. This convinced Breton that there could, after all, be a specifically surrealist branch of painting—one in which painting and poetry were joined in a unique synthesis.

Breton still owns several Miros: the *Figure 1927*, one of Miro's few dramatic pictures, and *The Trap*. (He had, unluckily, to get rid of *The Hunter*.) *The Head* is the biggest of all the paintings in Breton's studio, and it shows how immensely important to him was the 'tumultuous entry' of Miro in 1924, the year in which surrealism was born.

When I first called on Breton in his studio Tanguy's *Proteous' Wardrobe* (1931) had a great effect on me. It seemed to explain exactly what Breton meant when he spoke of a picture "opening a window upon the unknown". Here if ever, I thought, was a 'mental landscape'. Tanguy came to surrealism and, to an even greater degree than Miro, he abandoned the objective in favor of the subjective. He even refused ever to give any explanation of his paintings, and carried their secret with him to the grave. Dali owes several of his 'inventions' to Tanguy. Dali's work was, in fact, entirely un-original until he joined the surrealist group, but he

did manage to create around an ambiance of the most extraordinary delirium. Breton owns one of his finest works: *William Tell*. In this, lyricism and eroticism join in frantic alliance; and, much as one may deplore Dali's natural bad taste, it can never be denied that his visionary humor has about it a certain ample magnificence.

Other painters who nourished Breton's faith in surrealism were: Victor Brauner, above all, Matta, Wifredo Lam, and Wolfgang Paalen. Breton owns some of Brauner's best works— *The Strange Case of Monsieur K.* (1933), in particular—and Brauner was the first to bring to surrealism a universal symbolism. The group as a whole comprised a number of people who were not merely different from, but in certain respects opposed to, one another. What linked Dali's academic *trompe-l'œil* technique to Matta's revolutionary palette was not a shared aesthetic position but (as Breton constantly insists) a shared ethic; and this was made up, primarily, of the capacity to say "No" to certain propositions.

Breton's studio is a rendezvous of the unique, and there clings to it a last vestige of the Baudelairean dandy. Styles, periods, whole civilisations rub shoulders there, with poetical imagination as their one constant factor. A heightened awareness of life links Tibetan statues to paintings by Mexican primitives, Hopi dolls to Gallic coins. The Hopi dolls are the latest arrivals. Breton brought them back from a three months' visit, in 1953, to the Hopi reser-

vation in Arizona. Carl Bach, a New York dealer, was the first to bring Red Indian art to the notice of Ernst, Matta and Robert Lebel when they came to the U.S.A. as refugees during the war.

The fashion for primitive art is usually held to have begun at the period of Picasso's *Demoiselles d'Avignon*, but Breton likes to point out that it was Gauguin who first drew attention to the beauty of Polynesian fetishes-and, of course, introduced them into paintings such as his *Poèmes Barbares*. African primitive art, for all the brilliance of its execution, has never quite satisfied Breton, and he turns for preference to the more lyrical, more imaginative, more fantastic art of Oceania.

Breton has in his studio a large ancestor-figure from New Ireland, and has placed it in front of three of his most 'important' pictures: Marcel Duchamp's *Portrait of Washington*, Chirico's *The Child's Brain* (1914), and the violent, convulsive *Head* which Picasso gave to Breton on the day in June 1940 when France capitulated. The statue presides, therefore, over three significant aspects of modern art—and, especially, over Duchamp, who gave up painting in 1912, when he was only 25, after having brought more than one daring venture to a triumphant conclusion. From time to time, and from one motive or another, Duchamp makes a momentary return to painting. Once, between two games of chess (he is a master player), he took some lump-sugar-sized pieces of marble and put

them in a bird cage with a thermometer at the top of the heap. It was rather in the same spirit that he put together his Washington. In 1943 'Vogue' offered a prize for the best portrait of Washington. Duchamp tore a piece of blue paper with gold stars upon it in such a way that its outline was that of Washington's profile. This he mounted on a piece of white material that had been streaked with red, so that the whole composition evoked, more or less, the Stars & Stripes. He did not get the prize... perhaps because the picture betrays his lack of regard for the concept of the 'national hero'.

The Child's Brain is one of Chirico's finest works. It was one of the pictures which Chirico left in Paris when he went back to Italy at the outbreak of war. Like Derain's *Portrait of Chevalier X.* it gave Breton a 'feeling of reading the impossible'. The naked man has the weight, the blindness, the anonymity, and the immobility of a sphinx whose riddle none will ever guess; the picture generates, too, a feeling of extreme claustrophobia which ends by hypnotising the visitor. It symbolises, perhaps, some element in life which defies analysis.

This picture and the Douanier Rousseau's *Still Life with Cherries* are the twin magnetic centres of Breton's studio. The Rousseau, a little-known work, was bought by Breton in 1937. True naivety, in which may be descried man's original innocence, has always fascinated Breton, and he owns many other pictures by *naif* artists: notably the *Ogoun-Ferai* or God of the Voodoo war, by the self-taught voodoo priest Hector Hyppolite. Madness also fascinates him for its power to unveil the farthest recesses of human nature: some of his drawings by Aloyse, for instance, (Aloyse is mad), can stand comparison with Matisse. Breton also has two pictures by the 'medianimic' or metapsychic painter Joseph Crépin. "Pictures of the marvellous" was Crépin's name for them. It was at Martigny-en-Gohelle that this former Pas-de-Calais coal-miner painted the extraordinary pictures in which forms and symbols are disposed on the canvas with an exact and delicate symmetry. What is amazing is that these pictures have marked Egyptian affinities—most obviously in the pyramidal motif which often recurs in them.

Ogoun-Ferai, God of the Voodoo War, by Hyppolite, a naif painter from Haiti. Breton had visited Haiti and has a great interest in voodoo and primitive painters.

104

André Breton sitting among the mysterious jumble of his collection in his Paris apartment rue Fontaine. On the table and shelves : primitive sculpture, rock crystals, voodoo objects. The still life of fruit, left of center, is by the Douanier Rousseau.

(Breton went to the villages in question, walked about them by night, and at last happened on the explanation of these 'Egyptian' obsessions. They were, in point of fact, transpositions of the shapes cast on the night sky by the pyramidal architecture of the mines.)

Breton's collection has been devised, as far as his circumstances have allowed, to help him to resolve all the unexplained contradictions of human nature. Such has been his Grand Design since 1924, and to it have contributed, in their varying ways, the mischievous and childlike simplicity of Miro, Max Ernst's sense of private mythology, the glacial serenity of Tanguy, Picasso's violence and aggressiveness, the tender naivety of Rousseau, Dali's delirious humor, the visions of Brauner, the extreme intelligence of Duchamp and Matta's flamboyant lyricism.

More recently he has bought some pictures by Charles Filiger, Alfred Jarry's favorite artist ; these point to a new departure in his researches. (Jarry's one and only piece of art criticism—in the *Mercure de France* for September 1894—was about Filiger). Filiger, who died at Plougastel-Daoulas in 1930, was altogether an extraordinary figure. (He once turned an 'art-lover' out of his house and shouted after him "Call yourself Vollard, do you ? Speculate in pictures, do you ? Get the hell out of here !") He was at once a mystic and an ironist, and it may well be that he had a decisive influence upon Gauguin. (He attacked Gauguin to his face and praised him warmly when his back was turned). Breton's bedroom is ornamented by, among other things, three Seurat drawings which Félix Fénéon once gave him as a New Year present. Not far from them are hung several gouaches by Filiger—projects for stained-glass, it would seem—which reveal a delicate sweetness of vision, allied to a fine sense of proportion and formal balance.

Filiger is, to date, the latest of Breton's re-discoveries. His work appeals as much to intelligence as to sensibility, and it is one more proof, if proof be needed, that Breton has still the eye for a picture that he had when, as a boy of fifteen, he gazed enraptured at the Matisses in Bernheim's window. And where this eye has led him, no other man has been.

My friend Brancusi

BY HENRI PIERRE ROCHÉ

*"If you want to remain my friend you must never write a word about me while I'm alive",
the sculptor used to say to the author of this article*

Brancusi lived and died in Paris in
the Impasse Ronsin, an oasis from which
nearly all the studios, save his and a
few that were protected by it, had
been cleared away.

It had once been a flourishing artists'
colony, and through him it had become
famous. He had lived there for nearly
half a century, like a peasant on his
land, dressed as often as not in white
airman's overalls, doing his own marketing and laughing with the market-wo-
men, small of stature, frugal and fastidious, climbing gradually from poverty
to a belated affluence.

"Millions," he said towards the end,
"are like peanuts—when you have them."

He had two doctors, one orthodox,
the other not, two diets, and two refri-
gerators, each with its different stock,
one for himself and one for his friends;
and he had found, by experiment, the

Brancusi always claimed that no one knew
how to photograph sculpture, so he bought
a camera and started taking his own
works. The picture opposite and the one
on the following page, by the sculptor
himself, date from before 1925. For many
years they were fixed to a wall of his tum-
bledown Parisian studio ; they faithfully
reflect its curious atmosphere. Shortly
before his death in 1957 the sculptor gave
them to his old friend Roché. Recognizable
on this photograph are Princess X *in*
bronze (center) flanked by two versions
of Bird in Space, *one in marble, the*
other in bronze. In the foreground : Leda.

Photographed in Saint-Germain just out-
side of Paris in 1923 : Henri-Pierre
Roché, Brancusi and John Quinn. *Quinn,*
an American lawyer collector, was an
early admirer and patron of the sculptor's.

things he liked best. Mumm demi-sec, for instance, and whisky with plenty of Vittel water and a little honey.

He had a slang all his own. *Ah, les vaches !* meant "Good Lord !"

I used to visit him there from 1915 to 1957. "Yes," he would say. "You can bring your friends, or anyone who'd like to come, provided they're amusing and unaffected, but never a critic, and never an art-dealer, and if you want to remain my friend you must never write a word about me while I'm alive."

He would never give me his opinion of another artist, or of a beginner.

When young he was like a nimble smooth-haired fox with mischief in his eye; open-hearted but no great talker, and reserved in the extreme if not immediately sure of his ground.

The first work of his I ever saw was the big-bellied bird. He felt how much I loved his polished bronzes, and as I couldn't at that time buy any, he gave me one—a child's head, rough-surfaced in parts. It became one of the two centre-pieces of my home, and caused a great commotion there. No one liked it. Artists came specially to laugh at it. Some of them are still alive and would not care to be named.

It is difficult to imagine to-day that the *Princess X.*, that poem in white marble, translated into polished bronze in all its fantasy and purity, was accused of being a phallic symbol and turned out of the Salon des Indépendants on the opening day, although one or two people protested, because "The Minister's coming, and we really can't show him *that* !"

Brancusi's admirers were few in number and slow to increase, but one of them, John Quinn, suddenly made it possible for him to work as he pleased, in peace. Brancusi trusted the judgment of ordinary people and was not at all annoyed when one of them stood in

◄ *A corner of Brancusi's studio photographed by the sculptor. In the center of the picture, his* Endless Columns *in wood ; on the right,* Chimera. *On the bases in the foreground :* Beginning of the World *and* Child's Head *; on the round base,* Leda *in polished bronze. In the background,* Bird in Space *and, extreme left,* Princess X.

The Roumanian sculptor shown at the Saint-Cloud golf course near Paris in 1923: from l. to r.: Brancusi, Jeanne Forster *(an American poet), his friend the composer* Erik Satie *and* Henri-Pierre Roché.

front of a polished bronze and said "Why, it's even more beautiful than a fireman's helmet !" He was very good-natured about showing his studio at no. 8 Impasse Ronsin (he moved to no. 11 later). I must have taken over a hundred carefully-chosen people there during the last forty years, and each visit added something to the ritual. Brancusi had an infallible intuition and knew instantly what his visitors were thinking. What was said was irrelevant: what mattered to him was the authentic immediate reaction. When this was favorable it acted on Brancusi like a vitamin-injection.

He began with a brief summary of his development, illustrating it with a packet of big photographs of his early work—from the anatomy-study he had made for the Ecole des Beaux-Arts in Roumania to the naturalistic busts and torsoes which—much to his annoyance —made the cultivated visitor pronounce the names of Rodin and Michelangelo. "Beefsteak merchants !", he would cry, "I was in the beefsteak trade myself once. Year after year I used to do these anatomies, likenesses, copies... it came easily to me and I thought I had quite a knack for it. Then one day I got ashamed. And when I was asked to make a funerary monument for a devoted husband and wife I did something that, without being at all like that particular couple, was like all the couples who have ever loved and been joined together. And this is what it looked like".

And he showed a photograph of the vertical couple from the Montparnasse cemetery: two people embracing face to face, leg to leg, arm to arm, eye to eye, squinting almost... If the visitor sensed the difference between beefsteak and non-beefsteak, and preferred the second, the whole studio was laid open for him. Here are some names of sculptures, without dates: *The Fish, Socrates, The Sorceress, The Return of the Prodigal Son, The Negress, The Sophisticated Young Girl, The New-Born Son, The Leader, The Spring Chicken, Adam & Eve, Mademoiselle Pogany, The Beginning of the World, Sculpture for the Blind*, the two (and later three) *Penguins, The Seal, The Cocks, The Unending Columns*, the two *Young Girl* torsoes, one in onyx with pink kiss-marks on the hip, and the other pear-shaped, with no thighs. Later came the series of *Birds in Space*, a theme that Brancusi never wearied of during the second half of his life; beginning with the vase-shaped bird that stood upright like a goose, he turned in the end to birds which, as he said, pierced the vault of the heavens.

The first of the white marble birds in this series stood on a cone of the same white marble which, though embedded in the bird, was in some way foreign to its being. Brancusi worked for a year on the living, palpitating stalk which seems not only to support the bird but actually to launch it into the air. It was as difficult as the bird to get right, he said. "But now it's definitive": all the same he later made one or two very small amendments to it. It was the most strenuous moment in all his career, and the bird is, little as he knew it, the emblem and prototype of the interstellar rocket.

Some years later he made his *Leda* in polished bronze, a sculpture that turned slowly, never-ceasingly, on its base, and in which the rest of the studio was reflected, as if in a mirror of gold. Its undulatory motion was such that one grew giddy as one watched statues and human beings mingling within its mythical forms. It grew ever more marvellous in my eyes.

If you felt at home in his world, and your surprise and joy were such as to drive out all conscious cerebration, then Brancusi would delight in your delight and, without saying so, would be grateful to you. Such visits sweetened his life: he didn't care at all whether you bought, or not: those things could wait.

In 1926 or thereabouts I took an American girl to see him. She was deeply moved. He showed us two bronzes he'd just finished polishing—a *Mademoiselle Pogany* and the torso of a young boy. She fell in love with the first, and I with the second. "I can't live without it," she said, "and somebody else might get it. I want to buy it at once". I felt the same way about the torso, and we bought the two pieces then and there.

Another time I took a young Indian prince whom I had known at Oxford. He and Brancusi liked one another, and the visitor studied the sculptures with the rapt calm of a fairy-tale character. He was not rich, at that time, and after a while he took out his pocket-book and began to do sums on the back. Why? Because he wanted nothing less than the three major, sister works which were there: a big *Bird in Space* in black marble, one in white marble, one in polished bronze. A trio unique in the world: he was working out what he could afford. Later he decided to house them in a temple specially designed by Brancusi, twelve feet by twelve in area, on the grass in front of his palace, with neither doors nor windows and an underground entrance. A temple of meditation which would be open to all, but open to only one at a time. In the interior there was to be a square pool of water, with one side for each of the three Birds and on the fourth a tall oak figure of Buddha by Brancusi. It would be so laid out that the gold Bird would stand in the direct line of the sun, on a certain sacred date, as it struck though a circular hole in the ceiling. Sketches for this temple were soon ready, and payment for the sculptures was spread over the next two years. The prince bought nothing else in Paris.

The birds were sent off, but they left such a gap in the studio that Brancusi was quite downcast and reproached me bitterly for having been the cause of their departure. Time went by, and Brancusi was invited to India to supervise the building of the temple. He had been pleased with the samples of the local stone that had been sent to him. He liked the idea of working with Indian stone-masons and intended to do some of the cornerstones himself. He had made a plaster model of the temple and some sketches for a fresco for the interior.

When he got to India the young monarch was too ill to receive him and, after waiting in vain for more than a

month, he came back to Europe, consoled only by the fact that he had made friends with an elephant. In the end the prince got better, but the finances of his country were in serious disorder, the monies destined for the temple were spent elsewhere, and the war of 1914-1918 broke out. The temple of love and peace was never built, and the three birds are still waiting for their aviary. Twenty-five years after his first visit the Maharajah, as he then was, came to see Brancusi; and together, in silence, they sat cross-legged, as they had many years earlier, and looked at the model of the Temple.

Brancusi had a white husky dog, which he called Polaire. Beautiful and remote as the Frozen North, she would refuse even fresh meat if it were not from Brancusi's own hand. Nor did she like visitors to interrupt their tête-à-tête; if the visitor was a lady her jealousy was pitiable to watch, and if her Master were to kiss the visitor's hand she would punish him by sulking and fasting for the rest of the day. This went on for a year until one day Polaire was run over and killed by a motor-car. I said to Brancusi how sorry I was, and thought I saw the shadow of a tear in his eyes: but all he said was "Yes, it was terrible. But now I can work again!"

Brancusi liked beautiful women, and they liked him, but he was discretion itself; never did his men friends intrude on a rendevous. We could, at most, form certain hypotheses.

Brancusi was respectful, attentive, sweet-tempered and indulgent, where women were concerned. He loved them to bring him flowers, and they loved to do it. His studio was never without flowers. He had many close women-friends, all very different from one another, and it was a great joy for him to receive them. Champagne flowed, and the lively conversation went on for hours. Towards the end he became a Sage, a director of consciences in his way, always smiling, always full of mischief and yet—also in his own way—deeply in earnest. With his lively eye and curling beard he had the air of a legendary seducer or improved Jupiter.

Erik Satie was a very close friend of his, alike as a creative artist and an artisan of integrity. Tough nuts both, they never showed the profound influence which each had upon the other. They were continually laughing and joking together like schoolboys. Sometimes at night, when I went out walking with them, Satie would stop under a gas-jet and note down a phrase of music that had occurred to him. Brancusi was dazzled by Satie, who taught him to fence with words, to have confidence in himself, to put things lucidly. Brancusi was Socrates' disciple. Only once did Satie speak to me about Brancusi's work—his genius, tenacity, courage, purity—but he did it in such a way that respect and gratitude shone through every word. Brancusi once spoke of Satie in much the same way, but neither would have done it in front of the other. There was no need. But at the end of the day each would seek the other out and the joking would begin again.

Brancusi had a hard time at the beginning of his Parisian career, and he owed his rescue to an American collector, John Quinn, who was already buying Brancusi in New York in 1915, and owned about thirty by 1925. He it was who made possible Brancusi's triumphal success in New York a quarter of a century later.

John Quinn was a lawyer, of Irish descent, and had a sense of humor all his own. One day he conceived the idea of taking Brancusi, Satie, and myself to play golf on a fashionable course. Brancusi was eager to try, and Satie followed his lead. Their complete ignorance of the etiquette of the game had consequences which John Quinn never tired of describing. Brancusi's driving, for instance, had a technique all his own: he would take aim from a distance, make a violent preliminary swing which never connected with the ball, correct his aim and lash out a second time. Never did this second shot fail. Satie, in bowler-hat and topcoat, and carrying an umbrella, preferred not to play himself. "I can see more of Brancusi that way," he said. He followed him round all afternoon, never losing an opportunity—and they were many—of pulling his leg. But Brancusi didn't resent it, for he was developing a passion for golf; and thanks to his long use of hammer and axe and a certain native precision he made good progress.

Brancusi envied the god Milarépa because he could make hail fall where he pleased. And he venerated him for the wisdom which he came to acquire.

But one must stop somewhere. I'll talk of those things another time.

Brancusi's Bird in Space *and a young admirer photographed at an exhibition in Zurich.*

Seventy-five

People and places form the imagery of the artist's life,
they are described here by a close friend

According to normal standards it is too early to attempt to establish a biographical record of the life of Pablo Picasso. There are many good reasons why it should not be done, the first being that there is ample time in store for one who has so often astonished the world by new departures in his work, to do so again in ways so disconcerting that they might alter all former statements about his past activities.

The act of creation achieved by him daily is to Picasso a continual challenge. For him the arts are not an exercise in aesthetics calculated to produce perfection, they are his life. Life and work are so intimately connected that it is impossible for him to remain idle. This condition is as true to day as it was fifty years ago. His memory is vivid and images that haunted him in his childhood reappear with such freshness that they might have been dreamed of for the first time over-night. It is therefore by no means pointless to try to trace these images in the surroundings and among the friends that he has known.

The seventy-five years preceeding Picasso's birthday on the 25th of October (1957) have seen changes unprecedented in history for their far reaching effects on our ways of living. During this time the inventions of Science have been greedily absorbed with little question as to their desirability, this is a commomplace well known to all, but we may already, owing to the universal fame that Picasso has now achieved, be inclined to forget that the revolution that has taken place in the arts during the same period was not received with the same approval, and that the work of Picasso, particularly in the early years of his life, was treated with derision or considered to be a danger to society.

In the general outcry against revolution in the visual arts there is only one innovation that has escaped disapproval. The developement of photography and its descendants, the cinema and television has always been considered a respectable form of progress, perhaps because it relies to such a degree on scien-tific technique and therefore escapes being entirely branded as an art. The photographer has become biographer and in the case of Picasso we are greatly helped, not only by the fact that he is not averse to being photographed but also that several distinguished photographers have become his intimate friends.

Before the camera became ubiquitous there were not the same facilities. Photographs were rare and of many events we would like to be able to visualise there is no trace. Among them are the banquet given in honor of the Douanier Rousseau in Picasso's studio at the Bateau Lavoir and the marriage of Picasso with Olga Koklova at which Apollinaire and Max Jacob were witnesses. But fortunately there are other means of following pictorially the biography of Picasso. From early days his own facility in making rapid sketches in which he

Picasso at Vallauris in 1955. He has always loved dressing-up, now as in the past he enjoys astonishing his friends by the variety of his disguises and his uninhibited clowning. Caps and hats are part of the fun.

112

BY ROLAND PENROSE

years young

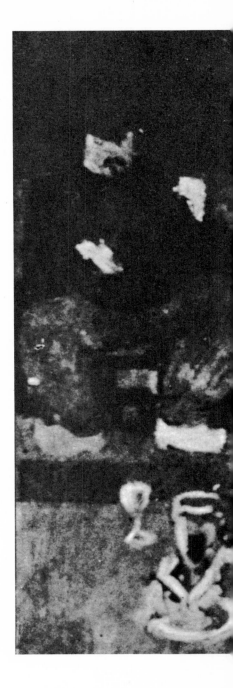

Brother Pedro de Cristo, Almoguera y Gonzalez (1773-1855), Picasso's paternal great-uncle, was major brother of the venerable company of Hermits of Our Lady of Bethlehem. Picasso's father, José Ruiz Blasco, painted the garland of flowers on the glass covering the picture.

Left :
José Ruiz Blasco, aged 32. Picasso's father taught painting at the Malaga, and later at the Barcelona, School of Fine Arts. He was his son's first master, but soon realised that his son's talent surpassed his own. He died in Barcelona in 1913.

Center :
Picasso's mother, Doña Maria Picasso de Ruiz, was born at Malaga in 1855 and died at Barcelona in 1939. Shortly before she died she wrote her son: "I can believe anything of you... If, one day, I heard that you'd celebrated Mass, I'd believe that too".

114

Lola, the artist's sister. (Charcoal, 1899). Howard Samuel coll. (England). Señora Lola de Vilato is three years younger than Picasso. She is the widow of a psychiatrist, lives in Barcelona, and has in her house some important early pictures of her brother including a series painted in 1917.

"Harlequin with glass" (39½"x35⅛") Detail. Paris, 1905. Here Picasso sees himself disguised as Harlequin. Most of his numerous self-portraits date from before 1919.

Center :

Pablo, aged 7, with his sister Lola. Picasso has an extraordinary visual memory. He recently added these notes to the photograph: "Lola's dress black, blue belt, 'me' white suit—navy blue coat, blue beret."

Right :

Pablo, aged 4, already full of assurance. Here, too, Picasso remembers exactly the color of his clothes "vermillion red tunic and kilt, gilt buttons, bronze shoes".

was encouraged by his father provided him with the means of describing his surroundings and his thoughts. His letters to his family, in childhood and later to his friends, are richly illustrated and up to the cubist period self-portraits are abundant. That he was conscious of his own appearance, not only as he saw himself in the mirror but also as others saw him, in profile, in conversation with his friends or at work, we have ample proof. Gertrude Stein claimed that the power of his eyes was such that he could see around corners. Certainly, that he can see himself from outside himself we can have no doubt. He enjoyed picturing himself in all kinds of situations, real or imaginary. We see him wrapped in his heavy overcoat, travelling to Paris with Sebastian Junyer, walking with his dog on the Ramblas or lying on the beach palette in hand, clothed in a toga. His delight in changing his appearance by disguises is apparent in the variety of head dresses, caps, top-hats, berets, and broad brimmed sombreros that he has fancied.

If we supplement these drawings with those made of him by his friends, we begin to have a view, not only of the superficial appearances of those who frequented with him "Els Quatre Gats" and the "Lapin Agile", but we can better understand their preoccupations, loves and hates.

There is only one period in the life of Picasso when the two forms of records at our disposal, the self-portrait or the rapid sketch in early days and more recently the photo, fail to overlap. During the years of the great cubist discoveries from 1910 to 1914, he abandonned descriptive or realistic drawing and since at that date the facilities for photography had not developed sufficiently, there is a dearth of visual records. For instance there are quantities of sketches and portraits of Fernande Olivier and also of Olga Picasso but of Eva (Marcelle Humbert), the companion of Picasso during the greater part of these years, there are only two photographs known. Although her name appears in many cubist paintings inscribed not unlike a

lover's declaration carved in the bark of a tree, Picasso never painted her portrait.

A record of the places where Picasso has lived is more easily established. Painters with few exceptions are not travellers. Their art is static and their equipment usually cumbersome. Picasso has never hunted landscapes, he has been content with light that excites the eye and a good climate. Never has he taken much interest in the picturesque, but throughout his life, originally by chance and later by choice, he has returned continually to the sea. Malaga, his birthplace, Coruna, Barcelona are followed later in life by Cadaqués, Biaritz, Dinard, Royan, Collioure and the Côte d'Azur as places where his imagination could look from a window giving on to the sea. In summer the dazzling enjoyments of the beach have for many years colored his thought. The sea, itself the home of creation, provides an atmosphere which is stimulating to him and appropriate for his work. Like the fishermen of Antibes he prys by night

116

Self-portrait in 18th century costume. Picasso dates this 1896. It is the earliest record we have of his love of dressing-up.

▲ Picasso and his friends in Barcelona at the Café "Els quatro gats" (The Four Cats), c. 1900. From right to left: the painter Sebastian Junyer, Angel de Soto and Picasso in a large peasant's hat from Cordoba.

▲ "Picasso with pipe in a peaked cap". Ink and watercolor. 1904. When he was first in Paris, Picasso had a cap with shiny peak of which he was especially fond. It figures more than once in drawings of the period.

into the secrets of the rock pools. He seeks beneath the surface with the same vision that formerly penetrated and dissected the guitar and the glass of absinthe.

The sea is the appropriate background for woman. As its waves break and refashion the rocks and pebbles into fantastic sculptures, so Picasso tears to pieces and reshapes the female form. From the sea emerges, not Venus but the woman he loves.

The only city that has been able to entice Picasso away from the sea and hold him absorbed for many years is indeed Paris. Among the many reasons responsible for this, undoubtly the main inducement has been friendships that have formed a web of associations from which it becomes difficult to escape. To Picasso, his friends and his loves are the sources of his inspiration even more than

the objects and the landscapes around him. He suffers the deepest depression and anxiety if he finds himself cut off from them. They are constantly in his thoughts. When he learnt of the death of Maurice Raynal, he confided in a friend who was staying with him that he was in the habit of going through the names of his closest friends each morning and that, to his great remorse, that day he had forgotten Raynal. At the same time he requires even friendship to bow to the exigencies of work. Friends can be asked to wait or to leave but the imperative call of his desire to express himself in work must be answered without delay. If this cannot happen he suffers bitterly from a sense of frustration.

In the choice of his friends Picasso has shown in general a marked preference for poets rather than painters. It

Picasso arriving in Paris. Pen and colored crayon. 1900. Mrs. Heywood-Lonsdale coll. (England.) Here Picasso shows himself wearing incongruously a bicycling costume with broad-brimmed felt hat, carrying his easel in front of the Moulin-Rouge.

Picasso in 1905, photographed in Paris with Fernande Olivier, who shared his companionship for the next six years.

is not that he is insensitive to the skill and the companionship of fellow artists and craftsmen, he loves those who are genuinely creative but finds no interest in those who theorise about art. The conversations he enjoys are those in which wit and paradox are the means of sounding the depths of truth. In this form of eloquence those who have a habit of expressing themselves in words are more adept than those whose medium is paint.

At the same time there have been long and fruitful friendships between Picasso and other painters and sculptors. Gertrude Stein writes of the first meeting between Picasso and Matisse and of the strong contrast in their characters. Picasso speaks of how he heard Matisse and Leo Stein laughing behind his back when he first showed them the freshly painted canvas of the *Demoiselles d'Avignon* but they had in common an overwhelming interest

in each others work. From early times they exchanged paintings and during Matisse's last years of illness in Nice, Picasso often spent long hours with him in conversations which were unfortunately never recorded. It is common to hear talk of rivalries between Picasso and Braque, but no two friends of such long standing and with such momentous associations in the past can laugh together with more understanding of each other and each other's work. That Picasso enjoys companionship in his work was never more evident than in the days spent with Derain at Cadaquès and with Braque at Céret, at Sorgues and at Avignon. The same spirit flourished around him when, due to Cocteau's introduction to Diaghilev, he produced his designs for the ballet, working back-stage with scene painters and dressmakers, even adding color at the last moment to the dresses of the ballerinas just before they made their appearance on the stage.

With his wife Olga, Diaghilev the great impressario, and Edwin Evans the English music-critic, in 1924. It was in 1917, when designing scenery for the Russian Ballet, that Picasso fell in love with Olga Koklova, a junior dancer in Diaghilev's company.

118

The artist at Mougins, south of France, in 1937, in front of the monumental Hispano-Suiza which he has owned for over twenty-five years, often motoring between Paris and the Mediterranean in one night.

Beach party at Antibes in 1925. To the left is Olga, in ballet costume. In the centre, behind Picasso, Comte Etienne de Beaumont, famous animator and patron of the arts, and to the right the Comtesse de Beaumont. For once, Picasso is the only member of the group not in fancy-dress.

For some years Picasso was much in the fashionable world. Here he is, dressed as a toreador, at the Beaumonts' ball in 1924. To the right, Olga: to the left, Mme Errazuriz, a Chilean-born hostess, one of the first to realise that old furniture and modern paintings may go well together.

"Already this first day, we felt for each other a great sympathy," wrote Max Jacob describing the first time he called on Picasso in 1901. The same immediate response was felt by those other poets who met him three years later in the turbulent atmosphere of Montmartre. Apollinaire, Salmon, Reverdy and a dozen others were all impressed by the strength of his personality. His companionship opened to them a new sense of vision and a liberation from preconcieved judgments. Cocteau in 1933 spoke with gratitude of how he learnt new values in the early days of their friendship. Fifteen years later Paul Eluard declared that he considered himself happy to be alive in this century above all because of his meeting with Picasso, "bon maître de la liberté".

The poets and painters who share Picasso's intimacy extend beyond the limits of our own time. He has enlarged this community of the great into the past by portraits that he has made of them as though they had been present for a sitting and by illustrations and adaptations of their works. He extends his fraternity of genius to Gongora, El Greco, Buffon, Cranach, Delacroix, Ingres, Cézanne, Rembrandt, Poussin, Mallarmé, Jarry, Balzac and many others of his choice. They are his companions, his associates in his work.

Just as Picasso never becomes the victim of a successful idea in his painting, he never exploits his friendships. He has always accepted the risk of being misunderstood and of having to part company even with those he loves most. When in 1907 he painted *Les Demoiselles d'Avignon* he accepted the possibility of losing both his reputation and his friends at the same time, and indeed for a while it seemed that he had done so. Allowing nothing but his instincts to guide him, he showed his capacity of questioning his own achievements as well as the most respected conceptions

of beauty. Realising his great powers, he also knew the danger of his position. He could say with Max Jacob: *le doute, voilà l'art.*

In accordance with tradition, Pablo in his childhood sat beside his father in the arena under the ferocious Andalusian sun, watching the rites of *la mise à mort.* Evoking the symbolism of the bullfight his compatriots have called him the Toreador of painting, but Picasso is more complex. It would be more true to say that he is both toreador and bull in one. He occupies the arena alone wrestling with the duality of his own nature. He is the monster walking upright, he is the hero disguised with the mask of the beast, who both triumphs and dies. A duality which is resolved only by the enclosing circle of the arena; world in which the action takes place or eye by which it is observed.

In spite of the great variety in his work, Picasso never forgets his discoveries. Throughout the long panorama of his work it is possible to trace the re-occurrence of images that reappear like actors for whom he has conceived definite roles. The horse, the bull, the ape and the owl from the animal kingdom are joined by harlequin, mother and child, the faun, the minotaur, the bewildered old man who is victim of his own conceit, and woman in the startling radiance of her nakedness. Though at certain times they have been neglected owing to his preoccupation with visual problems, they emerge later with added significance.

The events of Picasso's life and above all his loves are reflected throughout in his work, as in early days when,

Picasso in 1932

The meal

Picasso and Dora Maar photographed by
Roland Penrose in 1937 when they were
staying at Mougins with the poet Éluard.

Picasso and Braque at Vallauris in 1954.

◄ "Portrait of Dora Maar" 25⅝"x 21¼". 1937.
(Dora Maar coll., Paris.) An unpublished
portrait of the young woman who appears
in so many of Picasso's pictures from 1936
to 1946. She was his model, in particular,
for the famous double-profile portraits.

"Françoise Gilot with Paloma and Claude", 1951. An unpublished drawing from Françoise Gilot's collection.

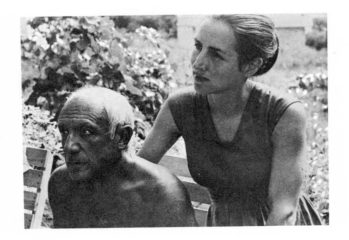

Picasso and Françoise Gilot at Golfe–Juan in 1948.

Picasso and Claude at Golfe–Juan in 1948.

126

In 1955 Picasso organised a corrida at Vallauris. This picture shows him with Jean Cocteau on his left. On his right, Jacqueline Roque, who figures in many of his recent pictures; behind him, his daughters Paloma and Maia and his son Claude.

with the arrival of Fernande Olivier, the dour theme of the beggar enclosed in the solitude of his blindness gave way in 1905 to the gaze of soft eyed madonnas, while at the same time harlequin, the families of the saltimbanques and their motley crowd appeared on the scene. The drawings and paintings of the early years of his marriage reflect the arcadian hopes of a world freed from war. They were soon to give way, as confidence turned to doubt, to savage distortions of the human form. Through the agonising years of the Spanish war followed by the dark hopelessness of invasion and the occupation, the presence of Dora Maar illuminates both his life and his work. Again, at the end of the war, the prospect of a new life enriched by the companionship of Françoise Gilot influences the great idyllic paint-

ings that now hang in the Château Grimaldi in Antibes. They are followed by pictures which show with unique insight Picasso's understanding and love of the child. The perilous adventures of the first steps of Claude and Paloma and the passionate seriousness of their play has been observed and revealed with startling accuracy. Latest of all, the spacious interiors of La Californie are animated by the presence of Jacqueline Roque.

Among the most enduring friendships, those of Jaime Sabartés and Daniel-Henry Kahnweiler must be placed in a category of their own as those who have consistently helped Picasso in the material affairs of his life while the names of Max Jacob, Apollinaire, Cocteau and Paul Eluard will always be closely associated with definite periods: Max Jacob with the early days of

hardship in sordid hotel rooms and the Bateau Lavoir, Apollinaire with the heroic years of cubism, Cocteau with the glamor of the Russian Ballet and Eluard with the poetic phase, surrealism and wartime as well as post-war political activities.

Judging by the complete dedication of Picasso to his art, it would be easy to assign to him the life of a hermit such as that lived by his ancestor Brother Pedro de Cristo Almoguera in the mountains of Cordova, but he combines with his passion for the arts an appetite for life, an eager curiosity and a profound humanity that endow him with a plenitude comparable to the abundance of his creation output. The genius of Picasso is dependant on the unrestrained flow of his imagination, generous, passionate and full of understanding.

Jean Arp

BY MICHEL SEUPHOR

Arp's work has been a part of modern art for the last half-century. He himself has few remaining examples of his first manner; his natural modesty and a gnawing dissatisfaction with what he created drove him to destroy what he produced almost as rapidly as it came into existence. His family recalls that when they were living in Strasbourg the big Alsatian stove was frequently fed with Arp's paintings and bas-reliefs. It was only through ruse that his brother François, who now lives in Paris, was able to save some of the 1914-17 output, including some charming, minute etchings done in Weggis in 1915. Arp had retired to this Swiss village in 1909 after academic art instruction at Weimar and Paris. He met Paul Klee there for the first time.

Since these early, historic pieces are so rare, it is all the more remarkable

that a large painting by Arp, a grisaille dated, I think, 1907, was recently returned to the artist who had not seen it for about half a century. It represents a group of naked figures, summarily treated with large curving lines and unexpected angularities. It's an amazing work, for its date, and amazing too for a man of Arp's age (he was twenty at the time). The same style recurs in even more opulent state in the drawings he published in *Der Sturm* in 1912. The grisaille painting had been all these years and throughout two wars in Germany; it was sent back to the artist as a surprise by an old friend.

Arp was born in Strasbourg on September 16th, 1887, and he is therefore just seventy years old. Known as "Hans" during his early years, he changed to the French version "Jean" at the time of the First World War when, to escape mobilization into the German army, he caught the last train out of Germany to Paris and from there went on to Zurich. At that time he was working on abstract collages and designs for embroideries and carpets using geometrical motifs. He exhibited his first abstract works at the Tanner Gallery, in Zurich; these were generally composed of rectilinear forms. The artist has subsequently explained that he was

Arp has lived since 1926 in Meudon, near Paris, in a small, neat house designed by his late wife, Sophie Taeuber Arp. The little surburban garden is studded with his sculpture, to the surprise of passers-by. His studio is at the bottom of the garden; here he has a complete repertory of all his works in plaster. A man of simple tastes, he is an early riser and a prodigeous worker. The photograph shows him building up a form by adding wet plaster to a wire foundation.

Constellation *(commas and full stops). 1944. Characteristic painted wood relief. 43½″×55″. Basle Museum of Art.*

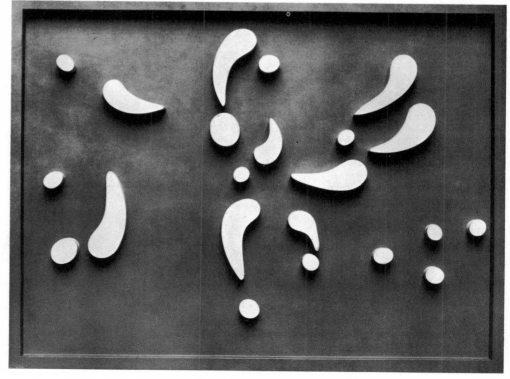

not then familiar with the juxtaposed rectangles used so extensively by Mondrian and van Doesburg in Holland. Soon he was to abandon this orderly method of proceeding, preferring the

Crucifixion. 49¼″ × 49¼″. 1915. This picture belongs to Arp's brother Fran ois and is one of the few remaining of a series of paintings and reliefs carried out between 1914 and 1917. Arp was then working in Strasbourg, and most of the work of this period was consigned to the big Alsatian stove which warmed the whole house. In recent years Arp has stopped painting completely. Sculptures, reliefs in two colors and collages take all his time.

chance effects achieved with "rudimentary, irrational objects, mutilated or

broken" which announced the first symptoms of the Dada spirit.

Arp's important role in the Dada group, founded in 1916 with Tzara, Janco, Ball and Hulsenbeck is described elsewhere in this book. For a while Arp's work reflected once again a more rigorously geometrical and abstract construction under the influence of the talented Swiss woman who was to become his wife, Sophie Taeuber, an artist who combined simplicity with real richness of invention. Together they made large collages comprised of straight forms. Later, also together, with van Doesburg, they decorated a cinema dancing hall at Strasbourg which is no longer in existence.

From this same early period date the abstract wood cut illustrations and the first polychrome reliefs. Then Arp began creating rounded forms resembling mysterious vegetables. The reliefs were the links leading him on imperceptibly to sculpture in the round which entered his œuvre in 1930. He was to turn his attention increasingly to the great processes of nature, infusing organic forms with the spirit of growth and change. He has described his sculpture as signs, condensations of nature, related to trees, stones, clouds and sky, transformed by the act of artistic creation.

Summer metope. 1946. 56″ × 25⅝″. Oak. Collection Arp.

Arp's collaboration with his wife is of immense importance to his art. She died accidentally in Zurich in 1943, and Arp has re-lived, ever since, every detail of their shared life, realising ever more vividly how much he was helped in his work by Sophie's presence and her exquisite modesty. In the late twenties she had drawn up plans for a small house, and the Arps moved to suburban Meudon, just outside of Paris. Her studio there was above his own, and few of his visitors knew of the important body of work that she steadily built up, day by day ; she needed to create, but asked nothing for herself and had no great faith in her powers. (She first

This big grisaille is one of Arp's earliest works. Painted in 1907, it was hidden by a friend of Arp's throughout the Nazi régime and the war of 1939-45. The curving lines and sharp angles of the figures were daring for the period.

exhibited in Paris in 1930, in the "Circle and Square" exhibition which I arranged with Torrès-Garcia.) Many of her paintings are still in her Meudon studio, and nothing pleases Arp more than to be asked to show them. Only now is it beginning to be clear how great were those powers of hers: perhaps doubt is an essential component of artistic creation. It is only later in life that the value of an artist's first efforts becomes clear to us: and it's easy enough at that late stage to read into their fragility the look of solid foundations. The element of risk disappears and in its place we see "historical necessity". The insolence of youth merges into the mummified seriousness of age. Arp is well aware of all this: not for nothing did he call one of his collages of 1914 *Before I was born*.

Arp was, in fact, not "born" in the true sense till many years later—1929, for instance, when he produced his first white reliefs, and later, with his first round-boss sculptures. The part he had played in the uprears of Dada and his subsequent flirtation with the surrealists had no deep influence on his slow, unwavering evolution.

People often say that Arp's work is, historically and in spirit, a continuation

Superimposed sections. *1947. Black-patined bronze. Height 39". Open-Air Sculpture Museum at Middelheim, Antwerp.*

of Brancusi's. Seen from a distance and superficially this might seem to be true. Arp's work could be called a richer and more highly developed pendant to Brancusi's. Brancusi had, it is true, established what matters most in his art before Arp took seriously to sculpture. But neither in its origins nor in its spirit does Arp's work really sustain this interpretation. Its roots are in Arp himself, and we can trace them right back to 1914. In spirit, too, he is radically unlike the great Roumanian. Brancusi begins with the object as it exists in nature and proceeds to inter-

pret and transpose until nothing nonessential remains. Form is loved for itself, by the end. But Arp proceeds quite differently. He perfects his forms by an autonomous, closed-circuit procedure, starting and ending with form, and working, one might say, from within to without, as if inventing a new fruit. It's a procedure of free auto-formation, in complete detachment from the objective world and from any traditional concept of sculpture. Thus does he reach the inmost recesses of the heart. Insidious conformism has no hold upon Arp.

When Arp was born, his native Alsace was still a part of Germany, German was his first language. When he started

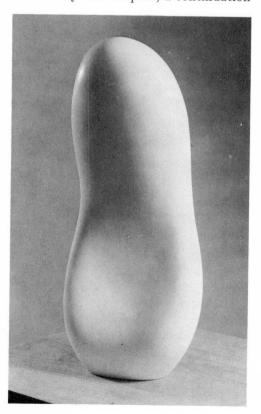

Silent. *1942. Height 13¼". White marble. Mrs. John D. Rockefeller III coll. N. Y.*

131

to write poetry however—his body of poetical works is important—he used both German and French, and as a man he has always preferred to live in Paris; when he was twenty-one he opted for French nationality. He loves to travel, and has been twice to America, twice to Greece, and on several occasions to Italy (he won the first prize for sculpture at the Venice Biennale in 1954), Holland and Germany. For a holiday he prefers Switzerland, and often stays in Ascona or Basle with Marguerite Hagenbach, who has a remarkable collection of abstract art. But he always comes back to Meudon before long; and there, in the house still haunted by his wife's presence, he has an old servant-assistant who rejoices in the name of Dante Pisanelli.

Arp is a simple man, and if his personality has a strong poetic element it is by virtue of his continual astonishment that the world is less simple than he is. "It's senseless", he says at every opportunity, "completely senseless"; and in his quiet and determined way he works to set things right. Candor ends by conquering the world; and Arp's candor is inexpugnable, in that it has no internal contradictions within it. He

has retained intact, by some special dispensation, the simplicity of childhood. It's difficult to run through any book

Sophie Taeuber-Arp. Parasols. *Relief in painted wood. 1938. 35⅛″ × 25¾″. Kröller-Müller Museum, Otterloo.*

on Arp and not be struck by the homogeneity of his work. Yet everyone knows that Arp is a many-sided person—poet and essayist as well as sculptor—and

that he has taken part in several mutually irreconcilable art-movements and been a friend of Max Ernst, Tzara, Breton, Kandinsky and Mondrian. Arp alone has managed to box the compass of modern art without losing the sharp edge of his own personality. He has, for instance, been a leader of abstract (he prefers to call it "concrete") art without ever losing touch with figuration. Nor is there anything disappointing or unworthy in the result : Arp is always of Arp-quality.

Arp likes clear ideas and well-defined forms. But a well-defined form need not be hard to the touch : a cloud can be well-defined, and Arp has never hesitated to annex the clouds which take his fancy. But in so doing he betters them, gives them an aristocracy of his own devising : when they re-appear it is as *An owl's dream*, a *Pagoda*, or a *Shepherd*. A composition of curves and straight lines is given the name of *Early Morning Geometry* and at once begins to smile and hum a tune. As with Klee, poetry slips in everywhere : creation is its other name—creation, commotion, the unknown.

In a book collecting his poems and essays entitled "On My Way" published

Below : Spatial development of Ptolemy, *sculpture in Hautville stone. 1953. Height 41⅛″. Burden coll. New York.*

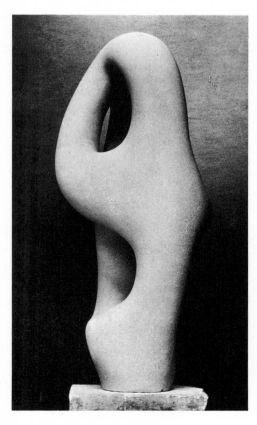

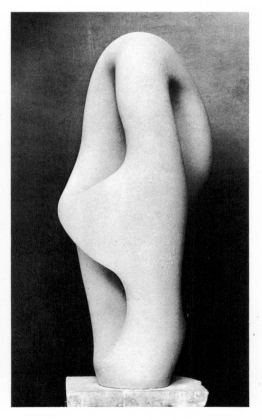

The living room of Jean Arp's house is as orderly, chaste and gleaming as one of his works. The sculptures—of stone, metal or marble—stand on white bases on the polished floor. Wood reliefs in sober colors hang on the white walls. Arp is shown here preparing pieces of cardboard for a collage; he obtains the smoothly rounded forms he loves by sand-papering the curved outlines.

in 1948 (George Wittenborn Inc.) Arp wrote: "When I exhibited my first 'concrete' reliefs, I issued a little manifesto declaring that bourgeois art was sanctioned lunacy. These naked men, women and children in stone and bronze, set up in public places, gardens and forest clearings, indefatigably dancing, chasing butterflies, shooting arrows, offering apples and playing flutes, are the perfect expression of a crazy world. These gibbering figures should no longer be allowed to sully nature. Like the early Christians, we must go back to essentials. The artist of today must let his work create itself directly. We are no longer concerned with subtleties. My reliefs and sculptures merge themselves

into nature. But if observed more closely, they reveal the work of a human hand. That is why I named a number of them 'Stone Shaped by Human Hand'."

Arp's first patrons were Belgians. Later came the Swiss and the Americans. There are now a great many collectors of Arp in both North and South America.

French people do not buy Arp as yet, although some of his few enthusiasts in France are encouragingly young. Not long ago a troop of boy-scouts happened on Arp's house, which lies in a steep and isolated lane on the edge of the Meudon forest. They were fascinated at once by the bronzes and marbles in

the garden, and eventually plucked up courage to enter the house and ask to be shown more. They were made cordially welcome by Arp, and when they went away it was with a small sculpture that he had given them for their meeting-hall. Thus it was that a suburban scout-troop stole a march on our most "enlightened" local collectors.

Arp won his place in the history of modern art by work of many kinds: but in spite of the polychrome reliefs during the Dada period, the clocks and "holed pictures" which followed them, or the great light reliefs of a little later, it is in his sculpture that he shows himself a major artist. There his particular turn of mind is most strikingly,

133

most legibly displayed. He has a profound sense of the mystery and the polyvalence of things. Perhaps it is to his passion for the pre-Socratic thinkers and the early Christian mystics that we

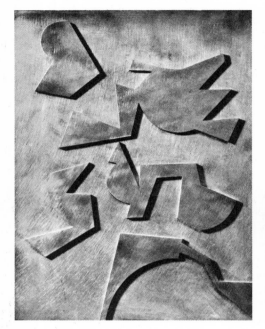 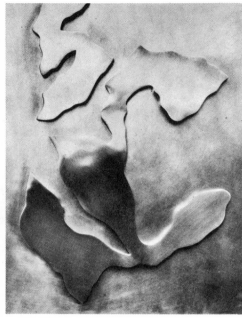

Upper left : Constellation. *1955. Bronze* 13¼″ × 10¼″. *Arp coll.* *Right :* Configuration (a memory of Athens). *1955. Bronze* 29⅛″ × 23¼″. *Annenberg coll. U.S.A.*

must trace the rich and noble character of his forms.

These forms are always simple, with the simplicity of clouds and fruit. Clouds inspired one of Arp's most telling remarks : "It's a waste of arrows to shoot them at the clouds", he said. "Yet many sculptors are wasting their arrows in just this way. If you want to charm the clouds down into your studio you must play violin-music on the drum, or beat a tattoo on the violin. Then you'll see the cloud come down in ecstasy and ask for nothing so much as to be turned to stone. That's how the best sculpture gets done."

Arp is full of humor, as you can see, but his humor is never bitter or sharp. The laughter to which it gives rise is relaxed, long-lasting : armchair laughter. Humor is indispensable to society and proves what cannot be proved by any other means. There is such a thing as a *mystique* of humor and Arp and Schwitters are two of its 20th-century masters.

No one can tell what posterity will

Near the studio's stone wall: Sitting figure. *1937. Direct carving in limestone. 13″.*

think of Arp, or of any of us. A work of art cannot, after all, be judged by rule or rote. It has its own rules. But we have still the right to love or withhold our love, as we please, and it is here that

passion and adventure step in. Arp, like Mondrian and Malevitch, must be taken whole, as he is, or not at all. He cannot be explained. Any attempt at analysis is, in itself, an act of betrayal. Arp's every sculpture is a compact of love,

obeys no laws but its own, and makes no concessions at all to its time. That is why we cannot understand him without running his risks and loving his work as he himself has loved it. To love his work in this way is to share in its creation. I have known Arp for more than thirty years, and during that time I have watched his work becoming more and more completely "itself and not another thing". As happened with Mondrian and with every other true artist, his work has one inexhaustible theme, and that theme is : his own nature. Rembrandt and Van Gogh never tired of self-portraiture ; nor, in their very different ways, have Arp, Mondrian, Schwitters, and Miro. They have never ceased painting themselves, pursuing a single theme, as if reconquering a paradise lost and always on the point of being regained.

Arp's patient pursuit of the unattainable is a sign of true greatness, an eternal beginning-anew. Masterpieces cannot be improvised, and the artist's secret message can only be delivered in complete disinterestedness and by the slow conquest of himself and his private mystery. Discipline is not as important as humility before what cannot be expressed and gratitude towards the material which does what it can and has so often the savor of a forbidden fruit.

The garden of Arp's small house at Meudon is filled with sculpture. This one near the street in gilded bronze is called Pagoda fruit *(1934). Arp wrote in* On My Way *"Art is a fruit which is born of man, just as fruit grows on a tree, or an embryo in the mother's womb. But whereas all fruits have forms intrinsically their own, the human fruit we call art nearly always embodies a ridiculous resemblance to something else...It is reason that has inflated man's pride with the fond belief that he is lord over nature and an infallible criterion in himself. Reason has turned him into a tragic figure... I love nature, but not its substitutes."*

Where there is forbidden fruit there is paradise, and Arp seems to me to rule over a kingdom where all is always "Set fair". A debonair monarch, he rules with a universal harmony in mind, and such is the noble goodness of his nature that he never so much as mentions his enemies' names : brief and rare, therefore, are his quarrels, for he disdains to be drawn. Mondrian had the same slow, golden nature and the same apparent cautiousness. And in reality they complement one another, for all the

Two painted wood relief Clocks : *right,* 21⅛"×10⅞", *Hagenbach coll., Basle; extreme right,* 29⅛"×29⅝", *Liège coll.*

seeming difference between them. Mondrian's province is the earth, and he parcelled it out as a master of proportion designs a building. Arp's province is the

sky. He has made of it a playground as indispensable to us as Mondrian's ennobled earth, and as pure. The one is Attica incarnate, the other Arcadia.

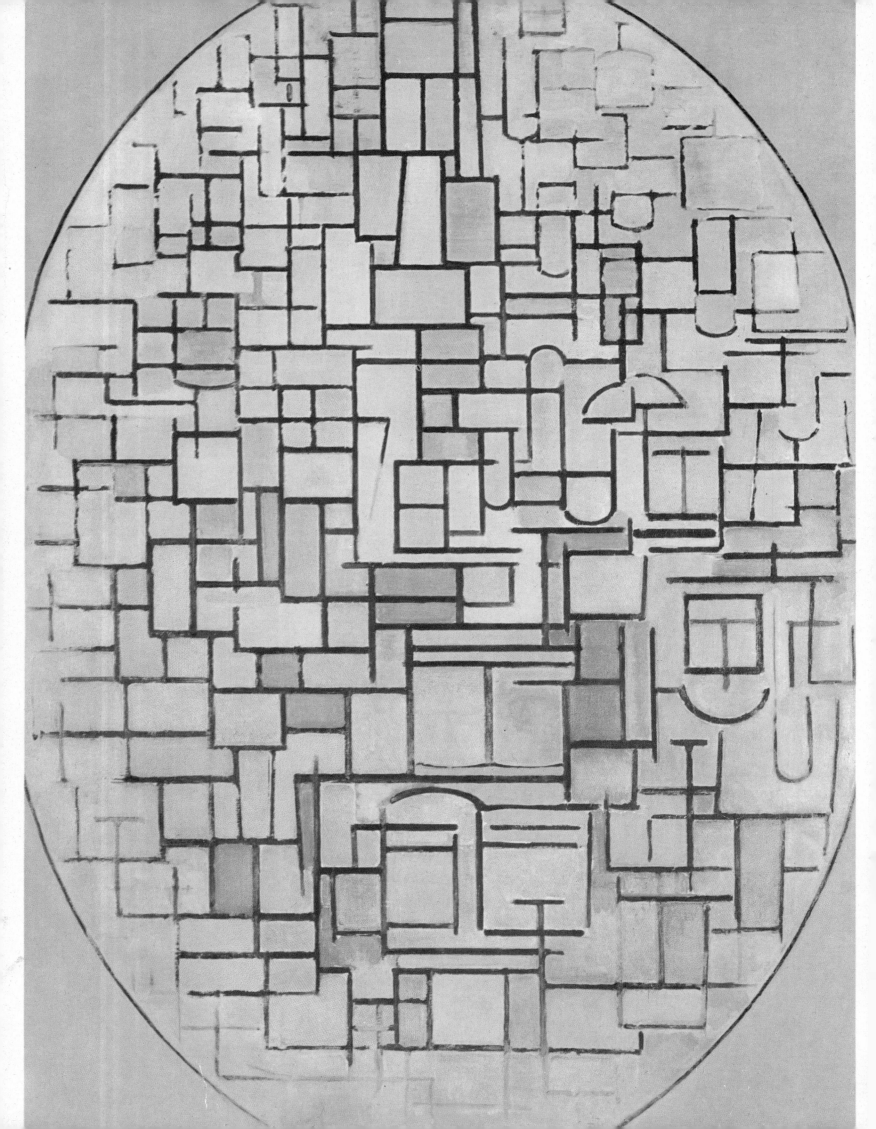

A militant museum

BY MICHEL SEUPHOR

Amsterdam is rich in the art of the past, but, thanks to the Stedelijk Museum,
the art of to-morrow also finds its place

What is a museum ? A center where a city keeps its treasure. A jewel-box, one might say. But a profitable one, for most of the world's museums take an entrance-charge and do very well out of it. Even where entrance is free, the museum may well attract foreign visitors, and those visitors will spend money in the city concerned. Sometimes the crowds are so dense as to give the museum the air of a cosmopolitan fair-ground—although the word "museum" would indicate an altogether much graver scene. But alas ! Such Muses as may be present are present in wax. Nothing remains of their inspirational power ; a museum is, in fact, a place where dead art is lying in state.

Temporary exhibitions are one way of dispelling this atmosphere and restoring some semblance of life to museums. The nineteenth-century "religion of art" finds new expression in these ephemeral manifestations, and so numerous are their devotees that sometimes they have to file past the exhibits in solemn line—attentive, obedient, hushed.

So much for the museum as our fathers knew it. But what of the new art—the art that bursts out of the studios, bobs up in the dealers' windows, and sometimes even gets past the solemn portals of the Museum itself ? It has the irresistible appeal of Life : and as, to the sedentary Muses, life and scandal are synonymous, we are faced with a situation in which the Muses take fright at the Museum.

A prime example of this is the Stedelijk Museum, Amsterdam. Its activity is tremendous. When I was last there I saw no fewer than six temporary exhibitions. They could hardly have been more varied : paintings and drawings by the Danish painter Mortensen, a suite of rooms given over to Israeli painters, another devoted to the work of five American artists now resident in Europe (Alcopley, Chelimsky, Fontaine, Parker, Levee), an important retrospective exhibition of Franz Marc, a collection of Germaine Richier's sculptures, and a group of recent paintings by Vieira da Silva.

Nor must one overlook the permanent collection, which includes memorable groups by Van Gogh, Cézanne, Chagall, Delaunay and Mondrian. Mondrian's retrospective exhibition, in 1946, included 160 paintings and was one of the great moments in the life of the Museum. It's amusing, though, to run through the titles of some of the Museum's temporary

A. Allebé : Going round the Museum. *This canvas shows one of the rooms of the Stedelijk Museum in 1870. Allebé, a Dutch painter, was Director of the Academy of Fine Arts in Amsterdam at the end of the last century, when Mondrian was a student there.*

exhibitions : The Free Book, 1940-45, Drawings by French Masters, Swiss Posters, Young French Engravers, South African Art, 150 Years of French Fashion, Thirteen Parisian Sculptors, Twelve English Painters, Life as is lived in Sweden, Polish Popular Art, Expressionism from Van Gogh to Picasso, The Gobelins, Nineteen Painters from Haiti, Surrealism and

◄ *Mondrian :* Composition III. *1914. 55½″×39″. Stedelijk Museum, Amsterdam.*

Above : Two glimpses of the Museum's new wing, which is reserved for temporary exhibitions. The right shows a Gonzalez exhibition, the left a show of young Dutch painters. The walls are of glass, with adjustable blinds. Moveable screens make it possible to vary the lay-out of the interior in accordance with the needs of each exhibition. The light comes mainly from above the windows, accompanying rather than contradicting the progress of the day outside.

Abstraction, The Domnick Collection, The Dotremont Collection, Religious Art, Van Gogh's French contemporaries, Eight Abstract Painters from the Argentine, Children's Art, Japanese Calligraphy : ancient and modern, English Ceramics, and retrospective exhibitions of Bonnard, Braque, Kandinsky, Hokusai, Klee, Kokoschka, Léger, Toulouse-Lautrec, Rouault, Miro, Vuillard, Matisse, Degas and Le Corbusier. The list could go on indefinitely, for the Stedelijk Museum has held, since the Liberation, no fewer than 195 temporary exhibitions.

The man behind all this is the alert and ubiquitous Mr. Sandberg who, since 1945, has been the director of the Stedelijk Museum. He has a lively, venturesome, and sometimes, it would seem, an absent-minded way of carrying on his directorship. But the absent-mindedness is more apparent than real : it is the manner of a man who is open to all things and yet aloof from them. Under the German occupation Mr. Sandberg published a little anthology of maxims culled from many of the world's great writers. One of them was "Blessed is frivolity when it preserves us from doubting". No author's name was quoted, and for a long time I attributed it to Sandberg himself : but now he tells me that he took it from a French writer whose name he has forgotten. I still think that it suits him perfectly and might, in fact, have been his family motto. For what it means is : Blessed is the frivolity that makes the great enterprise seem less of a burden, blessed the sense of fun that accomplishes so much more than the sense of duty, and blessed the laughter that breaks down the barrier between one idea and another. Barriers of that sort have little chance in the Stedelijk Museum, now that Mr. Sandberg is in charge of it.

Rare is the museum, rare the artists' colony, where Mr. Sandberg is not known. His great shock of white hair, slight figure and expressive face are familiar everywhere. Missing nothing, slipping in here and slipping away there,

Julio Gonzalez : Monserrat. *Wrought iron. Stedelijk Museum.*

he has the touch of gold where museum-ventures are concerned. Jonkheer W. H. J. B. Sandberg was born at Amersfoort, a little town in the centre of Holland, in 1897—just twenty-five years after Piet Mondrian was born there. He studied in 1919 at the Amsterdam Academy of Fine Arts, travelled in France, Germany, Switzerland and Italy from 1920 to 1923 (with long pauses in Pisa, Rome, and Paris—where he worked at the Grande Chaumière). In 1927 he spent some time in Berlin and Vienna. In 1928 and during the next ten years he worked in Amsterdam as typographical adviser, while studying psychology at the University of Utrecht and, at the same time, doing the duties of an assistant at the Stedelijk Museum. At this early date he was already organizing avant-garde exhibitions—among them a retrospective exhibition of Theo van Doesburg, the Dutch "De Styl" theorist,

It is to Mr. Sandberg's great experience as typographer and lay-out expert that we owe the striking beauty of the Museum's catalogues. He takes a great delight in their preparation, and he knows that they are all that remains when a temporary exhibition, however dazzling, has come to an end. Too often, museums issue catalogues which simply call aloud for the waste-paper basket, but there is nothing of that sort at the Stedelijk. People collect its catalogues ; some go so far as to take out an annual subscription to them. A similar scheme is in operation at the Museum of Modern Art, New York, but the special character of the Amsterdam venture derives from its very moderate expense. This applies as much to the Museum itself as to the catalogues. Young people, students, artists, teachers and members of any large group (employees, for instance, of a big store or a shipping line) can

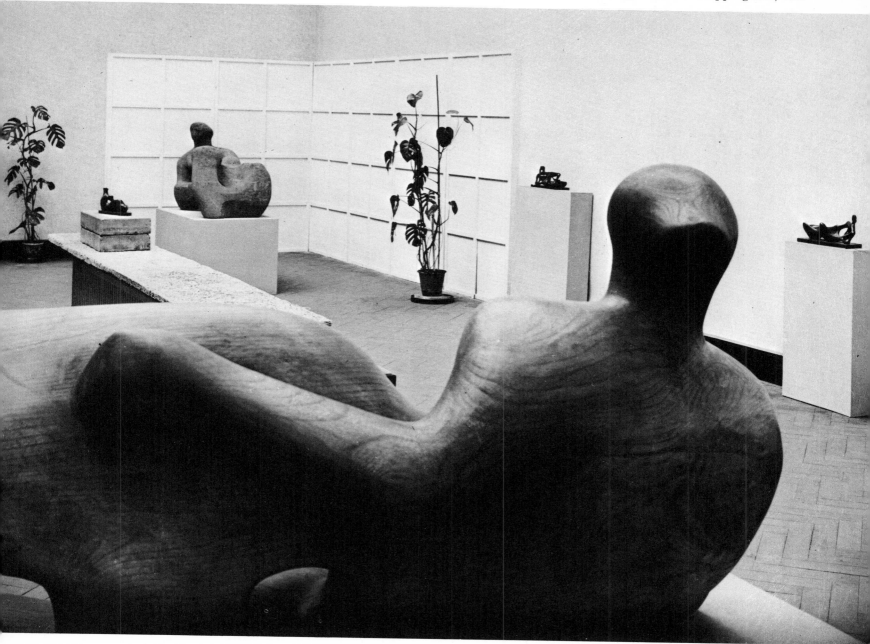

One of the re-designed rooms in the original Stedelijk building. Screens of varying color and texture break up the wall space. This photograph was taken during a Henry Moore exhibition.

and one devoted to Moholy-Nagy, who had lately fled from Germany as a refugee from the Nazis.

buy the right to go to every exhibition in the Museum for some sixty cents a year. The catalogue subscription, which

entitles the subscriber to some twenty illustrated catalogues a year, comes to about four dollars. Ten thousand people subscribe to the Museum itself : substantially fewer to the catalogues.

The Museum is also very active in other fields. Reproductions, for instance : since 1952 it has put reproductions of modern art at the disposal of many schools and colleges, and has also arranged for them exhibitions of reproductions. Conducted tours are led, whenever possible, by artists. The Museum attaches great importance to children's art, and has often shown children's paintings and drawings and reproduced them in color. Schoolchildren are allowed to experiment as they please, every Wednesday and Saturday afternoon, with painting and sculpting materials. But the most remarkable of Mr. Sandberg's innovations is undoubtedly that of the guided tours for the blind, who are encouraged to handle the sculpture as much as they like. Many say that those visits have been a great joy to them. (Even Brancusi, I believe, gave his consent to it, despite his reluctance to have

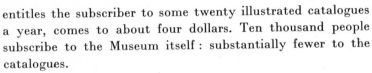

The Stedelijk Museum's reserve store is especially remarkable. The pictures, some framed, some not, are hung on sliding metal grilles, and can be examined or photographed in ideal conditions.

Above, to the left, a cast of Duchamp-Villon : The Horse. *1914.*

his sculptures touched. Many years ago I was in his studio and made as if to touch the *Mademoiselle Pogany* : he held me back, saying quietly : "Don't do that—it annoys them". Brancusi was right, and I unworthy. *Our* hands do no more than act out the clumsy desires of the eye : but the hands of the blind have a spiritual quality.)

These manifold activities involve, of course, a great deal of administration, and Mr. Sandberg, who is so often abroad in search of new exhibitions, needs to be able to leave the Museum in sure hands. As his admirable second-in-command he has Mr. Jaffé, and beneath him is a team of no fewer than seventy persons. Mr. Sandberg is the first to admit that, where so much has to be done so quickly, mistakes are bound to creep in. The catalogue of the De Stijl retrospective

exhibition, for instance, is full of obvious gaps, and the French translation of the well-chosen texts is often erratic, and sometimes quite meaningless. On another occasion there was what might be called a positive lack of information : the exhibition called "Modern art, old and new" showed works of art side by side with modern industrial products, but denied the visitor that minimum of explanatory comment which would have made certain essential distinctions clear : the difference between walking and dancing, for instance, or between a flint axe-head and the design engraved on the shaft, or between what is useful and what, in art and life alike, is gratuitous. A public which is not taught these distinctions will end by not "seeing the point" of free aesthetic creation ; even the very existence of the Museum will then be threatened. But enough of such things : as Balthazar Gra-

war, when the pictures were hidden away in an underground shelter beneath a dune. As there was not much room there, Mr. Sandberg decided to make some trellised big screens, fit them with rollers, and hang the pictures like an enormous mosaic—sideways up, if need be, so that not an inch was wasted. These moveable screens were formed up in two serried ranks, with a narrow corridor in between. This system was later adapted for peace-time use in the Museum itself. The storage space remains small, but the curator has complete freedom of manoeuvre and can inspect at will any one of the hundreds of canvases on the screens.

Holland is, one might say, one enormous sea-borne invention, and the element of ingenuity is as strong in the museum-world as it is anywhere else. Fancy plays a great part in Dutch life—in the International Congress of Twins which was

The Stedelijk Museum has, among many other things, an important Chagall group, which fills an entire room in the original Stedelijk building. Above, left : Self-portrait with seven fingers. 49¼″×42¼″. *1913. Right :* The Musician. 39½″×62½″. *1912-13*

cian says, "It is a debasement of criticism to dwell on one failure and ignore a hundred successes : such a man would only notice the sun when it was in eclipse".

A place where the sun is never in eclipse is the Stedelijk Museum annex, which was completed a year or two ago. Its glass walls are so built that the light is always even throughout the building : night and day, winter and summer. It is the Museum's greatest achievement, and I doubt if there is anywhere in the world an exhibition building more nicely adapted to contemporary concepts of display. (This will be clear, I hope, from the photographs which accompany this article.) And the remarkable thing is that this most modern of museum-buildings is based on a drawing of Noah's ark by Jan Luyken, the Dutch 17th-century painter.

The Museum's reserve store is also, in its way, a remarkable technical achievement. Its system was developed during the

 *Opposite : Younger Dutch sculptors are made welcome in the garden of the new Stedelijk wing.*

dreamed up by one small town, or the fact that in Amsterdam it was decided, after lengthy Parliamentary discussion, to fire a salute of twenty-one guns every sixth of December to celebrate the solemn entry of His Majesty Saint Nicolas.

Mr. Sandberg had an idea of this quality, not long ago. Walking past the original Stedelijk Museum building, I noticed that a solid wooden platform had been built at the level of the first row of windows. Staircases gave access to this, but there was no sign that any work was being done there. What was it for, I wondered ? One of Mr. Sandberg's colleagues told me that it was a new idea of his : passers-by could climb up, if they felt like it, and have a free look at what was going on inside.

The moral ? That the gate-crasher must be made welcome, and fancy not be turned away. In the living museum there must be a place for what some would call madness, and others inspired improvisation.

"I am not a revolutionary painter", Georges Braque has said.

It seems a surprising remark. For was not cubism one of the most revolutionary movements in all painting? An old order, which had held fast since the Renaissance, was overturned; a new logic of space took its place; the painter, free from the constraints of the external world, claimed for himself a total liberty.

Yet so transitory is the revolutionary element in art that people who are sensitive above all to the inward and meditative element in Braque's work have likened him to Chardin. His pictures are not, as a rule, dramatic. Their sensuality is almost always discreet. He is above all a still life painter, and it is with an air of tranquil reflection that he arranges and re-arranges his interiors, kitchens, studios, and salons; everything in them bears witness, moreover, to a feeling for order, and comfort, and taste. An intimist, one might say, and the intimist is rarely a revolutionary.

There's no reason, of course, why there should not be revolutions in the world of objects, as much as anywhere else: but the word is really out of place in any discussion of novelty in the fine arts, because a revolution is generally based on hatred and violence and aims to overthrow an old order of some sort. But the young Braque knew quite well that the great painters of the past are "all our contemporaries". It was the future that he reserved for himself. For personal reasons he happened to dislike the Mona Lisa, but it never entered his head to mutilate the picture, whereas the self-styled 'revolutionaries' amused themselves by giving the Mona Lisa a moustache or making nonsense of

Woman playing guitar. 1917. 88⁴/₅" × 44⁴/₅". Basle Art Museum. Braque often used musical elements in his cubist compositions. He is very fond of music; when a young man he played the accordion.

Georges Braque

BY GEORGES LIMBOUR

the tranquil master who has created a new world with old materials

the Angel of Rheims by dressing her up in Carnival costume. Braque was never for burning down the Louvre; even to talk of doing so took up time better spent at the easel. The futurists thought themselves revolutionaries, and it may be that their commotions served some purpose. But how dead they are to-day!

Braque is no more of a revolutionary in politics—or in industry, for that matter—than he is in painting. Radical social change has little appeal for him, and he takes no part in politics. Technical 'progress' is something he holds in little esteem, and as for plastic or other synthetic or substitute materials, he detests the whole lot of them: in clothes, especially, and in things used about the house, he prefers traditional 'natural', materials and the methods to which our ancestors devoted so much time and love. His craftsman's nature is in revolt against the very idea of plastic materials, in which the element of surprise is ruled out from the start. Braque likes materials—wood, for instance, and marble—which have a life and a sensibility of their own. Plastic gets dirty, but it doesn't get old. It *can't* mellow as Braque and his pictures have mellowed; the meditative element has no part in it. Braque's is a civilisation of wood and earth and linen and silk: an age of stone, not of imitation stone. He has a horror of cement. (It should be said, all the same, that the house which he had built for himself in the Rue du Douanier in Paris was designed by Auguste Perret, the great master of reinforced concrete).

All this makes it understandable that he doesn't want to be taken for a revolutionary. A demiurge is not a revolutionary. Braque has simply created a new world with old materials.

He was born at Argenteuil on May 13th 1882. He was as if destined to paint, for his grandfather had a house-

Braque brings back to his studio shapes found in nature which please him: shells, leaves, bones. Here on a shelf in his Parisian atelier is a bone, right, and a plaster moulding of it transformed into a pitcher, center. Another jug by Braque is on the left, next to a stuffed frog. On the wall, a horse's head in gilded plaster made in 1942.

painting business, and his father set up in the same line, in 1890, in Le Havre. Nothing revolutionary, therefore, about young Braque's vocation—more especially as it was already the custom for members of the family to submit pictures to the Salon des Artistes Français. Georges Braque was to do no more than perfect and glorify these traditions. Till he was 17 he went to the local

lycée, and studied at the Ecole des Beaux-Arts in the evenings. He was a vigorous, lively young man, with a healthy appetite for singing and dancing and sport and a great fondness for Le Havre.

Le Havre, as he knew it, no longer exists. Largely destroyed in 1945, it has been rebuilt by Auguste Perret—in cement. Braque never goes back there.

143

A view into Braque's studio in Paris. On the floor, sheets preparing a color lithograph of birds, a favorite theme of the painter's since several years. Finished lithographs, also of birds, by the easel and on the left. Framed picture on floor is a beach scene of Varengeville, Normandy, where Braque has a house. Tacked to the studio door: an enlarged reproduction of a Corot portrait (Christine Nilsson) and photographs of a harvesting machine reminiscent of shapes that appear in the artist's works (see page 146).

But in Braque's boyhood it was pleasant enough: that we may judge from engravings and prints, and from pictures by painters like Dufy and Othon

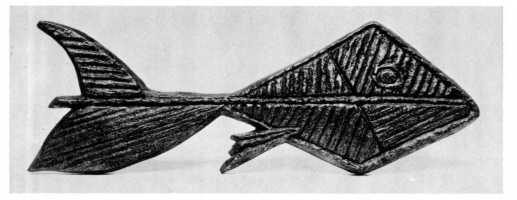

Fish. 1942. Length 14¹⁄₅". Braque has made few sculptures, until now they have been of small dimensions. Besides this fish he has also sculpted horses and birds.

Friesz who were friends of Braque at that time. It was built along the sea, and its most animated and characterful street led out on to a vast esplanade from which could be seen the *avant-port* and beyond, the estuary of the Seine. The jetty was not of stone or cement. Like the fishing-boats, it was built of massive tar-soaked oaken beams. The quayside was full of tumbledown houses and sailors' bars, and if you wanted a monkey or a parrot you were sure to be able to buy one there. There was a street of ill-fame. The docks were not apart from the town, as they are in many ports; they came right into it, and sail-boats were tied up within ten paces of the flower-shops. And right there, on the esplanade, protected by a row of ancient cannon (taken from the British in times gone by) was the Museum. Once the property of François I, the building contained a token representation of Courbet, Boudin, Corot and Toulouse-Lautrec: this Braque came to know when still very young. The Museum is built in cement to-day, and it's grown considerably larger. There are even some Braques in it. But at that time it had no Impressionist pictures, Braque got to know of these in the pages of *Gil Blas*. There was a Museum in the town proper, and something that especially impressed Braque, there was that disquieting object, an Egyptian mummy. The image of it came back to him when, many years later, he painted those 'still-lives with death's head' to which he gave the traditional title of *Vanitas*.

From the parrot-and-monkey quay one could take a broad-hipped and high-funneled paddle-steamer to Honfleur. These pitched agreeably and trailed behind them a great white foam-crinoline. Honfleur had not yet been spoiled by organized tourism and clogged with the alluvial deposits of the Seine. It was, in fact, the place beloved of Jongkind and the Impressionists. Braque would step off the steamer with bicycle under one arm and paint-box under the other and pedal off at top speed up the surrounding hills. (He made, as a matter of fact, several long sojourns at Honfleur—in particular in 1904, when Dufy went with him.) To the north of the jetty was a beach where the stones, black and white, were like marble and there was as yet no oil-fuel to spoil their lustre. Stormy winds from the north west swept across this beach in winter, and in summer a wooden breakwater was

Woman with mandoline. *1937. 65³/₅″ × 34⁴/₅″. Museum of Modern Art, New York. This canvas belongs to a series of interiors with feminine figures painted in the late thirties, but it is similar in theme to the cubist compositions with musicians including the one reproduced on page 142. A picture within a picture is added by the still life.*

Braque is neat, organized and ingenious. On his work-table sheets of corrugated cardboard hold his pencils and drawing materials. A glass holds leaves, right.

built in front of the wooden-walled Casino Marie-Christine and bathers, Braque among them, would dive into the sea from the end of it. Both Friesz and Dufy recorded the look of this breakwater, with its flags flying in the breeze and the striped tents all around it. From it you could see the beginnings of the white chalk cliffs that went up as far as the Somme. These were striped, here and there, with black silex.

How far did this landscape influence Braque? He painted some pictures of sail-boats as they lay moored to the quay, but it was in Antwerp, in 1905, that he painted the harbor-scenes which mark the beginning of his personal achievement. Cliffs, and the boats that lay on the beach below them, were to become a favorite theme of his, but one that he did not attempt till later, at Etretat and Varengeville. Dufy was a painter of the picturesque, a master of outward appearances, and as such he drew great inspiration from his native Le Havre. But what is interesting in a painter is *what he leaves out*: Braque breathed in his fill of the wind-blown harbor-town, and he loved swimming, bicycling, boating and even boxed from time to time. Rude, untroubled health was his reward; but when he came to paint there was little

Bronze sculpture. 1939-1955. 8²/₅″×16″: Braque likes to pursue a theme in different mediums, creating many variants. The horse harnessed to a chariot appears also in his lithographs and in his illustrations for Hesiod's Theogony. *Although Braque's sculpture has always been small in scale, he is planning a very large version of this subject. He has placed a sheet of white paper behind the sculpture here, in his studio, to have its outline clearly before his eyes as he works on other things. Note the leaves in the background—Braque keeps his atelier and his house filled with plants and flowers —and the resemblance of his chariot to the harvest photographs on his door (page 144).*

It's possible, too, that his apprenticeship taught him to have a great feeling for interiors, and thus for the *intimiste* in painting. He never lost this intimacy with household objects. But his apprenticeship was no sooner behind him that he threw open the windows and began to paint landscape.

In 1902, with his military service out of the way, he took a studio in the Rue Lepic, came to know Picabia, Manolo, Marie Laurencin and Maurice Raynal, and kept up his friendship with Friesz and Dufy. In 1905 the first fauve pictures began to appear. (Matisse's *Luxe, Calme et Volupté* was shown in the 1905 Salon d'Automne). Braque had yet to show any of his pictures, and he went off to Antwerp with Friesz for several months. It was then that his fauve period began (views of Antwerp). It continued in 1906 at L'Estaque and La Ciotat, where he painted landscapes and a few nudes. Braque is the most considered of painters; he thought long over each picture, and never was his color as violent or as arbitrary as that of some of his contemporaries. Order and construction were his watchwords, and when he came upon Cézanne's work he began to push its principles to their logical extreme.

The year 1906 was marked by several decisive events in Braque's life. D.H. Kahnweiler came to see him, introduced him to Picasso, and took several of his canvases for the gallery which he then had in the Rue Vignon. In the following year Picasso painted his *Demoiselles d'Avignon* and Braque his *Grand Nu* (Cuttoli coll.). Braque's first exhibition was held in 1908 at Kahnweiler's gallery. He showed the work of his Cézannesque period : *House at l'Estaque, L'Estaque Viaduct, Dungeon at La Roche Guyon,* and some harbor and shipping-scenes. They were sober in

in common between what he put on the canvas and the rough, extraverted pleasures of his young manhood.

We mustn't forget, either—for musicians, scores and instruments all play a part in Braque's work—that Braque took flute-lessons in Le Havre from Raoul Dufy's brother Gaston. (Twenty years later this same Gaston Dufy gave piano lessons to Jean Dubuffet, who loathed the sea and seems to have had none but unpleasant memories of Le Havre.)

In 1900 Braque went to Paris to complete his apprenticeship as painter-decorator. (Laberthe's were his employ-

ers.) Historians have set great store by the technical competence he acquired at this time : how to make and mix his colors, how to paint what looked like wood or marble, how to become a judge of wall-paper and lettering. And of course it's true that Braque is a deeply professional person who loves to see work well done and is in no sense an improviser. But one can lay too much stress on "Braque the Artisan".

Before a canvas with birds, one of the tables made by the artist to hold his supplies. Paints are mixed in tin cans.

The tennis players. *1932. 6″×8²/₅″. Pen and wash. Private coll., England. This theme and its expression of movement are unusual for the artist; the swirling lines and heads like arrows suggest speed. Braque painted* Women bathing *at the same period.*

color, and the pictures were built up in levels, like terraces. Braque was looking for subjects or elements which could be broken down in geometrical terms. 'Pure landscape' no longer satisfied his demands. No longer was the picture subject to what the painter 'saw' in the world outside: it was the painter's idea of what the picture should be that summoned in from outside the elements which were to be the pretext for the picture. The reign of the still life had begun. Musical instruments and scores, curved elements and rectilinear elements, all began to make their appearance: fruit and fruit-dishes, likewise.

Braque and Picasso had become firm friends and were working in close association. They spent the summer of 1910 at Céret and that of 1911 at Sorgues, where they were joined by Pierre Reverdy, the poet.

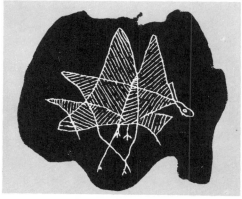

Engraved plaster. 1939-1940. This technique was invented by Braque: plaster is coated with black and the drawing incised into it, leaving a white line.

From 1910 onwards Braque may be said to have passed from his pre-cubist period to the period of cubism proper. The *Girl with Mandoline* is the first of the cubist musicians. Painted in an oval, a shape which Braque was to favor especially, the picture is almost ascetic in color: greys and ochres predominate, and there are elegant modulations of color which cause the light to vibrate. The problem of color has, in fact, become secondary. What preoccupies Braque and Picasso is form: volume and space. In the *Guéridon* of 1912 which is now in the Paris Musée de l'Art Moderne, certain elements have been isolated, more or less, from their physical supports, and play, therefore, a purely plastic role—the S-shaped slots from the belly of the violin, for instance, and the topmost part of the same instrument, and scattered notes of music; or, again, that motif which we find also in André Masson's first cubist paintings—the scroll of paper which makes, as Juan Gris said, a 'plastic rhyme' to the scroll of the violin.

Braque and Picasso had re-composed

sense of the words unimportant, when a label or the title of a newspaper or musical composition is in question. Some severe persons detest the idea that these pictures have within them an 'allusion', whether literary, poetic, or anecdotal. But in the famous *Aria of Bach* the sense of the words *does* count

the more tangible for being sensed, as it were, indirectly.

The physical substance of Braque's pictures was becoming richer and richer. Sometimes they were painted on a foundation of plaster: the thickness varied, and the outer crust was smooth and granular by turns. For some years he inhabited a world of silence and contentment in which the traditional resources of Dutch still life—lemons, pears and oysters, especially—were allied not to the Bible but to the newspapers of Braque's own day.

But in 1922 he went back to the nude, and there appeared the monumental *Caniphores*, basket-bearing women of Greek ancestry. Braque's many visits to the Midi had never robbed him of his taste for his native Normandy, and more especially for the Dieppe region. In 1928 he built himself a country house at Varengeville, with a big studio in the garden, and ever since he has spent a part of every year there. The house does not, be it noted, give on to the sea. Braque would not care to have the sea continually present. The house is, therefore, some way from the cliff-edge, and looks south towards the Caux plateau, a monotonous stretch of country enlivened only by the birds which were one day to become one of his favorite subjects. Braque at Varengeville went back to his seaboard subjects—cliffs and boats drawn upon the pebbly beach. Cliffs and boats alike were treated as if they were guitars or fruit-dishes. Certain folds of the cliffs even remind us of rolled-up scores or newspapers. Even the sea, in the *Etretat*, is handled as if it were wallpaper. These works are sombre in color, with plenty of black. Yet the particular light of Varengeville is always present.

In 1930-31 Braque drew, it may be, upon recollections of the seaside scene for his *Tennis Players* and *Women Bathing*. The latter are quite different from the Canephori, and are, indeed, the most audacious that Braque had yet put before us. The sea takes only a secondary place in these pictures, and before long the bather became the *Recumbent Nude in an Interior*, and the landscape a landscape of wallpaper and still life. Before long these peopled *Interiors* became Braque's major preoccupation. The figures themselves derived in part from the illustrations he had made for the *Theogony* of Hesiod, and there are also double-faces, faces seen simultaneously from the front and the side, just as in other and earlier pictures there are double-jugs, double-guitars, and double-vases, with one light face and one dark one. The figures of this period have an ambiguity, a touching and sometimes sensual mystery, which is new in Braque's work, and the interiors themselves—pianos, easels, whole canvases even—have a contained rich-

Plaster, painted and engraved. 1939.

their universe, therefore. A few more novelties still to come, and they would have realised what is, to date, the loftiest achievement of 20th century painting.

Letters were the next to appear in cubist painting—as independent objects with the same significance, the same authority as a bottle or a pipe. From 1911 onwards Braque included letters and figures in his work, and at Sorgues he went further: he introduced directly on to the canvas brute elements from real life—fragments of newspaper, pieces of brown packing-paper, and later small pieces of ready-made wall-paper. (One of his *papiers collés* of the Sorgues period incorporates a poster from the Tivoli Cinema, where "La Petite Fifi" was then showing.) The magic of the *papiers collés* is manifold: to begin with, they introduce into the composition a fragment of reality, and as such are the *nec plus ultra* of naturalism in painting. Then the fragment in question is absorbed in and transfigured by its surroundings. Newsprint and packing-paper lose their utilitarian and vulgar character and become picture-ingredients, colored planes. Or perhaps they are not absorbed, and for this reason assume the character of a provocation to the eye. The brown packing-paper plays the role of *inimitable matter*, and, by standing out in low relief, diversifies the surface of the picture. Nor is the

for something, and Braque has drawn them by hand.

It was also at this time that Braque introduced sand into his pictures and used the motif of playing cards. The whole future of modern art was changed by these innovations. All kinds of foreign and heterogeneous elements were added to pictures. Sand was followed by seashells, string, nails, etc... Surrealism went further—though, of course, Max Ernst's collages were aimed at quite a different target.

When war broke out in 1914, Braque was mobilised as a sergeant, wounded in the head, and trepanned. It was to be three years before he was well enough to go on painting. When he did so, his cubism had entered a new phase. Color had come back, and was used in broad planes. The planes had become regular and stable. Carpets, linoleum, paving-stones, mosaics, rear walls, wall paper and boiseries all had an importance equal to that of the central objects—fruit-dishes, mandolines, human beings. The human beings had not, for the moment, any psychological significance. Sometimes, as in the *Guitarist* of 1917, they merely set the scale for the decorations on the wall. Even the *Café Bar* of 1919 is quite empty: yet what would it gain by the inclusion of clients or *patron*? The silence and immutability of the picture are such that the presence of human beings is all

Atelier IX. *1956. 57¼″×57¼″. The artist has painted a great series of Ateliers since 1939. The same elements appear in most of them including a palette and a large jar. This one with its subtleties of muted greys is particularly fine. Maeght coll., Paris.*

ness that is one of his greatest and most disturbing achievements. ("Art is meant to be disturbing", Braque says.) The still-life series continued : the billiard-table, least wieldy and most challenging of subjects, made its appearance. Up-ended and broken into X-sections, the monster was soon tamed. The billiard-table was, in fact, the last item in his Interior vocabulary. Later there were a few flower-pieces, although these prov-ed difficult to assimilate in cubist terms.

One of Braque's more recent and greatest themes is the Studio. These are without figures, but their ingredients are in other respects those of the artist's everyday life. Many are square in format, and for that reason all the more difficult to bring off. Braque has always liked unpopular formats—ovals, to begin with, and then long thin canvases, vertical or horizontal, and finally squares. His own palette, when introduced into the Studios, becomes wing-shaped or turns into a metaphorical bird. Real birds also insert themselves, and stand upright on a table, or fly unconcernedly across the crowded picture-space. Eventually they leave the studio and mount on their own towards the sky. The theme of birds in the sky was the one that Braque chose when he was asked in 1951 to decorate the ceiling of the Salle des Etrusques in the Louvre. In 1956 his exhibition at the Galerie Maeght in Paris included several studies and some large compositions on bird-themes.

Braque's work, as we have seen, is of many sorts and kinds. But it has one constant aim: the conquest of a new conception of space, in which the artist re-instals the ingredients of his pictures and gives them not only the rarest richness of physical substance but also a spiritual content. Braque's example has influenced many painters over the last half century, and many of them were very unlike himself. De Staël, for one, had the highest regard for Braque. It was perhaps as a result of his many visits to Braque at Varengeville that he turned back from complete abstraction to the pursuit of the recognizable object.

Braque has shown that objects are inexhaustible, that there is no limit to what can be made of them, and that their world is one which can always be re-invented.

Right and opposite page: Braque in his Paris atelier, under white curtains which filter the light. As always, he is dressed with casual elegance. The display of pictures was not arranged for the photograph; Braque works on many canvases at once and keeps certain finished ones around him for reference. The bird theme is repeated throughout the studio: in a large canvas with a sky background on the left, in transparent sheets preparing a lithograph on the floor, in finished lithographs on the easel and on the back wall.
When painting the artist sits on a child's chair (behind table in foreground). Painting equipment is laid out in perfect order, placed low to be within easy reach. His devoted assistant-secretary hands him what he needs to avoid exertion on his part, like a trained nurse helping a surgeon.

Pevsner on Constructivism

AN INTERVIEW BY ROSAMOND BERNIER

The Constructivist movement issued out of the rich ferment of artistic activity that bubbled up in Russia during the first two decades of the century. Its founders, Antoine Pevsner and his younger brother Naum Gabo, forced by political events to leave their country, went on in Germany and later France (now Gabo lives in the United States) to create sculpture that is ranked as masterpieces of abstract art in the collections of important museums throughout the world.

Although Pevsner has lived in Paris since 1923 he has both through choice and circumstances remained removed from the artistic centers and gatherings of this capital. He is in the curious position of having a great international reputation while remaining relatively obscure in his country of adoption. He sees few people, fewer still are allowed to penetrate his small studio.

In the first months of 1957, the French public had an opportunity to familiarize itself with Pevsner's work at a retrospective exhibition given at the Paris Musée d'Art Moderne. To learn something of the artist's career and his ideas about his own sculpture and sculpture in general, I went at that time to call on Pevsner one rainy afternoon in his little apartment on the rue Jean-Sicard.

The artist and his wife greeted me with typically Russian hospitality. We sat on over-stuffed blue armchairs, Pevsner with his back to the window—a small, slight man with the high forehead and the pallor of an indoor intellectual—receding grey hair, the ghost of a white mustache hardly visible. He was wearing a long grey sweater almost to his knees and bedroom slippers. Mrs. Pevsner sat by the upright piano ; she is very musical, has a contralto voice and plays the piano, a handsome friendly woman, obviously capable, who preserves clippings and remembers the names of collectors. Pevsner speaks willingly and

at length, in a pronounced Russian accent,—a single-minded man with intense convictions who not only wishes to but insists on expressing them.

Seeing that he had no objections to being quoted, quite the contrary, I took out my pad and started the interview.

Rosamond Bernier : *I know that while your brother started as a sculptor, you were at first a painter. Will you tell me about your early years ?*

Antoine Pevsner : I was born in Orel (Russia) in 1886. My father had a copper refining business and my two older brothers were engineers. I never cared about the family business. Later on I came to use the same metal that my family manufactured, but for plastic expression. I went to art schools—the School of Fine Arts of Kiev (1902-1909) and the Academy of Fine Arts of St. Petersburg (1910), but I found nothing there to interest me. Far more important than anything else to my formation was the impact of Greek and Byzantine art through the primitive icons of my country.

I travelled a good deal in Russia to see this art. A decisive moment for me was my visit to a Novgorod monastery, where I saw an icon of Jesus holding a Bible, in the cell of one of the monks. I studied this for a long while and was struck by the eyes that appeared to look right at me. Then I looked at the hands of the figure and remarked it was impossible to tell if the Bible were bent backwards or forwards. I looked again at the eyes, and to my terror I saw they were no longer looking at me, but appeared closed. As I changed my position, the eyes of the icon seemed to open and close, and so did the Bible. I was not a religious man but I was troubled by this mystery. I stayed in the cell, trying to understand the phenomenon, and finally grasped that it was due to the use of reversed perspective.

Antoine Pevsner in 1920, in the park on Tversky Boulevard, Moscow, where the first Constructivist Exhibition was held.

Primitives did not know the laws of perspective later discovered during the Renaissance, but produced an effect of space by a reversed perspective with forms appearing sometimes open sometimes closed. Afterwards this use of receding and projecting planes was to become a vital part of my work.

R. B. : *Were you familiar at that time with the developments of modern art in Paris ?*

A. P. : We had the unique opportunity in Moscow of seeing the most recent French painting, not only the Impressionists but Matisse and the Cubists, because of the Morosov and Stchoukine collections. As a young man I met

Matisse when he came to Russia to visit Stchoukine. What I saw of French painting drew me irresistibly to Paris.

R. B.: *When did you go ?*

Mrs. Pevsner: In 1911 for the first time. He stayed there until 1913, then came back to Russia for a few months.

A. P.: When I first arrived in Paris I was very struck by the Eiffel tower. *Au fond*, Jean Eiffel was the first Constructivist !

R. B.: *Did you see the Cubist painters in Paris ?*

A. P.: I observed their work but I was not intimate with them. I felt from the start that Cubism was a limited movement. The fact that it is difficult to tell the works of Braque and Picasso and some other Cubist painters apart is an indication of its weakness. It was a catastrophe that Cubism determined

in fact I was disgusted with the situation of sculpture that to me was simply imprisoned by mass.

R. B.: *What made you change your mind about sculpture ?*

Mrs. P.: The outbreak of the war reunited him with his brother Gabo. Gabo had been a student in Munich. When the war came the Germans let him go provided he left for a neutral country, so Gabo went to Norway.

A. P.: My family sent me to join him in Oslo. Preoccupied as I was with my own problems of painting, I could observe his sculptural experiments with a certain detachment. I soon saw that his evolution toward his first constructions opened up a whole rich field of new possibilities. We were both working on problems of depth, trying to create depths in space. Together we began to

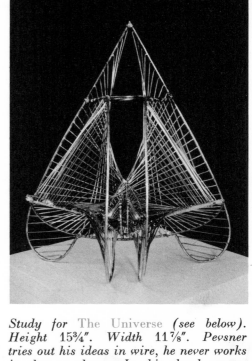

Study for The Universe *(see below). Height 15¾". Width 11⅞". Pevsner tries out his ideas in wire, he never works in clay or plaster. In this sketch we see the concept of enveloping outer forms and a central nub in its original state ; this was to be modified in the final version.*

A. P.: Then the Soviets officially favored the most avant-garde art movements. We were given every encouragement. I was made professor at the Beaux-Arts. (Kandinsky and the painter Malevitch also taught there.) I had 150 pupils. The state museums bought our work. There was an atmosphere of fervent optimism. We all felt we were building a new world—no more ugliness of cities compressing and depressing mankind. Beauty was to be for everybody. You will see that this state of affairs did not last long...

All through 1919 Gabo and I were framing the expression of our ideas to

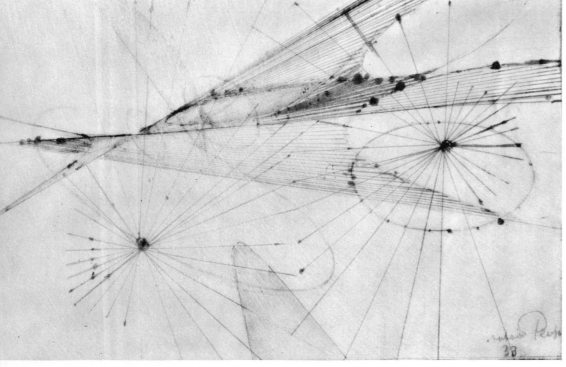

Drawing. 1933.

certain forms once and for all : a guitar always looks alike, so does a table, and so on. The same limitation exists with the Futurists—this reducing of a subject to a formula.

R. B.: *I have heard that Modigliani and Archipenko were your friends at this time.*

A. P.: Shall we say they were acquaintances.

R. B.: *All this time you were still painting ?*

A. P.: Yes, but it is inaccurate to say that such works as my 1913 Composition (see photograph) were in any way influenced by Cubism. The linear quality and the separation of planes derives from primitive Byzantine art. At that point I was not interested in sculpture—

formulate our ideas of Constructivism based on a philosophy of space and time. We sought how to use empty space and to get rid of compact mass. We worked quite independently from anyone else.

Mrs. P.: In 1918 the new Soviet government invited them to come back to Moscow.

Right, and following page : two views of The Universe *in its definitive state. Brass and oxidised tin. Height 28". Pevsner coll. The artist has evolved and refined the first design (see above) and the nub is now considerably smaller. Pevsner's curves are built up of metal wires laid side by side. In themselves these are rigorously rectilinear. It is this method of assemblage which gives the sculptures their veined texture.*

be published in the form of a manifesto. It was ready in August 1920. The government presses printed it—there were no other presses functioning—on sheets a yard square, and the government had it plastered all over the walls of Moscow. The tone was poetic, exhilarating, in keeping with the aspirations of the Soviet leaders of the time.

We announced the only way to liberate art from its impasse was to destroy compact mass and look for empty space; we negated mass as not being an expression of space. We declared that art must cease to be imitative to discover new forms.

We wrote: "We will construct our works." We called our pronouncement "Realist Manifesto." The word "construction" was seized by the others, and we were called Constructivists.

Mrs. P.: At the same time as the Manifesto, there was an exhibition of Gabo and Pevsner's works.

A. P.: Not in a gallery—we wanted to make it available to everybody in the freeest way—but in a public park in the center of Moscow on Boulevard Tversky, in an orchestra shell. These events were of tremendous influence.

At that time, so soon after the Revolution, few materials were available. That is why the Constructivist works of the period were out of poor materials—bits of wood and crude metal. It was only later that we were able to experiment with fine materials. There are sculptors today who work in crude metal, but they are still back in the very first days of Constructivism—they don't realize that we used those poor materials because we had nothing else.

R. B.: *Who were the other Constructivists?*

A. P.: There were no others. Gabo and I invented Constructivism. I have told you how it happened. Write it down, it is very important to get things straight and often people do not. Remember,

Portrait of Marcel Duchamp. *Construction in celluloid and zinc.* 37″×25″, 1926. *Yale University Museum.*

Gabo and I are the only Constructivists. Others, such as Tatlin and Rodchenko claim to have created Constructivism also. This is untrue. They took over our ideas but applied them falsely to a functional art with practical servitudes. We had always made it clear both in our discussions and our Manifesto that we were for a pure art for art's sake. Tatlin and the others put on an exhibition the year after our Manifesto and called it a Constructivist exhibition—it was just an imitation. And for all his utilitarian theories, Tatlin never created any designs that actually could be realized; his maquette for the III International monument, for instance, would never have stood up if it had been built.

R. B.: *Did you have anything in common with any of the other Russian artists?*

A. P.: At one point we were close to Lissitsky, and we shared the pure art approach with Malevitch who was a sensitive and intelligent man.

R. B.: *How long did the government maintain a sympathetic attitude?*

A. P.: By 1921 Lenin's health was failing and Stalin's power rising, bringing with it a narrow-minded rejection of anything but the most naturalistic realism. We began to be called "makers of art for decadent capitalists." The split between "applied art" and "pure art" became increasingly bitter. One day I came back to my atelier to find it

155

closed; the same thing happened to Kandinsky and Malevitch.

In 1923 the Soviet government sent an exhibition of Russian art to Berlin, Gabo and I had works in the show. With attending this exhibition as a pretext I left Russia with my wife, and we never came back. Gabo did the same thing.

R. B.: *I believe you made your first sculptural constructions in Berlin?*

A. P.: My researches to do with certain laws of perspective and depth and the separation of planes led to constructions built with transparent surfaces. The projections were planned in such a way so as to break up the light and shadows that would color the work in different tonalities—rose, blue, violet... My constructions are colored not by paint but by the spectrum itself. All the colors of the spectrum exist in Nature. They become visible when certain atmospheric conditions produce a rainbow. Gabo and I knew that it would be possible to capture these colors and retain them in a work. We used the air itself, enclosing it by certain angles, certain degrees that permit the accumulation of the spectrum. Some of my early works have the construction of prisms.

Mrs. P.: We stayed in Berlin nine months, then came to Paris. And we have been here ever since. Pevsner became a French citizen in 1930.

A. P.: Gabo and I had an exhibition in Paris in 1924 at the Galerie Percier. We made the first Constructivist stage design for Diaghilev's Ballets Russes in 1927, for *La Chatte*, in brass and bronze with a free-standing figure projecting out.

R. B.: *Did you go on using transparent materials?*

A. P.: I gave up plastic materials. For one thing they were too fragile.

Mrs. P.: And they no longer responded to your preoccupations.

A. P.: From the early 1930's I worked with metals. At first, elements of flat surfaces entered into some of my constructions, but these have been completely eliminated.

What is most important about my present work—and it has been true since the 1930's—the principle around which all my sculpture is now constructed, is the exclusive use of straight lines. You will see how pieces such as my *Developable Surface* of 1938 have curved surfaces, as have all my forms (*Developable Columns*, 1942, *Spiral Construction*, 1944, and so on ..) but

Fresco. Brass and oxidised tin 20¾″ × 28″. 1944. Pevsner coll. In Pevsner's sculpture the planes are calculated in such a way as to break up the light acting like a prism. The result gives the impression of varied colors.

these curved surfaces are built up exclusively of strips of straight lines placed one next to the other.

Other sculptors, to make a curve, would take a straight line then bend it, or punch out a circular or curved form from a solid mass.

(He picked up a round copper ashtray to demonstrate his point, tapping deprecatorily on the flat surface with his finger.)

This ashtray is a solid, without life, its round shape stamped out mechanically by a machine. When I make a curved form, it is alive. I have spent over a quarter of a century to learn how to negate a flat surface.

Until Gabo and I revolutionized the concept of sculpture there had been no evolution of sculpture since the Greeks. There was always the tyranny imposed by materials; the tyranny of the mass. The Greeks would take a block of marble and carve a figure out of it. Have you ever noticed what happens when a shadow falls on a Greek figure? It cannot penetrate the statue, the shadow falls to the ground. Ancient sculpture was not inhabited by light. But in our work—Gabo's and mine—light and shade weave through the work itself. Our sculpture absorbs light and shade like a sponge.

R. B.: *Do you feel that the Renaissance brought nothing new to sculpture?*

A. P.: Nothing. While Giotto and Mascaccio brought new concepts to painting, taking into account the expanding horizons of science, anatomy, perspective, mathematics—the constitution of painting materials themselves was evolved and developed—sculptors continued in the same direction as Praxitiles. Always the same way of treating materials, always the same block of marble, that eternal cube. Michaelangelo? Just another Greek. And it has gone on like that, of necessity since the materials used—marble, stone—imposed the mass, therefore, always the same subjects... a woman, an animal... just a series of copies. Look at Maillol—still the same thing, no creation in space.

R. B.: *And Rodin?*

(Pevsner shook his head negatively, clasping and unclasping his very white hands with the large, well-formed knuckles.)

R. B.: *You do away with the entire œuvre of Rodin?*

A. P.: He brought nothing, with the possible exception of his figure of Balzac.

R. B.: *Brancusi?*

A. P.: He is someone I respect, *un homme considérable*, but he did not really bring anything new. It is as though he found a bust of Phideas covered with moss under some bushes where it had been for centuries. He scrubbed and scrubbed to clean it until all the features were rubbed off, leaving it smooth. But it is always the same volume. The egg of Brancusi, his seal : polished surfaces, that's all.

R. B.: *What about Cubist sculpture ?*

A. P.: It played with the object, it broke the object, but the principles of sculpture remained the same.

R. B.: *Are there any artists of the new generation who are contributing work that is valid to your eyes ?*

A. P.: So many of them are creators of monsters, grotesque figures that only disturb. Man needs to be calmed, man is tired, he must not be confronted with horrors. Nothing in my work shocks or distresses. A work of art must bring harmony and peace. Simply to distort is not to create.

R. B.: *And the young artists who work in welded metal, are they carrying on the Constructivist tradition as established by Gabo and yourself ?*

A. P.: We won't mention them by name, but you know them : none of them are saying anything new, they are not true Constructivists. It is not enough to cut into metal to create something original. Maybe something will develop later, they have begun to catch on, but so far...

R. B.: *You find none of them of any interest ?*

A. P.: None of them, except, in a way, an American who works with wires, Lippold.

R. B.: *Have you ever accepted a pupil since your Moscow days ?*

A. P.: No, never.

R. B.: *Do you make preparatory drawings ?*

A. P.: Sometimes I do. But then a drawing can only show one aspect of a piece of sculpture, and my work always has many aspects—it is made to be seen from different angles, in different lights. So I do not always start from a drawing.

R. B.: *How do you make a maquette ?*

A. P.: As Gabo and I wrote in our Manifesto : "We will construct our works." I never model, I never dig into the material ; you know I never work in stone, only in metals. I build my maquettes with wires.

R. B.: *What kind of wires ?*

A. P.: Out of tin, bronze, different metals that are resistant.

R. B.: *Where do you find them ?*

A. P.: I order them from shops selling industrial products. I buy up large quantities at a time, usually ordering what I need to my own specifications. I use wires as fine as 1 mm., others of 2, or 3, up to 5 mm.

R. B.: *Do you copy the maquettes exactly, later, when you make the definitive sculpture ?*

A. P.: Not necessarily. For instance I decided once to make a work that would symbolize the World, my feeling of the Universe which is resumed in the figure of a woman and a child. (See photograph.) To express this feeling I worked out shapes in wire : an enveloping shape—the mother if you want—and an inner form—the germ, the child. When I started to work on the sculpture itself the forms modified themselves considerably (see photograph) but I retained the same essential idea.

R. B.: *How do you go about realizing a work ?*

A. P.: This is very hard to explain, each project requires a different approach. I had to devise my own method of work, my own materials, my own tools, because I had decided to do away with all existing technics. I gradually build up a piece of sculpture by assembling my wires or strips of metal and soldering them together. It is a very long and arduous process, it takes me at least a year to execute one work.

R. B.: *You must need special instruments ?*

A. P.: I use none of the conventional sculptor's tools—mine belong more to a mechanic's workshop, including containers of oxygen, gases, protective goggles...

R. B.: *Can't someone assist you with the actual assemblage ?*

A. P.: No, because a complete knowledge is required of how the different metals and substances react to the fire in the way I use them. I oxidize certain parts myself to vary the surfaces. I must be painter, engineer and sculptor.

R. B.: *Then your sculpture is not cast by a foundry ?*

A. P.: No, it would be impossible to make a mold for such shapes, each work is a unique piece that I construct myself, except, in a few rare cases. A certain part of the sculpture might be cast for me, such as the outside shell of my monument symbolizing *The liberation of the spirit* (see photograph).

R. B.: *It has often been said that your work is based on mathematical and scientific formulae, is this true ?*

A. P.: Most certainly not, and I am glad to have this chance to clear up this matter. Mathematics ? They do not interest me. My work has nothing to do with mathematics or science, although scientists say we are searching in the same direction. But they search for the laws of the universe according to calculations, while I base myself on pure art. I have told you that I build curves out of straight lines. A scientist will say that a straight line does not exist, a line that begins straight is eventually curved in space. This law, I use in my own manner. I constructed this principle for myself.

My sculpture uses no figures or formulae, although scientists try to find them in my work.

Mrs. P.: Once physics pupils came from the Sorbonne and took measurements of his sculpture.

A. P.: Not just pupils, professors.

Mrs. P.: The professors and their pupils searched and searched. Then they declared that indeed they could find no trace of a system, no formulae.

R. B.: *But your brother Gabo was an engineer and you yourself had originally been interested in science ?*

A. P.: That was long ago and has nothing to do with my *œuvre*. It is true that when I was a schoolboy my geometry professors were amazed because I could draw diagrams for concepts that had not even been explained to us. I have acquired considerable technical knowledge of physics and chemistry in order to work with my materials—but my work is only based on pure art.

R. B.: *Did you give up painting completely for sculpture ?*

A. P.: Now I only paint occasionally as relaxation, I don't consider painting my real work. I like to try out new surfaces, plastics treated with acids to bubble the surface, for instance.

R. B.: *I know you are represented in European and American museums, and in private collections, particularly in the United States and Switzerland. You have been living in France for over thirty years. Where are your works in this country ?*

A. P.: Only one collector owns my sculpture in France, M. Peissi (see photograph). But I have been very happy here. My wife and I live modestly, very quietly ; I am able to continue my work, we see few people. I have preferred not to have a dealer—which is why there is no one publicizing what I do. I have avoided exhibitions, except for a few international shows

We had talked for so long that by now the little apartment was filled with dusk, and no one had noticed. I got up to leave ; he and Mrs. Pevsner accompanied me to the small hall. "Don't forget your umbrella" warned Mrs. Pevsner. "Don't forget—Gabo and I are the only Constructivists" reminded the artist as I went out the front door.

Liberation of the Spirit. *Oxidised bronze.* ▶
Height 55¼". 1955-56. This work had its origin in Pevsner's study for the London Institute of Contemporary Arts' competition on the theme of "The Unknown Political Prisoner". Coll. of the artist.

Oskar Kokoschka

BY JOHN RUSSELL

The stormy career of a major expressionist painter of our time

Kokoschka plays with a paper snake at his home at Villeneuve, Switzerland.

The neglect of Oskar Kokoschka in France is a disconcerting phenomenon. In Germany, Austria, Switzerland and Czechoslovakia it is taken for granted that he is one of the most remarkable of twentieth-century men. He has excelled, after all, in so many fields. From his portraits and his empyrean land and townscapes a visitor from Mars or Saturn could reconstruct the look of Europe as we have known it and the presence of those who have made it exciting and memorable to live there. As an illustrator and a subject-painter he has known how to give universal application to his private dilemmas: like Byron and Rousseau, in fact, he is someone in whom his contemporaries are proud to see some part of themselves reflected. As a playwright he has been called 'the founder of the expressionist theatre' and as a *conteur* he has a compulsive quality which carried the

reader into a world as strange as that of Kafka or E.T.A. Hoffmann. As a teacher and an educational theorist he has upheld, often to his own disadvantage, the views of Comenius, the great Czech humanist. "Think for yourself! Study life at first-hand!" are the maxims which caused him to be outlawed from one country after another. To-day these same precepts attract hundreds of excited students each summer to his "School of Seeing" at Salzburg; but one need only run over the facts of his life to see how recently poverty and exile were the rewards of the man who preached them.

Oskar Kokoschka was born at Pöchlarn, near Vienna, on March 1st, 1886. He was of mingled Czech and Austrian extraction. His father, a goldsmith, was a craftsman of rugged and independent character who read Schiller's freedom-plays aloud to his children in the

evenings and preferred a life of vagabondage to the sacrifice of any one of his ideals. Kokoschka soon came to accept continual change of scene as one of the ordinary attributes of life. "I still find it odd to-day", he said to his biographer Edith Hoffmann, "to be treated as a 'foreigner', no matter where I am".

Kokoschka came to manhood at a time when Vienna was not only the capital city of half Europe but also a centre of commotion in the visual arts. The year 1908 should be remembered not only for the Douanier Rousseau banquet or the meeting of Braque and Picasso, but for the organization of the first *Wiener Kunstschau*. This was one of the rare moments in modern art-history at which everyone—artists, architects, stage-designers, masters and students alike—combined to present a common and harmonious front to a hostile world. (Nor was it provincial in tone : the *Kunstschau* of 1909 included work by Van Gogh, Toorop, Gauguin, Vuillard, Bonnard, Matisse, Munch, Max Liebermann.) But what astonished the public and caused Kokoschka's expulsion from the School of Arts and Crafts, where he was then teaching, was the plaster *Self-Portrait*. In this Kokoschka was inspired by Polynesian masks : as early, it would seem, as any of his contemporaries in Paris he had assimilated the disquieting power of primitive art.

Love and pity are the predominant characteristics of Kokoschka's later work ; and they bespeak a humanity so large that no outward circumstance can warp or sour it. But this was not the impression he gave as a young man : *Bürgerschreck*, terror of the bourgeois, was the newspapers' name for him, and the violent, anti-conventional, often erotic character of his work did, in fact, strike fear and dread into the Viennese public. Kokoschka has always been an

Wearing a striped apron, the artist attacks a large canvas with vigor. ▶

'outsider' where group-movements are concerned; but in respect of personal loyalties he is very much an insider, and it is characteristic of him that at the time when he was possessed by the unsung genius of Maulpertsch (1724-1796) his private affection was owed to

ented in his case with water, mountains or tall buildings, and lit with an even majesty that is particularly his own. Lac Léman was the first place to be thus handled, and it has remained his favorite and, indeed, his home: but the cataloguer has to reckon with fifty

music-hall notes, illustrations to his own plays, scenes from the New Testament, and here and there a strange and terrible scene of his own devising—the *Woman who Murders her Child*, for instance. There was nothing systematic about his work—he did not, for instance, join the expressionists in their conviction that certain colors provoke specific psychological reactions—and if his activities had anything in common with each other it was an immediacy of feeling, a tragic intensity of utterance. His associates took it for granted that, as Walden's wife wrote in 1911, "Kokoschka is an Old Master born late, a thing of wonder and terror".

In the self-portraits of this period we see a young man with one skin too few: the face which later broadened and thickened was still long and lean. Nothing could be less apathetic than Kokoschka's silences; but, even so, his friends in Vienna were amazed when he said to them, one day in 1912, that he was going to give a lecture. "*You* give a *lecture*? But you never have a word to say for yourself!" "I can do it all right when there are plenty of people there", said Kokoschka, "it's when there are only a few that I can't get going".

Old servant resting. *Pen drawing. 1919.*

the very different aims of Adolf Loos and his circle.

Loos (1870-1933) had been struggling since 1898 to make the modern movement in Austria of more than local significance. He was one of the first people in Europe to formulate the essentials of 20th-century style in architecture and decoration. ("The lower the standards of a people", he said, "the more lavish are its ornaments". And again: "The beauty of an object exists only in relation to its purpose"). Loos was the animator, among much else, of the *Kunstschau*: through him and his friends Kokoschka came to know what it means to live in the world of ideas. And Kokoschka has given us, in the portraits for which Loos secured him commissions, an abecedario of the Viennese avant-garde of the time. To one section, at any rate, of "*l'Europe aux anciens parapets*", he is as sure a guide as Proust.

Since the day in 1909 when Loos installed him in a hotel above Montreux, Kokoschka has been a great uprooter of himself, and for nearly every journey there has been, as commemoration, one at least of those canvases in which, as it seems, a great part of the visible world has somehow been put into one picture. Kokoschka the landscapist has the peculiarity that the scene treated is never restricted or enclosed. Like Rubens or Elsheimer he prefers—exacts, indeed—a vast, open prospect, accid-

years of inspired investigation, and Stockholm, Genoa, Jerusalem, Lyons, Bordeaux, Amsterdam, Avignon, Berlin, Florence, Salzburg, Hamburg, Venice, Istanbul, the Pyramids, Rome and the Matterhorn have all been the subject of paintings by Kokoschka. In these works Kokoschka is essentially an epic-painter—someone who sees with a condor's eye and has, too, the condor's power of treading the topmost air as others tread a pavement. No painter participates more vividly in his own work than Kokoschka; but his landscapes breathe an Olympian element, and it is only occasionally, in the handwritten quality of an individual figure, or the very personal tonality that hovers, in picture after picture, on the high middle ground between green and blue, that we realise that a master manipulator is, after all, at work on the visible world.

Hardly had he left the circle of Adolf Loos than he was drawn into its Berlin equivalent, which had as its centre Herwarth Walden, the editor of *Der Sturm*. It was in this valiant fortnightly (to which Léger, Picasso, Archipenko, Severini, Ernst, Klee, Marc and Delaunay also contributed) that Kokoschka published the portrait-drawings of Yvette Guilbert and others, the

Woman with bird. *1916. Oil. 33″×20″. Private collection, Berlin.*

Kokoschka won his audience at once. It was, on that evening in 1912, as it was when in 1956 he climbed into the pulpit of the Oude Kerk, Amsterdam, and spoke of Rembrandt in the church where Rembrandt's funeral service had been held—not even he himself knew quite what he was going to say. But the groping, unpractised, quasi-improvisatory manner never failed of its effect.

162

Dolomite landscape (Tre Croci). *1913. Oil 32⁴/₅″×47³/₅″. Private collection, Hamburg. Vast, open, mountain landscapes have been a specialty of this artist.*

Art is for Kokoschka predominantly a matter of communication—a way of sharing the secrets which make it possible to live. When he says to young people "Don't accept what you're told blindly—see for yourselves", it is the word *see* that counts ; and it is through art that people best learn to see. Kokoschka is someone for whom the act of seeing aright is the basis of rightness in all other actions.

Kokoschka in private life is a great forager in love and friendship, seeking and sought in his turn. Anyone so sensitive to human contacts must be haunted in youth by the concept of an ideal companion : wide is the field, and colossal the blunders, to which such a nature is exposed, and Kokoschka more than once crossed the far borders of the possible and sojourned for a time in regions trodden only by the romantic imagination.

His gift for the trans-fabulation of experience is vividly displayed in the masterpiece of his pre-1914 period : *Die Windsbraut*. It recalls the pictures done at Mürren and Cortina d'Ampezzo in the previous year ; but in place of the apple-green uplands there is now a great open sea on which two lovers are driven in an open boat. The mountain-landscape is a direct reminiscence of a journey which Kokoschka had made in the company of Alma Mahler ; and she it is who lies beside him in the boat. It is a picture which combines all the appurtenances of 19th century high romance with a lucidity that is Kokoschka's own : few visitors forget the open-eyed desperation of the man who, with his monumental queen upon his shoulder, is being carried he knows not where. Magnificence of mind and body means much to Kokoschka, who regards the Emperor Charles V as the greatest man in history, and in the *Double Portrait* (Christmas 1912) of himself and Alma Mahler there is something of royalty in her stance and bearing, and something, too, of the astonished consort in the painter's own aspect as he is edged to the far right of the canvas by his imposing companion.

With the outbreak of war Kokoschka sold the *Windsbraut*, enlisted in an exclusive regiment of dragoons, equipped himself with red trousers, blue jacket, golden helmet and a horse and set off for the front.

Never a man of the middle way, Kokoschka made two resolutions during his strange Army career : never to kill a "so-called enemy", and to overcome his fears by volunteering for the most hazardous patrols. Before he had been many months on the eastern front this policy resulted in his being shot in the head and wounded in the lung by a Russian bayonet ; and it was during the long and painful journey home, by way of the Ukraine and Poland in an open railway-truck, that he composed one of the most remarkable of his plays

163

Orpheus and Eurydice. In this, as in his life with Alma Mahler, it is Pluto, the man left behind, who dominates the action; eventually Orpheus frees himself from Eurydice and declares "I also other symbolic pictures — *The Power of Music*, in which a man closes his ears to the loved-and-dreaded sound, and *The Friends*, in which five members of the Dresden circle are seen pictures which he showed at the Biennale di Venezia, the German-Italian fascist press began to attack him; the Austrian Government offered him the Directorship of the Arts & Crafts

London, Tower Bridge. *1925. Oil. 30″×50½″. Art Institute, Minneapolis. Kokoschka, a great traveller, has taken many cities as subjects for paintings.*

confess with devilish joy that I hate you"; madness follows and in the end it is Eurydice who breaks free by strangling the madman. "In this last struggle, this last embrace, I free myself—at last redeemed..."

The effect of his wounds was that for some time Kokoschka wandered in a kind of between-world; neither soldier nor civilian, invalid or whole man, he was taken to Dresden, where he lived for the next seven years. There he worked on the cycle of symbolic pictures which had begun with the *Windsbraut* and continued, in 1915, with the *Knight Errant*. This latter, with its vivid portrait of the painter prostrate and deserted on the battlefield, is one of the most curious and touching of all his pictures, and one of the most contained and sober in color. There is nothing in it of the fine vibrant blue which, alike in the view of Stockholm and the Stuttgart *Frau in Blau* of 1919, is the color of Kokoschka's convalescence. To this period belong

in a cardgame which symbolises "the struggle of man against man, each terrifyingly naked in his passions, and all submerged by a color which binds them together".

In 1924 began a period of almost unbroken travelling. England, Scotland, France, Spain, Portugal, Switzerland, Egypt, Turkey, the Sahara, Palestine: all knew the vivid, restless, inquisitive figure. Such headquarters as he had were in Paris, in Pascin's villa in Auteuil; and in 1931 he had his first exhibition there —44 paintings, at the Galerie Georges Petit. Kokoschka has never cared much for the art-world of Paris—or for its methods—but it is worth noting that André Lhote gave the show a glowing review in the *Nouvelle Revue Française*.

After 1931 it was difficult for an artist not to be influenced by two things: the world economic crisis and the steady darkening of the European political skies. Kokoschka was no exception: as early as 1932, after Mussolini had manifested extreme dislike of the

School, and later withdrew their offer on learning that Kokoschka would accept "on one condition—that they accept my scheme for a general reform of the educational system according to rational principles which would restore peace to the world". In politics, as in most other things, Kokoschka was a natural anti-conformist; the man who, during the 1914-18 war, had published illegally two firmly anti-militarist lithographs was not likely to stand by when an even larger lunacy was gaining ground. In 1934 he went to Prague, settled there, and made the acquaintance not only of T. G. Masaryk but of Olga Palkovska, who was to become his wife. In July 1937 417 of his works, then in German public collections, were declared 'degenerate' by the Nazi authorities: and in May 1938 one of his pictures was formally cut into four pieces by the Viennese police.

In the autumn of 1938 Kokoschka and Olga Palkovska left for England, where they remained until 1945, and

Portrait of Else Kupfer. *Oil. 1910. 36″×28²/₅″. Zurich Art Museum.* ▶

where Kokoschka became a British citizen.

He had, of course, been to England before. But to come as an admired visitor is one thing; to arrive as a destitute refugee in time of nearwar quite another. Kokoschka was welcomed coolly in England, and even to-day his adopted country has yet to offer an honor of any kind to the most illustrious of its painter-citizens. *What we are fighting for* (the title of one of his wartime allegories) was never far from his mind, and Vengeance was not one of the things in question; in 1943, for instance, he gave the 1000 pounds which he received for painting the portrait of the Soviet Ambassador to the Stalingrad Hospital Fund, with the request that, if possible, it should be used to heal the wounded of both sides.

After the end of the war, Kokoschka continued to be haunted by the fear that the old, hand-made, humanistic civilisations had gone for ever. In his work, he proceeded with as much *brio* as ever. The President of Western Germany, the President of the Austrian Republic, the Burgomaster of Hamburg —these are tremendous portraits, as are those of Emil Bührle, Pablo Casals, Topazia Markevitch and Bettina Angehrn. His new house at Villeneuve, on Lac Léman, is the kind of high-lying, never-pretentious nest which fits him perfectly, and he has been able to execute for Hamburg University the *Thermopylae* panels—arguably the finest decorative paintings to have been done in Europe since the war.

Kokoschka remains obsessed with the fear that a proletarian, uniform, too purely technical society will come to instal itself in every country of the globe. To this he opposes, in his own person, the example of one who has always stood apart from group-movements of any kind and in doing so has learnt to think and feel and act for himself. Equality he loves, but he does not confuse equality with mere alikeness, and it is significant that for his first two commissioned stage-designs he has chosen *The Magic Flute* and *A Midsummer Night's Dream,* for in both of these there is an unaffected sense of the natural hierarchy of created beings. To know oneself, and one's place in the world, and to delight in both of them: that is Kokoschka's lesson, and it is because he teaches it with such infectious persistence that he is not only admired as a painter but loved as a human being.

Die Windsbraut (The wind's bride), a major work of 1912, depicts the artist and Alma Mahler (the composer's widow) driven by storms in an open boat.

167

The new School of Paris

BY GEORGES LIMBOUR

The significant names, the tendencies and the climate of the present generation

It's become an accepted thing to speak of the "Ecole de Paris", but it's not at all easy to say just what the name stands for. What the School of Paris represents now, who are the painters who comprise it, what are its tendencies and from which masters, old or new, it stems—all these are complex questions.

First, the painters who comprise it. There are hundreds, certainly : and by no means all are French—let alone Parisian—by birth and origin. They are of every nationality, and the only thing they have in common is that they all live and work in Paris. Even that may be questioned: for many of them work in the French provinces, and it was possible a year or two ago to speak of the School of Aix-en-Provence. Yet the painters concerned were still ranked as members of the Ecole de Paris, since they had made their débuts in the capital, still held exhibitions there, and came up from time to time to breathe in the atmosphere of the city. Nor is Aix the only provincial centre for members of the Ecole de Paris. Paris is no longer what it was even thirty years ago, and its restless, evercrowded, noisy and polluted atmosphere is very different from that breathed by Marquet, let us say; many are the painters who leave Paris in search of light, space, and air.

The foreigners come from every quarter of the globe : Central Europe, Israel, China, Japan, North and South America. The Ecole de Paris sponges up every kind of ambition and hastens

◀ **Jean Dubuffet**: Flee the city. *Assembled picture. 1956. 37½" × 28¾". Augustinci coll. Paris. Controversial figure, mostly interested in curious textures. After working such unconventional materials as asphalt, tar and gravel he now composes what he calls "assembled pictures" made up of multiple pieces of already painted canvas cut up then put together again.*

to forget the origins of such artists as make the grade.

Next : the 'masters', if one may still call them so, of the Ecole de Paris. Doubtless the great artists of the late 19th century—Van Gogh, Cézanne, Gauguin ; and their successors—Picasso, Braque, Léger. Yet there are many young painters who would claim descent rather from Mondrian, a Dutchman who had few Parisian affinities, or from Kandinsky and Klee, members of the Blue Rider group, whose headquarters were in Munich. So that it is not easy to trace the origins of the School of Paris, and indeed at times one might suppose the whole concept to be a myth, or an illusion, with no palpable sense behind it.

But that is not the case. The word 'school' may itself be inapt (it is, in fact, no more than a makeshift) but there is a reality behind it. It's a reality more easily felt than analysed, a reality of sentiment rather than of reason. Its character is affective. What binds these painters to one another is the atmosphere of Paris, its productive climate. No other city in the world has such a passion for painting. Nowhere else is the painter so highly regarded. The public for painting is enlightened, quick to seize on the new and the good, and so various in taste and temper that only very rarely does a good painter fail of support. He is almost bound to find recognition in Paris, and it is for this reason that Paris is the ideal place in which to work.

And this love of painting is gratified and assuaged by the galleries, daily more numerous, which cater for the painter and his patrons. No European capital can compare with Paris either for the enthusiasm of the lay public or the volume of traffic which results from that enthusiasm. Frequent public sales add to the climate of excitement about the arts.

François Arnal: *Born 1924 in the south of France. Builds up his canvas with thick areas of paint contrasting with other parts where the canvas is left apparent, sometimes mixes sand and other matter with the pigment. He studied law, gave it up to devote all his time to art in 1944. Has designed large abstract tapestries for a public building in the Saar.*

The Tower of Babel

Given the high proportion of foreign artists in Paris, it is only natural that the School of Paris should reflect

169

a great many varying and at times mutually contradictory tendencies. Sometimes the foreigner—Chagall, for instance—brings with him the folklore of his native land, or a more generalized national anxiety, nostalgia or conscious or unconscious ambition. The passions thus generated are not always harmonious, but the conflicts which result can be, and often are, beneficial to the School as a whole. Far from presenting a "united front", the Ecole de Paris is torn this way and that by the most spectacular dissensions—ideological disputes, that is to say, of which the most obvious is the now-historic combat between figurative and non-figurative painting.

One no longer speaks of 'schools', the vaguer term 'groups' is more in favor. But within these groups individualism knows no restraint. That is why it may be misleading to make even the most rudimentary classifications, and why the views which I advance here relate merely to the *tendencies* of the artists concerned, and not at all to their relative or comparative merits. Nor will my list of names be exhaustive; certain important painters will doubtless have slipped through the net.

Sam Francis: Black on yellow. *Urvater coll., Brussels. Born in 1923 in San Mateo, California. He studied medicine and psychology at the University of California. Has been an abstract painter since 1947, and has lived in Paris since 1950 where he is a leading member of what the French call "l'Ecole du Pacifique". His work suggests fluidity and space.*

Paul Kallos: The Window. *1956. 28¾" × 21⅜". Galerie Pierre, Paris. Born in 1928 in Hungary. Lives in Paris since 1950, when he started in the abstract manner. He had spent a year in a German concentration camp and studied art in Budapest. His palette is warmly luminous with gold lights recalling Bonnard and the tranquility of a summer afternoon.*

General characteristics of the new School of Paris

The School of Paris has taken on a new orientation since the Liberation. The character of this post-war 'school' is, in fact, quite different from that of the Ecole which had its greatest

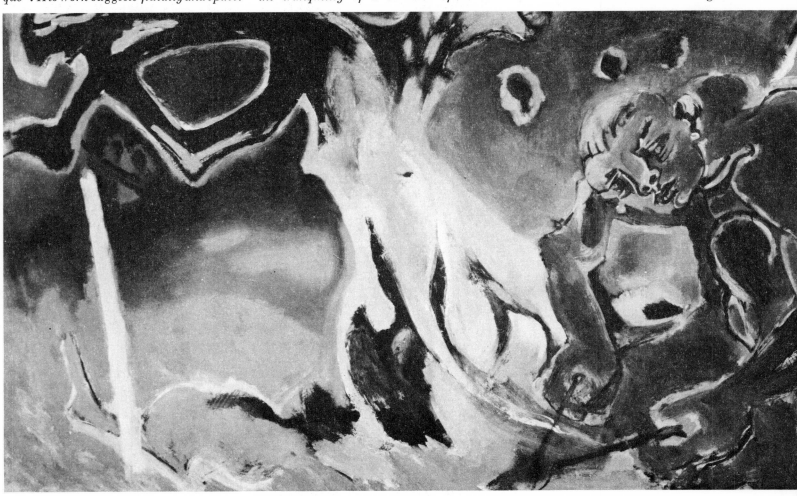

period before and after the war of 1914-1918. Fauvism, cubism and expressionism were the sources of that earlier school's authority and attraction: and, of these, expressionism was never specifically a French movement. Rouault, certainly, was one of its greatest champions, but it was essentially a movement rallying Germans and Belgians. Klee and Kandinsky had no influence in Paris at that time. Nor for many years did abstract painting appeal at all to Parisian opinion. Léger, perhaps, could be said to have got very near to pure abstraction at one moment, and Delaunay, after painting his famous Eiffel Towers, turned to a lyrical use of color that had little or no reference to the visible world. But the real abstractionists, like Mondrian and Malevitch, seemed quite foreign to the Ecole de Paris and made no impression upon it. Abstract painters like Goetz and Magnelli who are favored now by the evolution of taste worked then in complete obscurity—and, in Goetz's case, in great poverty.

It's important to note that although the first great masters of the Ecole de Paris allowed themselves complete liberty in their handling of the world of appearances they never denied that world its part in their pictures. Transformed and transmogrified the objects might be, and often were; but it was always possible to "read" the subject of

Constantin Macris: Lights in the trees. *1957. 32″×25⅝″. Galerie Pierre, Paris. Born in Cairo in 1919 of Greek parents, has lived in Paris since 1948; he studied drawing there in Fernand Léger's atelier. His abstract compositions in blond, milky tones are sometimes like landscapes, sometimes like walls with flat patches of color*

a picture by Braque or Picasso and to identify or, as Juan Gris said, to "name" the objects concerned—in spite of the public's indignant claim that their pictures were incomprehensible. The bourgeois public was scandalised then; today it has lost the capacity

◀ Edouard Pignon: Landscape with olive-tree. *1954-55. 94¾″×47⅜″. Galerie de France, Paris. Born in the Pas-de-Calais département in 1905. Has lived and painted in the south of France where he has spent much time with Picasso. A realist, his subjects are usually work in the fields or scenes with fishermen. He reforms his own perspective, flattening out space and rearranging the natural forms of such elements as nets, trees and hills.*

Zao-Wou-Ki: The river. *1956. 39⅜″× ▶ 39⅜″. Galerie de France, Paris. Born in Peking in 1920; has worked in France since 1948. Continues the Chinese landscape tradition in terms of twentieth century Paris expression. His deft, delicate and evocative canvases suggest hills, valleys, distances and imaginary flora.*

to be shocked or startled and it can no longer be said that "modern art" and its representatives are faced with a hostile world. This change is not entirely for the better. People will accept anything, it is true; but that "anything" may be quite worthless, and at times is actually fraudulent.

The element of figuration was nowhere more predominant than in the surrealist movement, which reached its height during the inter-war period. An extreme naturalism was often combined by the surrealists with the wildest play of fancy. But the new Ecole de Paris has witnessed the death-agony of surrealism.

ing with blobs and trickles of tenuous color that innovate new variants of impressionism.

Max Ernst: Arizona. 1955-56. 16¼"×13". Private collection, England. Born near Cologne, Germany, in 1891. A founder of surrealism, he has lived and worked much of the time in Paris, once had a house in Arizona and is now installed in Touraine. Already well known before the war, he has now become one of the "grand old men" figures of modern art. Since gaining international recognition by winning First Prize at the Venice Biennale of 1954 his success has been translated into practical terms. His strange evocations of an imaginary world of crystals, burnt forests or underwater vegetation have influenced many young painters. So have his textural innovations.

Representation of the outside world

We can say, first, that all members of the Ecole de Paris reject imitation or representation pure and simple and aim, instead, to re-create the universe in an original language of their own. Partisans of 'social realist' painting can therefore be ruled out from the start. This applies to all those who grouped themselves as "painters of reality" and present a view of the world which, though personal, is purely traditional. Neither techniques nor subjects, therefore, are new. We can safely put them on one side.

It is notable that certain figurative painters of today stem more or less from expressionism and are drawn to the *monstrous*, for instance Lorjou and Reyberolle. Realist subjects are most often mean and sad, expressed in paint that has a brutish, un-luminous quality, and in color that itself is confused and ambiguous. Such uncertainty, both in choice of subject matter and technique, reigns in figurative circles that at a recent exhibition in Paris several painters considered as "avant-garde" submitted "Crucifixions" in styles derived from the cubists !

While the majority of the new generation in Paris prefers the abstract idiom, certain painters working from reality as a point of departure are

After the Liberation many painters, including some of the best, turned away entirely from figuration and relied instead upon a personal handwriting or sign-language to express their world. These signs were so abstract that they were impossible to identify ; their connotation was entirely private. They ended, in fact, by becoming their own reality, whereas the cubists never ceased to have some relation, however remote, with the reality of everyday life. It was at this point that postwar abstract art may be said to have begun.

We must remember that the first Ecole de Paris had, as a whole, reacted against impressionism. Cubism, especially, ruled that forms should not be dissolved or volatilised in light. Rigorous construction, precise and solid forms, were the order of the day. The new school has a less exacting sense of form ; some of its members are more sensitive to color than to line, proceed-

Kandinsky and Mondrian have had many admirers since 1945. Bonnard, too, has quite regained the high place which cubism had for a time denied him. Sometimes Braque and Picasso are handled none too gently by certain champions of the rising generation. It remains true that there is no such thing in either phase of the Ecole de Paris as a fixed "age-group" ; some of the outstanding figures of the between-wars period are still alive and undoubtedly an old master like Picasso qualifies as one of the youngest painters of them all.

Hans Hartung: T56.16. 65"×45". Private collection. Born in Leipzig in 1904. Has been an abstract painter since 1922. Was naturalized a French citizen in 1945 after fighting in the French Foreign Legion and losing his right leg. He spreads a violent outburst of lines against a luminous background, creating a spatial play of light against dark. Hartung has had frequent shows in Paris, Germany and New York.

Alberto Magnelli: Rising forces Nº II. *1951. 51¼″×53¾″. Private coll. Paris. Born in Florence in 1888, he is a pioneer among the abstracts having been a non-figurative painter since 1915 (with a return to reality for some twenty years). He lives in Paris and exhibits there. He deliberately avoids lyricism and works in flat colors organized into precise, geometrical forms.*

essential to any survey of artistic activity in tnis city.

Balthus (page 188) is a case in point. This painter, who has one of the most authentic artistic personalities, works with precise representation. Its very

◄ André Lanskoy: Possibility of fire. *1955. 39⅜″× 38¾″. Louis Carré coll., Paris. Born in Moscow in 1902, has lived in Paris since 1921. He was first a figurative painter, producing scenes of interiors and still lifes in simplified compositions and bright tones. After 1944 he abandoned exterior reality for an exuberant abstract style. He can be called the most truly gay of the non-figurative painters, his work being devoid of tragedy and nostalgia.*

exactness exerts a curious fascination which comes in part from an element of surrealist strangeness and in part from a discreet perversity of outlook which could not have found expression at any time but the present. Balthus' technique derives from Courbet but his turn of mind and inspiration are of our own day.

A fine artist who before the war was known only as a sculptor has added painting, and also drawing, to his activity : Alberto Giacometti (page 187). His canvases recreate the same attenuated figures as his sculpture, also scenes of his atelier, still lifes and the street where he lives—all directly observed from life : he never works without a model. His principal effort

is to make the human figure emerge in its appropriate space embued with a hallucinating presence. Lights spring from a tight web of fine black lines, suggesting volume. This artist is haunted by the problem of the dimension of his figures, the relationships they must have between the space they occupy and the space around them. Color is, therefore, of secondary interest to him.

His pictures have a grey and ochre monochrome aspect with here and there a small touch of red. Giacometti's almost anguished search to establish a proportion between the human being and the empty space from which this being establishes his plenitude and consistency reveals a metaphysical pre-

occupation. The hieratic attitude of his statues, the almost religious aura he imbues them with contribute to giving his human figures the immobile attributes of divinities.

Borès (page 186), a Spaniard, is an entirely different case. He springs from cubism and strives to make his pictures like a harmonious beach reflecting ever increasing floods of light. He has evolved from a rather dark palette to a range of clear, transparent and serene tonalities. His forms are pure and allusive, sometimes constructed with large, circular rhythms. In his recent works *(Fishermen pulling in their nets, Women lying on the beach)* the subject, although apparent, is merely the pretext for an elegant play of light that goes beyond a descriptive or anecdotal character.

Pignon (page 170), a generation younger, has been a close friend of Picasso's and has undergone his influence. He has not lost contact with the reality that inspires him; contrary to the young painters with whom he exhibited before and after the Liberation, who have had an increasing recourse to the use of subjective *signs* to translate their impressions of the exterior world, Pignon's aim is to insert the shapes of the objects and people making up a landscape into a space that is personal to him, but which preserves the distinctive character of reality. His boats, fishnets and fishermen, his olive-pickers of the south of France, show him to be an artist courageously looking for a common ground where the richness of nature and the recreating powers of the artist can meet.

176

Bernard Buffet (page 187) among the figurative painters, became amazingly famous while still very young. The predominant feeling in his work is that of a would-be tragic despair. Color, drawing, and subject all work to this end, but his horror, despair and bitterness do not strike the observer as quite spontaneous. He seems, like his own acrobats, to risk nothing of himself as he goes through his routines, and the final effect is, to most observers, depressing and devitalising. How is it then, that he has so many admirers ? For two reasons, as I see it : one is that his wealthy and not over-alert public prefers its pictures to be immediately legible ; in this respect Buffet satisfies a craving with which other painters of our day have little patience. The other reason is that his pictures are believed by many of his admirers to characterise our "age of anxiety" By buying a Buffet, they think, they are really taking part in their time. This would seem to be the view also of those magazine and newspaper editors who have chosen Buffet as the spokesman of his generation.

Among these figurative painters is one who made his début after the first world war and may now therefore be presumed to be at his peak, André Beaudin (page 188). Beaudin has made rich use of his cubist inheritance, both as painter and as sculptor. His paintings (portraits, land- and townscapes, still lifes, animal-subjects, horse-racing scenes) are marked by a great severity of construction and reliance upon straight lines and pure curves. He is as pure in color as in form, and although he never aims to be "lyrical" his very reticence is moving.

Since Maria Blanchard and Marie Laurencin there have been few well-known women painters. Suzanne Roger is not well-known, but in her own way she deserves to be mentioned in the same category although on a very

different level. She first showed her pictures in 1925, and her *œuvre* has retained ever since a consistent distinc-

André Masson : Attack by birds. *Sand painting. 1956. 29⅝″×39″. Saidenberg Gallery, New York. Born in 1896 near Paris. Originally he exhibited with the surrealists when he expressed himself through "automatic" painting. He always has been interested in surface texture and has made pictures with sand backgrounds splashed with paint. He preserves some figurative elements in his present work but embues them with duality—a head that at the same time is the sea, a face that is part of the sky. Masson's subjects are cosmic forces, growth and germination. He is also a lithographer.*

tion. She too has known how to profit by the lessons of cubism. Her subjects are those things which, in life, delight or distress her : markets, fairgrounds, wedding-parties, burials, city squares, children in the schoolroom, craftsmen at work, cemeteries. When a crowded canvas is in question she has a natural elegance in her simplifications, and a real delicacy of touch in her handling of color. She is close to life, but recreates it completely.

Landscapes of the mind

When a painter interprets the external world, giving it a new appearance, he must—if he is representing people or

Pierre Tal Coat : Painting. *1956-1957. 35½″×18⅛″. Maeght Collection, Paris. Born in Brittany in 1905, his family were fishermen. Lives in Paris and Aix-en-Provence. His Provençal canvases suggest blinding light which swallows up objects and outlines, occasionally resembling blurred prehistoric cave paintings.*

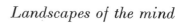

objects—make these recognisable, or "readable". But when painting landscape, he has complete liberty to transpose and transmute, to substitute the

Roger Bissière: Summer equinox. *1955. 51¼″ × 63¾″. Galerie Jeanne Bucher, Paris. Born in the south-west of France in 1888. Once a cubist, Bissière made strange tapestries during the war of odd bits of material sewn together. The play of cloth colors was to influence his painting; it led to abstract canvases.*

impressions he feels, the purely imaginary image, for reality. The elements of landscape become so vague, so fluid, so ill-defined, that the final picture offers us merely a general idea of landscape with no particular, limiting details. Why bother, in such a case, to refer back to the visible world at all? If, instead of evoking that world, we have arrived at the point of abolishing it, what is the point of calling it landscape? Would not "mental landscape", at any rate, be a more appropriate name? And, of course, some painters do speak of 'landscapes of the mind'.

Max Ernst (page 172), one of the inventors of surrealism, created imaginary and fantastic landscapes—his calcined forests, for instance. He produced an impression of strangeness by the use of new textures and surfaces, notably the smearing of wet paint by pulling off paper placed on top of it. Such techniques, and many others developed by this artist, were often to be taken up in the future. Ernst has taken his place since the war as one of

the outstanding contemporary painters.

Another important surrealist painter, André Masson (page 177), made his début in the middle 1920s. Then, from recollection of individual places, he devised his first vehement, lyrical, largely imaginary landscapes. His subject was the germination and unfolding of Nature (in this many others were to follow him later) and he aspired to represent the flux and flow of life, to make visible the invisible forces of the world, and to portray in point the vast, slow, impalpable movement of the universe. His *Indian Spring*, for instance, painted in the U.S.A. in 1943, cannot be 'read' distinctly, but there is no disputing the power with which the secret and irresistible forces of Nature are brought to our notice. Jackson Pollock, for one, was greatly impressed and influenced by Masson, and Pollock, as we all know, was of great influence himself.

Maurice Estève: Captive. 1954. 22″ × 18⅕″. *Born in central France in 1904. Studied and lives in Paris where he exhibits with the abstract painting groups. Uses bright, pure colors including red.*

Of those who first became known at the end of the last war, I shall cite first a group of artists who are friends of one another and show in one or other of the same group of galleries. Colorists one and all, they have profited by the lessons of their seniors. Originally it was easy to read their landscapes, interiors and still lifes, but gradually the identifiable elements became fewer and fewer and were absorbed entirely into the general impression. Signs, or emblems, took their place.

It was in this way that Bazaine (page 180) became one of the best colorists and landscape painters of our day. Touches of meaningful color stand, in his pictures, for trees, rocks, rivers, beaches, and (as in a recent show) Dutch landscapes. It was not a case of "Back to Impressionism" but rather of a new kind of impressionism.

Tal Coat (page 177) is another subtle master of light. He has learnt much from the Chinese. The pictures he paints in Provence allude to the hills, ravines, cliffs and rivers of that region, but these appear in the form of long broad dark undulating bands of color, each and all bathed in the golden light which is peculiar to this artist.

Manessier (page 181) has travelled the same road. The heightened color and mystical light of his pictures derive in part from his long sojourn in Brittany (his themes are often based upon ships, harbors, marine landscape) and in part from a preoccupation with religious subjects. These latter he treats not representationally, but symbolically, by the use of the Cross and an imaginative handling of color. His *Passion*, which was shown in the 1957 Salon de Mai, is a transposition not of a "thing seen" but of a "thing felt"—the exteriorisation, that is to say, of an

178

Maria Elena Vieira da Silva: Naval Yards. 1955-56. 19¾″ × 19¾″. Priv. coll. *Born in Lisbon in 1908 where she was brought up by private tutors and studied music and sculpture. She came to Paris as a young girl, worked under several masters and finally evolved her very personal manner of painting. Her "mental landscapes" are delicately assembled planes and facets establishing imaginary distances often inspired by urban scenes and the sea. She is one of the best known members of the new school of Paris and has works in various museums and private collections. The artist is married to the Hungarian painter Arpad Szenes and lives in Paris.*

179

inward experience. Spiritual states or
moments of being are these painters'
subject. Kandinsky expounded the
theory of pictorial expression which
had as its base the mystical implications
of color. Yet it is not from Kandinsky
that these painters derive : their paintings—Manessier's *Alleluia*, for instance,
—come from the heart and are, in fact,
hymns of color.

Any painter who is not in a perpetual
state of grace runs many risks when he
sets out to devise a sign—or emblem-
language of his own. For the signs may
not, after all, make themselves clear
to us and the language, therefore, may
not 'come through'. The picture may
remain no more than an imposing,
enigmatic, largely meaningless object.
Singier (page 184), for instance, may
be thought to stick too closely to Klee
in his personal 'language' : and if we
try to discover the exact relationship
between Estève's fine color (page 178)
and the title he has given the picture
we may have to turn away unsatisfied.

To say that Ubac (page 185) was
a "landscape painter" would seem

absurd to anyone who had not grasped
the sense of those words as applied to
the new School of Paris. Yet Ubac
knows how to coax the northern light
on to his curiously matt and cloudy

suggestive of rain-soaked places and
a wilderness of rocks. Yet there are
people who prefer to see in Ubac's pictures nothing more than a texture of
extreme refinement.

Alfred Manessier: —12º. *1956. 57½″×45″. Private coll., Paris. Born in the Somme*
département in 1911. Studied architecture in Paris, worked under the abstract painter
Bissière at the Académie Ranson which formed his early style. Although grouped
among the abstract artists, his point of departure is a personal vision of reality. He has
often expressed such religious themes as The crown of thorns *or* The carrying of the
Cross. *Another source of his subject matter is Brittany, where he spends his summers,*
particularly the play of light on the water there.

surfaces, and although it would be
difficult to give a name to his elongated
forms or blocks of color they are re-
cognisably the symbol of a particular
countryside : Flanders, the Ardennes,
or the northern suburbs of Paris. Sometimes he introduces a piece of real
slate into his picture, as if it were
a collage. At once the canvas takes
on a new meaning—vast, pathetic,

Auguste Herbin: Noon. *1953. 63¾″×*
51¼″. Born in the north of France in
1882. A pioneer among French abstract
artists, Herbin has been a non-figurative
painter since 1926 and has had conside-
rable influence on the young. He descends
from Kandinsky and Mondrian but is
less rigorous in his construction than
either of these masters. He uses flat sur-
faces, even colors and neatly delineated
forms. Has written on non-figurative art.

Many painters work mid-way between
the allusive and the abstract. Perhaps
Vieira da Silva (page 179) who is Por-
tuguese, evokes a metropolitan landscape in those pictures of hers which
are made up of innumerable glittering
facets of paint often in tones of grey.
The spectator is not sure of the subject
but stays on, fascinated by the subtlety
of her constructions.

In the same way, Zao-Wou-Ki
(page 171) suggests synthetic landscapes
with fresh perfumes of flowers and
orchards and the vast modulations of
forms and colors of mountains hazy in
the distance. This Chinese painter who
lives in Paris has collaborated with the
sculptor Germaine Richier (as has Hartung) ; in 1955 he painted a vertical
setting in lead for one of her sculptures
inspired from natural forms. By its
very lack of definition Zao-Wou-Ki's

landscape does not impose but allows interpretation; it accompanies without interfering with the sculptured form

—newspaper or wrapping paper— into his pictures and thus vary their texture; these were the first collages. He was

of the artists who has carried these experiments to their furthest point. Since 1948, he gave up traditional colors to compose a series of canvases with asphalt, tar and gravel. Into these unusual materials he scratched human figures. Later, he invented imaginary landscapes in "high relief" like geography models with thick ridges. His talent is, in fact, a talent for texture: the subject is of secondary importance. He is the only painter of our time who could be said to have caused a scandal, in the traditional sense of the word, and he did it by reason of the sheer enormity of his materials. "Base matter" has never been so transformed as in Dubuffet's art, and it might have been assumed that his lyrical approach to unexplored materials would be taken up eventually by other painters.

It is curious, but understandable, that the painters on whom Dubuffet had the most effect were the abstractionists. His work is, of course, figurative in the sense that there is usually a decipherable, and often a naively obvious, "subject" in them—people, animals, landscapes. But it is the unexpected texture, the physical variety, that dominates. Many of his admirers felt, in fact, that the "subjects" were merely an intrusion, distracting the observer from the sumptuous and original *matière*. Thus it was that the abstractionists have, as it were, annexed Dubuffet as one of themselves.

The development of abstract painting has carried with it a bubbling and fermentation of pigment, a rising of the paint surface, a heterogeneity of *matière* which turns the canvas into a veritable colored bas-relief. These are characteris-

Henri Goetz: Picture. *1956. 24″×30″. Private collection. U.S.A. Born in New York in 1909, studied at Massachusetts Institute of Technology and Harvard before coming to Paris in 1930; is a naturalized French citizen. He also is a pioneer among the non-figuratives, having worked in the abstract style since 1936. He uses successive planes to create impressions of space, somewhat in the manner adopted later by Soulages.*

before it. This very unusual use by a sculptor of a painting suggests new, and perhaps controversial, possibilities.

Two young artists who have lately come forward in this very general category are Kallos (page 170) and Macris (page 171). Both employ the "new impressionist" method and evoke landscapes of a private, light-filled sort: the first with a Bonnard-like sumptuousness, the second with golden and milky tones. Both, too, make a delicate and transparent use of paint. It is painters such as they who make us feel that landscape painting is confusedly, mysteriously alive and has still many secrets to reveal, many metamorphoses to undergo.

Preoccupation with texture

Till the cubist period, pictures were usually painted in thin layers of more or less smooth paint. Braque was the first to introduce extraneous matter

also the first to add sand, either as a background, or mixed with paint, to give a granular surface. He also used plaster. Expressionism, at the same time, made it accepted form to seek a rougher texture than had hitherto been usual. (The use of the palette knife instead of the brush leads automatically to a thicker texture). Certain painters researched into new techniques and materials, where formerly they would have experimented with form.

Dubuffet (page 168) is certainly one

Serge Poliakoff: Composition. *Private collection. Born in Moscow in 1906. Travelled in Europe, studied art in London and Paris. Met leaders of abstract art in Paris (Kandinsky, Delaunay, Freundlich); since the middle thirties has been a non-figurative painter. His work, based on simplified geometric forms, is characterized by the elegance of his colors —they are subtle and of a subdued sonority. Exhibits in Paris and New York.*

tics of what has lately been dubbed "lyrical abstractionism". Arnal, Appel

Pierre Soulages: Painting 1956. 51¼″×35⅛″. *Private collection. Born in South-Western France in 1919. He uses black with great dramatic power, crossing straight bands one over the other against a luminous background. He exhibits in one-man shows in Europe and New York and has designed scenery and costumes for the stage.*

and Hosiasson are some of those who work in a veritable tempest of paint. The first two use colors of a frenetic violence including a savage red. To distinguish between these painters and make some estimate of their comparative merit is no part of my purpose here. But I feel bound to say that texture in itself, especially when it is composed of oil paint alone, does not seem to me enough to sustain the observer's interest for long. Dubuffet knows this, and it

Giuseppe Capogrossi: Surface Nº. 160. *1956. 57½″×45″. Galerie Rive Gauche coll., Paris. Born in Rome in 1900. Studied law, then painting. Has worked in Paris, now lives in Rome; exhibits internationally, has been represented for many years at the Venice Biennale. His work consists of imaginative variations on a decorative abstract theme.*

is for that reason that he tries to spiritualise his texture by conjuring from, or into, it a living creature or a reality which can touch us on its own account. Too great a turbulence of paint may begin by exciting us, but there comes a time when we long for the storm to blow over. (There lies the significance of the transparent textures employed by Kallos and Macris.) Every volcano cools in the end, after all.

Abstract art

The frontier between abstract painting and allusive painting is not easily defined. Certain painters generally considered as abstract indignantly deny the classification and it may be that some of those whom I shall now put in the abstract group will not be pleased to see themselves there. But painting as a whole benefits by these confusions, in that they serve to throw into relief its richness and variety and pointful ambiguity. Abstract pictures are, after all, very often rich in suggestion: light, color, dynamic form, texture—all hint at analogies in the universe outside.

They owe their origin to something—some impulse in the known world, a burst of feeling, a conflict, a super-abundance in some part of the painter's psyche. Old pictures sometimes record and spring from a single moment in the life of the eye; abstract pictures, on the other hand, may be literally an "abstract" of many thousands of such moments. A good picture of any kind originates in a tension in the painter's being which only the act of painting can relieve. Painting which is a mere gratuitous game can never be more than ornamental—and such is, in point of fact, the case with many abstract pictures.

A first group of abstractionists comes to mind: those who use geometrical forms and paint with flat surfaces, such as Dewasne, Herbin (page 181), Magnelli (page 175), Mortensen. It is a kind of abstraction which now shows its age and will probably die out before long.

Others, like Capogrossi (page 183), embellish their pictures with clearly-defined ornament and make up pleasing color-schemes which seem to compete with the best carpets on roughly their own ground. In such paintings the problems are simplified, the element of depth is ruled out, and the space evoked is the space of the canvas itself and no more. Others, more subtle, aim to invent an imaginary space, to evoke depths and distances which have no parallel in life, and light their pictures now from one point, now from another.

Hartung (page 172) has gone furthest in the presentation of this type of imaginary world. He projects vehement strokes that seem to burst from an explosion through distant space. On deep backgrounds, he floats curving patterns recalling feathers or reeds. Glimmers of dusk or dawn light pierce between his dark forms. By the vigor and originality of his handling of space and light he seems to me to have out-stripped the painters with whom he used to exhibit—Schneider, for instance, who has abandoned himself to automa-tism and impulsive calligraphy. The surrealists also made use of automatism as a principle of creation, but both in their case and in that of the abstrac-tionists it tends to a certain monotony. Poliakoff (page 182), less turbulent by nature, has a certain quiet simplicity in his forms and a delicate and sure touch with color. Soulages (page 183), working with a palette knife, builds up large, dark bands in superimposition, creating an illusion of space. All these artists, be it noted, make great use of black. Ever since the Galerie Maeght held an exhibition, in 1948, called "Black is a Color", black has been in many a painter's color-box.

There is no doubt that the Russian-born Nicolas de Staël, who died at barely forty in 1955, influenced certain abstract painters. He was an impetuous creator who often worked all night. His canvases were extremely personal, organised in broad, flat bands of color. It is curious that while de Staël was a factor in bringing several other artists—including his compatriot, Lans-koy—over to the abstract camp from figurative art, he himself was coming back to the external world at the time of his death, attempting to find a new solution for figurative expression.

Lanskoy (page 174), is not a grave inquisitor of the universe, he paints for the sheer pleasure of the eye in clear color that expresses his own *joie de vivre*. In black and white, he can produce a kind of ivy-foliage in which varying thicknesses and granulation of texture lead to a delectable play of light. Where others of his contempo-raries strive for dramatic or tragic effect, he scores by a sure technique, grace of manner, and the feeling of

Gustave Singier: Egyptian nocturne. *1955. 39½″ × 25⅝″. Museum of Modern Art, Paris. Born in Belgium in 1908, a naturalized French citizen. For many years after he arrived in Paris he worked as a decorator. He descends from Klee and shows certain similarities with Manessier. His compositions create a dream-like atmosphere.*

Raoul Ubac: The North suburb. *1957. 43⅜″ × 42½″. Maeght coll., Paris. Born in Belgium in 1910. Came to Paris originally to study literature but followed painting classes. Joined the surrealist group as a photographer. During the Occupation he branched off into the completely different direction of painting and drawing tending towards non-figuration. This painting was suggested by the lights and the stones of a Parisian suburb ; these gave him the pictorial idea but he does not try for literal representation.*

Francisco Borès: Composition in white. *1953. 35″×45¾″. Louis Carré coll., Paris. Born in Madrid in 1908. Came to Paris in 1926 and has lived there ever since. At first influenced by the cubists and his compatriot Juan Gris, he then evolved a freer, more flowing style, working entirely apart from the artistic community. For some years his canvases have been characterised by their luminosity, sensitive elegance of simplification and handling of space. This serene still life in a high key, almost devoid of shadows, led to a series of beach scenes in which brilliance of light destroys the solidity of objects and people.*

freedom which emanates from his canvases. Not that Lanskoy 'imitates' ivy-leaves any more than Hartung's calligraphies are 'inspired by' the feathers or reeds which they sometimes evoke: 'inspiration' works differently. But there are, on the other hand, painters who consciously adapt motives from vegetable life and strive to give expression to the hidden forces of Nature. Atlan, for instance, seems to celebrate the secret mysteries of Earth.

Others look to light as a source of poetry. Matta (page 176), a one-time surrealist, disturbs us with his greenish vegetations, among which electric phos-phorescent charges shoot and explode. And a more recent arrival, Saby, paints strange grottoes, underground or under water, where the light is not of our world.

There has also appeared in recent years a kind of visceral painting, in which forms and colors seem inspired by the anatomical cross-sections which we find in medical literature. Such works make us all the more appreciative of the healthy vigor of a painter like Lanskoy.

We may perhaps conclude our brief survey of the multiple tendencies visible today with a mention of Riopelle's major compositions (page 173). They form a vast multi-colored network of long strokes, spreading out in all directions. This artist was born in a clearing of the Canadian forests and his work recalls the confused and tumultuous vitality of his native land. The eye loses its way, as if in a virgin jungle, when it tries to follow any particular path among the many thousands of possible routes which exist in a 'land-scape' of Riopelle. And, like the woodmen of Canada, he uses a knife to make his intentions clear. In his latest work Riopelle has opened the dense thicket of brushstrokes to clear the center of the canvas.

Pictures and their titles

Until the cubists the title of a picture did not as a rule have anything fanciful about it. Its purpose was to say what the subject was, and to allow the picture to be identified in, for example, a catalogue. But the title assumed a new importance when it became difficult to read the picture itself. In such cases the title could, as it were, put the public on the right road. The surrealists gave their pictures 'literary' titles, thus introducing an impure element into the commerce of eye and canvas. It would be amusing and instructive to make a study of the evolution of titles in the painting of the last few years. Some are based on humor or poetry. Some are definitely of practical use to us—whether they are descriptive *(View of Amsterdam)* or allusive *(Morning Star* or *Hallelujah)*. Most abstract painters content themselves modestly with titles that have no associations: *Composition, Painting*, etc. Ambiguity is impossible, in such cases, and the observer cannot be led astray. Others give their pictures titles which are quite irrelevant but may well amuse the... reader. Jean Dubuffet has a knack for titles. Like Erik Satie who gave amusing titles to his music *(Piece in the form of a pear)*, Lanskoy in the same spirit called one of his recent pictures *Consolation for pale people.*

But humor is a weapon that may well be turned against the painter, especially the abstract painter, so he does well to think carefully before inviting the observer to make fun in his turn.

Mathieu, for instance, an abstract painter in the calligraphic vein whose work usually attains colossal proportions, invents titles drawn mostly from

Alberto Giacometti: Annette. 36¹/₅″×26″. 1951. *Maeght coll., Paris. Born in Stampa, Switzerland, in 1901. This distinguished sculptor is preoccupied by the same problems in painting as he is in sculpture : space and depth ; color is a lesser consideration. In his portraits he strives to make the subject emerge from a monochrome background. Broken lines which seem to grope for the sitter establish a startling resemblance. He paints portraits, his street, his studio, always working from a model. His portraits require interminable poses for many months ; this one is of his wife seated in his studio.*

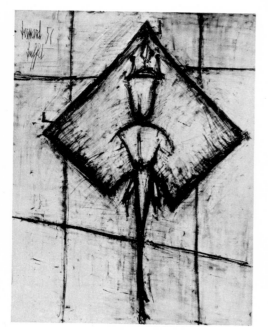

Bernard Buffet: Fish. *1956. Born in Paris in 1926. This young figurative painter has shot to fame since the war with his lugubrious figure pieces and still lifes, usually in tones of grey, black and white. His compositions are strongly linear, his people are always elongated and melancholy and seem to bear a curious resemblance to the painter himself. Many feel his original talent has been stretched thin by over-production. A certain cruelty is often found in his work, indicated here by the fish hanging from a nail.*

history ; they are ridiculous, rather than witty. Like Salvador Dali, he tries to turn his exhibition openings into theatrical occasions, appearing himself in medieval costume. But people soon get the measure of such antics ; it is the picture, not the masquerade, that counts.

Such, very briefly, is the look of the second Ecole de Paris. Certain formulae are already breathing their last ; other aspirations are beginning to emerge. But

Balthus *(real name Balthasar Klossowski)* : The Three Sisters. *1954. Private collection, Paris. Born in Paris in 1908. Balthus has worked completely apart from currents and groups of today; with courageous disregard for acclaim he pursues often obsessive images of adolescence, the curious atmosphere of certain Paris streets and the landscapes of central France where he now lives. These are expressed in a 19th century technique but reveal 20th century preoccupations. He was given a retrospective exhibition at the New York Museum of Modern Art in 1957.*

what counts above all in a school or group are the artists who comprise it. It does not necessarily follow that the figures who seem interesting to us at this moment, for one reason or another, are of equal value. In the years preceding the first world war Braque, Picasso and painters whose very names are forgotten now, were judged on the same footing. We are undoubtedly committing some of the same errors about many who seem to us today to be creating valid and daring works. And we may be overlooking what will prove to be the most authentic talents. Only the future will provide the necessary perspective.

Those who follow the painting of their own time take part in a fascinating adventure; they will know in some thirty or forty years time if their enthusiasms of today will prove perspicatious or fallible. And perhaps by then we will witness a third phase of that fascinatingly productive school, the Ecole de Paris.

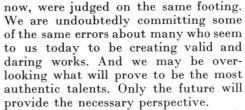

André Beaudin: The Evening Boat. *1956. 37" × 51 ¼". Private Collection, Paris. Born outside of Paris in 1895. Issued from Cubism; a close friendship with Juan Gris was to exert a formative influence. Using simplified geometric shapes he reconstructs Paris scenes, horses, birds, landscapes. His color, unevenly applied in transparent layers often letting the canvas show through, is of a restrained elegance. His work is limpid, sensitive and harmonious. He has illustrated books of poems by his friends and has made sculpture.*

LIST OF COLOR PLATES

Front-cover, Paul Klee : *The Equilibrist.* Detail.
Back-cover, Piet Mondrian : *Composition III.*
Jacket, Pablo Picasso : *The Meal.*

Color photographs

Carel Blazer : *Back-cover | page 136* — Conzett & Huber : *Jacket | pages 122-123 | 165*
Robert Doisneau : *pages 150-151* — Facchetti : *page 11* — Fleming : *page 121*
Giraudon : *pages 12-13 | 14 | 21 | 22 | 32 | 47 | 48 | 59 | 60-61 | 62 | 79 | 99 | 149 | 179 | 180 | 185*
Henn & Meyer : *Front-cover | page 89* — Hinz : *pages 166-167* — Lacheroy : *page 152*
Lacoste : *pages 80 | 100 | 124 | 173* — Inge Morath : *page 135* — Staatsgalerie, Stuttgart : *page 90*

This book was designed by Robert Delpire

Editorial Assistant : Monique Schneider-Maunoury

This book was printed
by the Imprimeries Réunies, S.A., Lausanne
It was finished
on August 15th, 1957